ROGER DOMMERGUE

HEIDEGGER'S SILENCE
AND
THE SECRET OF THE JEWISH TRAGEDY

ROGER-GUY POLACCO DE MENASCE
(1924-2013)

Roger Dommergue was a Franco-Luxembourg professor of philosophy best known for his controversial positions on the Holocaust. Dommergue supported revisionist theories of the Holocaust, questioning the number of Jewish victims and claiming that the Nazi gas chambers were a myth. He gave lectures and interviews in which he denied the extent of the crimes committed by the Nazi regime during the Second World War.

HEIDEGGER'S SILENCE AND THE SECRET OF THE JEWISH TRAGEDY

Le silence de Heidegger et le secret de la tragédie juive

1994

Translated and published by

OMNIA VERITAS LTD

www.omnia-veritas.com

© Omnia Veritas Limited – 2025

All rights reserved. No part of this publication may be reproduced by any means without the prior permission of the publisher. The intellectual property code prohibits copies or reproductions for collective use. Any representation or reproduction in whole or in part by any means whatsoever, without the consent of the publisher, the author or their successors, is unlawful and constitutes an infringement punishable by articles of the Code of Intellectual Property.

AUSCHWITZ: HEIDEGGER'S SILENCE 13
WHO WAS HITLER? 48
  Point of detail, certainly. 60
  Long live democracy! 61
THE FORGERY THAT TELLS THE TRUTH 68
NAZISM MUST NOT BE TRIVIALISED, MADAME SIMONE
VEIL? 79
  BUT WE'VE MADE IT COMMONPLACE... 79
FUNDAMENTAL NOTE 91
BEYOND ANTI-SEMITISM 92
  THE KEY TO JEWISH TRAGEDY: CIRCUMCISION ON THE 8TH DAY AND
  THE DARK AGES. 92
    A typical example from the 90s of the effects of circumcision on the 8th
    day: The financier SOROS. 101
    The constitution is more important than the nation 110
    Consumption for consumption's sake is a value in itself. 110
    The only reigning value is that of money 110
  THE TRUTH ABOUT RACE AND RACISM 112
    THE RACISM OF PSEUDO-ANTI-RACISM 112
  THE MARSHAL IN "1984 117
    Ubu circumcised king! 118
  AFTER THE ATTEMPTED ASSASSINATION OF PROFESSOR
  FAURISSON: 124
    THE 6-*MILLION-GAS-CHAMBERS* MYTH AND DOGMA OR REALITY? PR
    FAURISSON PUBLIC ENEMY N°1 OR INTERNATIONAL HERO OF THE
    XXTH CENTURY? 124
      Major psychological arguments 124
      Arithmetic and technical proof 127
      Psychological arithmetic technical 130
  THE MYTH OF INDEFINITE PRODUCTION AND THE
  CANNIBALISATION OF NATURE 131
    Overpopulation in the Third World is a disaster 135

UN STATISTICS 137
   THE MYTH OF PROGRESS 137
      True progress must be the perfect symbiosis of four perspectives: *138*
JUDEO-CARTESIAN GLOBAL SUICIDE 143
MARXISM, WHICH HAS KILLED AND WILL KILL AGAIN 146
TOLERANCE, TOLERANCE! 154
MUSIC THAT KILLS 156
ABOUT DR A. CARREL AND THE MANIA FOR RENAMING
STREETS AFTER HIM 166
THE ASTONISHING CHURCHILL 169
      Zionism versus Bolshevism, a struggle for the soul of the Jewish people
      By Rt, Hon. WINSTON CHURCHILL *170*
ESSAY ON JUDEO-CHRISTIANITY, JUDEO-CARTESIANISM
AND THE HOLOCAUST DOGMA 178
TOUVIER CASE 191
      Letter to Maître Trémollet de Villers (Paul Touvier's lawyer) *193*
      Touvier case: Letter to the President of the Versailles Court of Appeal. 205
      What Touvier should have said Why I chose the Marshal *207*
LETTER TO CARDINAL LUSTIGER, ARCHBISHOP OF PARIS 210
MADNESS AND GENIUS 214
      Memory *222*
      The genius mind is hierarchical *223*
      Logic and reason *224*
      Voluntary loss of attention *226*
      Intelligence *227*
      Fitness for work *227*
      The various attention deficits in the madman *227*
      Loss of willpower *228*
      Loss of moral sense *230*
      Loss of higher psychological elaborations *230*
      Abstractions *231*
      Discrimination of abstract values *233*
      Notion of identity *235*
      Summary *241*
      The evils of modern science *245*
      Modern science has no brakes and no end in sight *250*

What about Freud? *254*
    Attention, willpower and the moral sense of modern scientists *257*
PSYCHOLOGICAL ROLE OF THE SO-CALLED ORGANIC ENDOCRINES ... 263

    Adrenals: *263*
    Pituitary gland: *263*
    Thyroid: *263*
    Internal genital: *263*

WHAT DOES IT MEAN TO BE A FASCIST? 267
THE WORLD OF TOMORROW 270
UBU EMPEROR 273
DID YOU SAY ANTI-SEMITIC? NO? 277

    THE ULTIMATE SYNTHESIS OF THE GEOPOLITICS OF THE LAST
    MILLENNIA 277
    OTHER TITLES 291

*To the Jewish philosophers
present at the "Oceaniques" TV programme
about Heidegger*

Auschwitz: Heidegger's silence

Gentlemen,

This long presentation is motivated by a concern for synthetic truth. I give it to you without any hope of an intelligent and exhaustive response. Apart from Simone Weil, Bernard Lazare, Bergson and a few other fellow Jews, I have never met an intellectually honest Jew. I see nothing but their lies and bad faith oozing out everywhere. I wish I were not among the Jews, a rare exception capable of probity and synthesis

I followed your two 'Oceaniques' programmes, which were radically focused not on Heidegger, but on his SILENCE.

To raise the question of Heidegger's silence is in itself unconscious and I will explain this as clearly as possible.

Not one of you present at this broadcast has questioned for a moment Heidegger's superior intelligence. So why this hiatus? Why did he remain silent from 1945 until his death without the profound reason for his silence being perfectly integrated into the coherence of his intelligence?

Its silence is perfectly cohesive. It would be mine if the disturbing psychotic, paranoid, megalomaniac mentality of my fellow human beings didn't make me want to scream...

When Glucksman speaks of 'his vocation to contemplate the truth', *is he sure that it is the truth? Would he be following me to manifest his vocation?*

Everything that follows has been put through the relentless sieve of verification and Niagara of evidence by nine. I am therefore ready to answer all questions, provide documents, technicians and evidence, all of which can be found in the archives of the famous Zündel trial in Canada. It should be remembered that this trial irrefutably proved the conspiracy between Bolshevism and the Jewish bankers in the USA, and destroyed the myth of the Holocaust, particularly through elementary arithmetical and technical considerations, and the damning conclusions of the Leuchter report, confirmed by the counter-expertise carried out by the exterminationists themselves. Leuchter, an American engineer and specialist in gassing with hydrocyanic acid in the USA, demonstrated that no execution by gas had ever taken place at Auschwitz, Birkenau or Majdanek...

Glucksman says he appreciates all manifestations of intelligence! Indeed! Won't he label as stupid anything that doesn't fit into the flattering halo of his subjectivity? Worse still, isn't he going to NOT ANSWER, as my congeners have been doing for centuries on the strength of their financial and political power? I'm afraid so: the truth is branded as an insult, as moronic, as Nazism. It's even punishable by law and that's that...

The only reproach levelled at Hitler and endlessly repeated, amplified, hammered home, orchestrated even in the most popular films, and this since a few years after the end of the 2nd World War, is the so-called holocaust of 6 million Jews in cyclon B gas chambers. Auschwitz, that's it.

However, there is never any mention of the tens of millions of other victims of the war, the tens of millions of victims of Bolshevism, or the tens and tens of millions of victims SINCE the end of the war. We'll come back to that later.

But what do we now know about this problem, if we are honest and if we have studied it since 1979, when the FAURISSON affair first came to light?

We know that:

The "*6-million-gas-rooms*" dogma is as well established as the dogma of Redemption. Who would quarrel with a university professor who reveals that Pol Pot massacred 2 million human beings instead of 4? (the same Pol Pot who, as I write, is still alive and well and whom the international conscience has not brought before a Nuremberg tribunal worthy of him).

PERSON.

Why on earth would announcing the EXCELLENT NEWS that there were no 6 million Jewish victims and no Cyclon B gassings, if not for delousing, BE BAD NEWS TO BE SANCTIONED BY THE JUSTICE???

Who would be outraged if we were informed that THE CONCENTRATIONARY BOURREAUX AND SOVIET JEWISH CARCREARS (Frenkel, Yagoda, Kaganovitch, Rappaport, Jejoff, Abramovici, Firine, Ouritski, Sorenson, Bermann, Apetter et al.) only exterminated 30 million people under Stalinism instead of 60 million as is written??

PERSON.

In 5000 years of history, this case is unique: it illustrates the age-old phenomenon of the jeremiad. All those who give evidence of this juicy mystification are indicted and condemned.

Paul Rassinier, a Socialist MP and history teacher who was interned for years in German camps, came out weighing 30 kg and ended up dying as a result of his internment, was prosecuted for the books he wrote in pursuit of a truth that brought him nothing but trouble. As a socialist MP, an internee and a lay teacher, he had nothing to gain from this heroic demonstration of truth, and his books are immersed in the TOTAL CONSPIRACY OF SILENCE IN THE NAME OF DEMOCRATIC FREEDOM OF EXPRESSION...

Professor FAURISSON, who studied the problem for twenty years, and who had stumbled across this hoax by chance, was condemned, even though the jury "never disputed the seriousness of his work in debating with specialists and the public"...

HENRI ROQUES whose thesis on the GERSTEIN report was cancelled. An unprecedented incident, unique in history. This despite the fact that the best-known historian in the media, now a Socialist minister, Alain Decaux, had publicly attested to the excellence of this work! Moreover, this thesis could have been perfectly useless, since THE GERSTEIN REPORT WAS REJECTED AT THE NUREMBERG TRIALS. The thesis is nevertheless useful, since for half a century we have been able to rely on a document declared worthless by a court whose infallibility we are constantly told is infallible!

Everyone suspects that the Judges of a tribunal constituted exclusively by the ALLIES and which did not have at all the INTERNATIONAL CHARACTER with which it is claimed to be clothed, would not have asked for anything better than to use this report if they had been able to. But it was so grotesque that they had to give it up!

ERNST ZUNDEL, whose trial caused a stir in Canada, until the orderly media plunged the affair into leaden silence.

Not only was the myth of the Holocaust destroyed, and the "great specialists" ridiculed (going so far as to claim "poetic licence"), but it proved irrefutably that since 1917 and without a break, American Jewish financiers had financed Bolshevism.

Despite the considerable publicity this trial generated in Canada, not a word was heard the European media: OUR FELLOW HUMAN BEINGS HAVE A TOTAL STRANGLEHOLD ON THE PRESS.

The ANNALES RÉVISIONNISTES are being seized in the name of democratic freedom of expression, no doubt. No right of reply for Professor Faurisson, insulted on Polac's programme.

Meanwhile, on the same day, 70,000 democratically zombified young people are stripping off their pants to imitate a vile slut from the pseudo-song, a kind of ignorant, infantile and obscene residue... while pornography, drugs and pathogenic and criminogenic music are spreading VERY DEMOCRATICALLY.

SINCE WHEN DOES DEMOCRACY NOT ALLOW FREE EXPRESSION AND THE RESPONSE AND EVIDENCE THAT WOULD DESTROY ANY LIE???

Faurisson demands, implores, that an army of contradictors and a huge public be placed before him: HE CAN WAIT A LONG TIME.

One day an Orwellian law will be passed against him 'for thoughtcrime'. It was indeed passed on the sly some time after this book was first written. It is the FABIUS GAYSSOT law. This Stalinist law bears the name of a Jew and a Communist - no coincidence! We can discuss the Revisionists but not with them", said a Jew, thus showing his perfect good faith and his luminous intellectual probity.

Someone show me in 5000 years of Judeo-Christianity a single liar who demands to speak publicly in front of an unlimited number of contradictors!!!! It should be noted in passing that every normal human being is a revisionist FUNDAMENTALLY. A HUMAN being has a duty to question anything that offends his heart or reason and which takes the official guise of dogma or postulate. Everything else is zombism.

The bad faith, the hatred, the lies, the persecutions, the tear gas, the assassination attempts prove beyond doubt that Faurisson is right even before studying the arithmetical and technical aspects of the problem. What's more, he is called a "Nazi", a systematic reflex towards anyone who casts the slightest doubt about the truth of the sacrosanct myth of the *6-million-gas-chambers!*

Yet everyone knows that Faurisson is a man of the left, anti-Nazi and a member of the Union of Atheists, who proclaims his democracy but will not have the courage to defend it...

Nineteen-fourty-four absoluteness conferred on the dogma of the 6-million-gas-chambers is the irrefutable psychological proof of its imposture. If Faurisson were wrong, it would have been a long time since someone had arranged to prove it to him in front of the huge audience he demands: television would have been the ideal means of letting him express himself exhaustively and then demonstrating his imposture.

Unfortunately, this was done on Lugano television entirely to Faurisson's advantage, and *Storia Illustrata* opened its pages to him...

The arithmetic-technical aspect is even more convincing.

6 million (or even 4 million, assuming that 2 million Jews died as a result of the war, which is inaccurate) represent a country like Switzerland. They were exterminated en masse in 1943-44 in 7 concentration camps. We know the exact number of crematoria still in use and how long it took to cremate a corpse. In fact, advanced crematoria were not installed until the end of 1943, as extermination historian Georges Wellers himself confirms.

This means that cremation only became technically perfect from this date onwards. Prior to that, massive global cremations would have been incomplete and would have triggered typhus epidemics throughout Europe. What's more, if we operate the crematoria in 7 camps according to the known duration of Holocaust cremation (less than 2 years) and the known individual duration of cremation, the result is that the crematoria are still running in the year 2030! We know perfectly well how these furnaces work and what their purpose is. They are absolutely essential to prevent epidemics of typhus, plague, cholera and other diseases endemic in concentration camps.

ON THE OTHER HAND, THERE IS NO CYCLON B GAS CHAMBER CAPABLE OF EXTERMINATING 1,000 OR 2,000 PEOPLE AT A TIME.

In this respect, it is amusing to visit the Struthof gas chamber in Alsace, where hydrocyanic acid was vented freely after gassing, through a simple chimney less than a hundred metres from the commandant's residence! The chamber itself was only a few square metres in size.

Let's quote a key phrase used by the exterminationists: "after the gassing, we opened the door, the victims, still throbbing, fell into our arms and we cleared away the corpses...

"This is absurd because it takes 20 hours of ventilation and 5-gas masks carry out such an operation. Everyone can find out, as I did, about the hydrocyanic acid gas chamber used in the USA to execute ONE condemned man. Its incredible complexity, the considerable precautions to be taken when gassing a condemned man, show irrefutably that gassing 2,000 people at a time with this gas is TECHNICALLY INEPERABLE.

The fact that the tiny Struthof site in Alsace was mistaken for a gas chamber for half a century will go down in history as an example of the naivety of the masses, who will believe anything as long as it is reported in a newspaper or on television...

The same applies to the whole story, which is a technical arithmetic problem at primary school certificate level. It is certain that if a pupil at this level were given the problem and solved it in accordance with the assertions of the official propaganda, he would get a zero on his paper.

In 1949, at the trial of DEGESH, the company that manufactured Cyclon B, the firm's CEO, Dr Héli, and the physicist, Dr Ra, stated that gassing under the conditions described was IMPOSSIBLE AND IMPENSABLE! No one ever tells us about this trial, just as no one tells us that the Gerstein report, on which Roques based his thesis, was challenged at the Nuremberg trial! A well-known American Jewish newspaper, the AMERICAN JEWISH YEAR BOOK, tells us in its n° 43 on page 666 (!) that in Europe occupied by the Germans in 1941, there were 3,300,000 Jews! How many have left for Spain since that date! How many thousands were protected in the Free Zone, like my whole family? How many hundreds of thousands were found under their own names or under a false name! Faurisson estimates that there were 150,000 victims of Auschwitz, all ethnic groups combined.

That's what all the reasonable people who know about these issues have told me.

We can admire the conscience of the Exterminationists in this extract from Le Monde dated 22.11.1979: "Everyone is free to imagine or dream that these monstrous events did not take place. Unfortunately, they did happen and no one can deny their existence without offending the truth. We must not ask ourselves how such a mass murder was technically possible, IT WAS TECHNICALLY POSSIBLE BECAUSE IT HAPPENED (!!!).

This is the starting point for any historical enquiry into the subject. It is our duty to reiterate this truth quite simply: THERE IS NO, THERE CANNOT BE ANY DEBATE ABOUT GAS FIREPLACES" What mark would be given to a French paper by a student who followed such a line of reasoning? How can such an absurd text even be published?

It is typical of the twentieth century to accept the ridiculous in any publication, whereas you wouldn't accept it in a copy of 6 a sixth form. Didn't I hear recently that "the maternal instinct doesn't exist"? You have to see the tight dialectic that leads to such absurdity. It will lead motherhood to the same gulags as the dismasted logic of Marxism...

This was precisely the starting point for Professor Faurisson's historical investigation, as he stumbled across the subject presented to his students in a course on research into historical truth.

He could have chosen another subject, but there was so much talk about this one that he chose it. It was during the course of the study that the cat was discovered and he choked on it. Understandably, a shower like that made him want to tell the truth...

After 20 years of work, he discovered that gas chambers for 2,000 people had never existed anywhere. All he discovered were the tiny delousing chambers that used Cyclon B!

To the naive, illogical, stupefyingly concrete, childish and paranoid assertion, the absurdity of which is there for all to see. ("Don't even try, it's just the way it is! Mrs Paschoud, a journalist and history teacher, replies: "The gas chambers existed, so be it! I'd like someone to explain to me why, for the last 20 years, people have been trying so hard to harm Revisionists in their professional or private lives, when it would be so easy to silence them once and for all by producing just one of the countless pieces of irrefutable evidence we keep hearing about...

"Madame Paschoud has paid dearly for her sincerity and courage! These sentences of elementary common sense are perfectly in line with the insane text published by Le Monde and which we have just quoted.

Who says that at the 1983 colloquium held at the Sorbonne against Faurisson, (AND IN HIS ABSENCE!!!) Raymond Aron was forced to admit that there was NO EVIDENCE, NO WRITTEN DOCUMENT, NO TRACE establishing the reality of the homicidal gas chambers. EVEN THOUGH ALL THE CREMATORIA ARE STILL THERE.

In reality, there are many more clues about extraterrestrials than there are about the reality of the gas chambers, which would pose an insoluble FINANCIAL and TECHNICAL problem for 2,000 people. Did we not see the height of the 1984 grotesquerie: "a federation of journalists with 2,000 members (including l'Équipe!) urges the government to silence Professor Faurisson IN THE NAME OF HUMAN RIGHTS AND DEMOCRATIC FREEDOM OF EXPRESSION (sic!)! NO DEMOCRATIC FREEDOM OF

EXPRESSION IN THE NAME OF FREEDOM OF EXPRESSION...

Give the press, the police and the courts to Mr Lévy and his assistant Mr Homais, and they won't look so ridiculous any more, and that's the 20th century...

Better still. In the name of freedom of thought, secondary school pupils will not be protected from shabby clothes, criminogenic music, drugs, suicide, unemployment, pornography or incitement to debauchery from an early age, via condoms, BUT THEY WILL BE TAKEN A COURSE IN ANTI-REVISIONIST CIVIC INSTRUCTION.

The idiot who dares to say that 2,000 people could not have been gassed with Cyclon B in gas chambers, and that there could not have been 6,000,000 Jews in occupied Europe, will never get his baccalaureate. Whichever way you look at it, the problem is one of lies.

Six million people gassed in the crematorium left thousands of tonnes of ash that did not disappear completely. A hundred or so samples of just a few cubic centimetres analysed WOULD HAVE REVEALED THE PRESENCE OF CYANHYDRIC ACID.

I've never heard of any such analysis having been carried out.

Point of detail: I thought freedom had all meanings. But freedom has only one meaning, and that is the ABSOLUTE DICTATORIALITY OF MY CONGENERATES, a dictatorship that is all the more despicable because it hides behind the cloak of a pseudo-democracy that is in fact nothing more than an IMPLACABLE CRYPTODICTATURE.

Even supposing that Faurisson is wrong (which he is not, since we have all the evidence of the imposture of which the psychological behaviour towards him is by far the most important proof), there is nothing wrong or scandalous about his thesis; IT EXPRESSES EXCELLENT NEWS which touches nothing of the all too real suffering of those who endured the pain of the camps. Is there ANY people who felt the need to whine about the millions of them exterminated by an enemy that disappeared half a century ago? Do you need to be a doctor of psychology to understand that such behaviour is psychopathological, as well as a rather despicable and typical need to ensure the foundations of a fantastic political and financial swindle? But as Faurisson says, "if we learn that 6 million Jewish victims were not gassed, should we say so or hide it?

A pertinent question! Our congeners don't want Faurisson to express himself, to be contradicted by obvious technical and arithmetical realities...

Faurisson and those who want him to enjoy his democratic freedom of expression are accused of anti-Semitism.

Anti-Semitism is elsewhere. It was in the USSR, which the Jews found unbearable. They didn't take the time to denounce the regime's anti-Semitism: all they wanted was to leave as quickly as possible.

What's more, and this is a huge thing, they are practically the only ones who can leave the U.S.S.R. Soviet slavery is good for everyone else.

90% of Soviet immigrants to the USA are Jewish! Point of detail! Soviet Communism has since collapsed. This collapse was calculated by Jewish finance, which wants to introduce the market economy into Russia. If this collapse had not been deliberate, it would not have happened because the USSR had the strongest army in the world...

Need I remind you of what HUMAN RIGHTS stipulate?

One wonders whether it is a question of human rights, which are flouted everywhere, or the exclusive rights of the Jew... No one should be harassed for his or her opinions. The free communication thoughts and opinions is one of the most precious human rights...

If these rights are abused by totalitarian Jewish financiers, Benezareff-style pornographers, Gurgi-Lazarus' music that kills, exterminating Marxism, abultifying and pornographic Freudianism, drug lords, the Mafia, parasitic hoarders and faggots, THERE IS NONE FOR ANY RESEARCHER OR TEACHER WHO HAS SOMETHING TO SAY.

Faurisson has the right to speak and everyone has the right to contradict him with PRECISE FACTS, EVIDENCE, DEEP STUDIES, DEEP ANALYSES, EXHAUSTIVE EXAMINATIONS.

All the rest is totalitarianism far worse than Hitler's, because his authoritarianism led to order, ideals and virility, while the other led to the purulent decomposition of the whole of humanity...

It adjoins Kaganovitch's and will eventually lead to it. The Jews will be forced (this text was written ONE YEAR before the Fabius-Gayssot law, hence the future) to have the political puppets they manipulate pass a totalitarian, radically anti-democratic law, which will condemn to prison and fines those who dare to question the sacrosanct concrete dogma of *6-million-rooms-to-gas*. I wrote to PIERRE VIDAL-NAQUET, more than a year before the enactment of this INEVITABLE law on the curve of Jewish hysteria.

UBU, CIRCUMCISED AND NOT JEWISH, IS KING OF THIS ORWELLIAN UNIVERSE.

No one can deny that the holocaust has become a true religion and that the democratic pyre threatens the miscreant.

Jacob Timmerman, a Jewish historian, says: "Many Jews are shocked by the way the Holocaust is exploited by the Diaspora.

They are even ashamed that the Holocaust has become a civil religion for Jews in the U.S.A. Leon A. Jick, another Jewish historian, comments: "The devastating quip that there is no business like the Shoa business is, it must be said, an incontrovertible truth".

Not a week goes by without the public being urged to "never forget". There are ponderous film screenings, simplistic broadcasts, and a hateful, psychotic hunt for the "war criminals", invalid old men in their eighties, of a regime that has been dead for 50 years. Popular adventure and action films are full of references to the evil Germans and the filthy Nazis, always portrayed as brutal torturers. Ah, to think of how the Russians behaved in Europe! Horrible behaviour, while the Germans, soldiers or officers, gave up their seats to the ladies in the underground!

We hear about Oradour-sur-Glane, a unique case in France, but we never hear about the CONTEXT of this affair: German soldiers mutilated by the resistance, a superior officer with his eyes gouged out, and the long time the Germans gave the guilty parties to denounce themselves before the just reprisals carried out by ALSACIANS! The word "reprisals" was not invented by the Germans and no general in any army would have accepted such an atrocity. Were it not the despicable torturers of German soldiers who, by not denouncing themselves, became THE REAL ASSASSINS OF THE HABITANTS OF ORADOUR?

If only we knew about Allied war crimes! If only young people knew how, even after 1945, Russians and Americans raped and massacred every German community in Europe...

WHEREAS A GERMAN OFFICER WHO RAPED IN ENEMY COUNTRY WAS IMMEDIATELY PUT TO DEATH.

That was the law. I have never heard of a German officer who raped in enemy territory. The mass grave of KOURAPATY in the northern suburbs of Minsk was discovered, containing around 250,000 corpses. They perished between 1937 and 1941, shot by N.K.V.D. troops.

We're not likely to hear about it every day in the media: they weren't Jews! And let's not talk about the one-sided teaching courses, the hypocritical appearances of political puppets at sacred holocaust worship events.

We need to refer to the Zohar's "the vile seed of cattle" to understand that Jewish victims are more valuable than others.

Do memorials, study centres and university ceremonies exist in the USA for the DOZENS OF MILLIONS OF VICTIMS OF THE JEWS KAGANOVITCH, APPETER, OURITSKI, FRENKEL, YAGODA, JEJOFF AND CONSORTS???

And yet Hitler's 6 million, even if true, is vastly exceeded! What kind of arithmetic is it that claims that 6 million is greater than 60 million?

Need we remind you of the mass crimes committed by the Soviets against Ukrainians, Balts, Chechens, Koreans and many others? The Ukrainian genocide claimed 6 to 8 million real victims.

Should we forget the hundreds of thousands of women and children and unarmed civilians murdered by the Red Army in 1945 in the East German provinces? The White Russians who joined the German army against Bolshevism and who, having been naive enough to believe that they would be welcomed back home, were executed by machine gun on their way home...

At last they want us to believe in the absurd equation: REVISIONISM= ANTISEMITISM.

They would have us believe that historical revisionism, which is perfectly normal (any historian worthy of the name is a PERMANENT REVISIONIST), is CONTRARY TO DEMOCRACY.

A curious postulate which amounts to positing the opposite: DEMOCRACY = NON-REVISIONISM.

This is the height of absurdity and silliness, because it amounts to saying that: REVISIONISM IS CONTRARY TO THE THE THEMES OF INTERNATIONAL JUDAISM!

C.Q.F.D.: Nobody can contradict that!

Ouch, ouch, ouch, those who say this are following in the footsteps of the worst anti-Semitism, which from Action Française to Hitler unambiguously asserts that:

DEMOCRACY AND MASONIC HUMANISM ARE JEWISH CREATIONS EXCLUSIVELY AT THE SERVICE OF THE JEWS.

L'Action Française even stated bluntly that this extended to all institutions, including education and the judiciary.

I have been told this by so many people, even though they are democrats, citing the Pléven and Marchandeau laws as examples, reinforced by the incongruous absolutism of the recent Gayssot law, which was easy for me to foresee.

The contempt for the law was evident in the Barbie trial.

He was sentenced to death in 1954 and could not be sentenced again for a similar offence. He benefited from the statute of limitations because 34 years had elapsed since his conviction, and it would take totalitarian legalism to get rid of the statute of limitations. As a Bolivian, he could not be tried in France unless he had been duly extradited. But he was abducted after some incredible shenanigans, including financial threats to the Bolivian government! A legal farce, a pseudo-legal, legalised circus, absolute contempt for judges and their conscience, contempt for JUSTICE.

Why not indict tomorrow a French octogenarian who had the misfortune to follow the Church and the Marshal?

Anything is possible in the dictatorship of horror that we are experiencing internationally. These lines were written some 15 to 20 months before the Touvier trial.

So, as expected, we were treated to this circus of justice and the media. Unheard of, while the world lies in the putrescent decomposition of JUDÉO CARTÉSIANISME, an unfortunate man who had opted for France' last clean regime is charged.

And all this while millions of people are strangled by unemployment, destroyed by the annihilation of all the values that make and preserve man... And this 50 years later. We'll come back to this later...

As for Barbie, had he behaved in the same way as a French officer, he would undoubtedly have been entitled to statuary honours, or at least urban honours. But his trial raises thorny questions. Barbie, condemned in advance, had nothing to lose. He knew all about the most unsavoury aspects of the Resistance, which he could have disgraced: he said NOTHING. He could have put the Jewish half-century on implacable trial, justifying his Hitler option: he said NOTHING. HE COULD HAVE CRUSHED THE PRAETORIUM AND TRIUMPHED SUPREME AND STILL BEEN CONDEMNED: HE DID NOTHING.

He kept his mouth shut! Why would he do that?

Wasn't he himself part of a circus carefully concocted to mystify the masses in whom anti-Semitism roars?

These Barbie and Touvier-style circuses are not going to distract the masses from their acute discontent with unemployment, nor from the anti-Semitism that this kind of spectacle exacerbates, whatever the Jewish paranoia may think...

Be that as it may, the policy being pursued against Faurisson, if it continues - AND THE HYSTERIA OF MY CONGENERATES WILL MAKE IT CONTINUE - will vindicate the worst anti-Semitic assertions of the extreme right, and IT IS PEOPLE ON THE LEFT WHO RELIEF THESE DEMONSTRATIONS...!

It is too often forgotten that Hitler wanted to exchange all the Jews of Europe for a reasonable number of lorries. It was the Jewish governments in England and the USA who preferred lorries to our fellow Jews, who would be much more useful to them as inflationary martyrs in the camps. The unfortunate thing is that the figure of 6 million is an arithmetical nonsense. In Jours de France, Bloch-Dassault pointed out that life in the German camps was no worse than in the Gulags, which were run by fifty or so Jews, whose photographs can be seen in Volume II of Solzhenitsyn's Gulag Archipelago, and who were responsible for tens of millions of massacres.

No one disputes this fact, not even Communist historians! I mention only for the record the tens of millions exterminated in the 1917 revolution, not forgetting the Tsar and his family, a revolution in which all the government teams and all the financiers who subsidised this delicious regime for human development WERE JEWS.

It bears repeating: are these tens and tens of millions of massacred people numerically less than the 6 million, EVEN TRUE, that our tired ears are constantly bombarded with by the media? And these people were not exterminated because they held all the levers of finance, parasitic speculation, suicidal systems and ideologies, but because they were brave anti-communist Russian nationals...

There's no need for the media to talk about these tens of millions every day, no need for the "international high conscience" to concern itself with them, no need to make a film entitled "SUPERHOLOCAUST": they weren't Jews!

So they are no more important than the boat people, the Biaffrans, the Eritreans, the Palestinians, the Christians in Lebanon...

For the whole world, on the other hand, it was eternal night and fog, those who died of hunger and typhus during the 3 months when Germany was collapsing. We forget to mention that, as a result of the Allied bombing raids, the situation was the same in the major German cities that had been reduced to ashes. Civilians were dying there like flies, and a single bombardment could claim 150,000 to 200,000 victims.

Of these martyred cities, there are no photos of children dying among the ruins or under the rubble. There were, however, photos of the camps from every angle, with captions that had nothing to do with reality: as the Allied bombing made it impossible to feed the internees, it was inevitable that they would starve to death! Who can believe for a moment that the Germans, seeing their defeat coming, could have left behind such a brand image?

Do we have such images of the horrors of the gulags???

Isn't it obvious that the living skeletons we are shown in photographs and films have nothing to do with gas chambers? How can we fail to see that famine and typhus are the cause of these distressing images?

THE SHAM OF THE 6 MILLION GAS CHAMBERS IS DECIDEDLY BLATANT: IT IS PSYCHOLOGICAL, IT IS ARITHMETICAL, IT IS TECHNICAL.

Assuming that the "*6 million gassedJews*" are true. What do we find in the fully "encircled" liberal-socialist world?

I deliberately do not use the term "JEWISH" because EVERYTHING THAT REMAINS FROM THE MODERN WORLD IS HERETIC AND CRIMINAL BEFORE THE THORA.

The use of the term Jew is a semantic abuse. The word has only one meaning and that is religious. The Jews can only be reproached for their silence in the face of the misdeeds of these impostors WHO ARE NOT JEWISH AT ALL: they are the "international sect of atheistic and speculative 8th day circumcision". We'll come back to this later.

Let's look at a few details:

1. All countries are subject to the fierce dictatorship of the dollar and crushed by huge, unpayable debts. International ruin is on our doorstep and it will be definitive when the hegemony of the bankers and their technocratic henchmen is accomplished by specious treaties such as those described in the false PROTOCOLS OF THE WISE MEN OF ZION. These treaties of the MAASTRICHT type, the G.A.T.T.[1] and those that will follow, will have the effect of definitively murdering the peasant class and reducing Europe to unemployment. Hitler, like Marshal Pétain, WERE FUNDAMENTALLY AGAINST THIS SUICIDAL SYSTEM WHICH TOTALLY DESTROYED THE TRADITIONAL MAN IN BALANCE WITH AN UNPOLLUTED NATURE.

He was against liberalism, which polluted the soil, bodies and souls, just as he was against Bolshevism, which exterminated tens of millions of human beings, reducing all living beings to the status of elementary matricular statistical units. THIS IS WHERE THE REAL CAUSES OF THE 1939-1945 WAR LIE, AND NOT ELSEWHERE.

Everything else, and we'll come back to this, is just a pretext for playing to the masses, who will be led by the 60 million to the slaughter.

2. Unemployment is a global scourge. Rockfeller's Club of Rome predicts that there will soon be one billion unemployed people in the world. Both Hitler and the Marshall eliminated unemployment in both countries by encouraging the birth rate, which was exceptional in Germany.

3. Sites, soil, forests, water, animal and plant species are being destroyed by industry and chemification. 5000 lakes are biologically dead in Canada, 2000 in Sweden. Forests are disappearing, devoured by advertising and monstrous ballot papers. Acid from cars and factories does the rest.

---

[1] Later to become the World Trade Organisation.

The Rhine was recently a dead river, and the Mediterranean is horribly polluted. Industry exists only through RADICALLY CIRCUMSTANT finance.

There are no financiers such as Warburg (who in 1914-18 simultaneously financed the Allies, the Germans and the Bolshevik Revolution), Hammer (who in 1941 alone owned as much oil as the 3 Axis powers), Soros (who destabilised a currency with a telephone call), Bronfmann, Holocaust preacher, alcohol king and owner of 3 billion 600 million dollars, who are not "circumcised on the 8th day". Those who are not have, on analysis, a derisory "range of action".

4. The exploitation of atomic energy threatens humanity with death.

Atomic bombs, Chernobyl, genetic damage, waste that cannot be neutralised or stored.

No one denies the importance of the physicists Einstein and Oppenheimer in the development of the atomic bomb, or that of S.T. Cohen in the development of the neutron bomb.

The philosopher Irène Fernandez, on the FR3 programme on 15 February 1988, informed us that Hitler refused to use the atomic bomb for humanitarian reasons. He would have used it as a deterrent, which would have avoided Hiroshima and Nagasaki!

The press recently revealed that Nazi atomic research was non-existent.

All this is in line with the draft treaty submitted by Hitler to England and the USA, under which civilian populations would not be bombed in the event of war. This treaty was rejected!

IT IS ABSURD TO SUGGEST THAT SUCH SPECULATIONS ARE THE PROVINCE OF THE INTELLECT, WHEN IN FACT THEY ARE THE PROVINCE OF SPECULATIVE GIFTS,

WHICH IS A COMPLETELY DIFFERENT MATTER. Science and finance, devoid of spiritual authority, DO NOT THINK.

5. There is hardly any drinking water left.

But Hitler was extremely concerned about ecology. He was well aware of the dangers of over-industrialisation, which he was forced to because of the dangers of war.

He had to deal with the economic situation.

The pill of Djérassi and Aron Blum (aka Beaulieu), abortion of Simone Veil and Rockefeller (with its veritable abortion factories), pornography of Bénézareff, the pathogenic and criminogenic music of Gurgi-Lazarus, with his infantile singers, reign throughout the so-called, grotesquely democratic West.

This suicidal niagara of the planet is taking place IN THE NAME OF FREEDOM, and nobody is laughing: zombism reigns, comatose and apparently irreversible.

But a university professor does not have the right to express the results of soothing research (the reality of which should delight everyone) because the subject displeases the globalist circumcisocracy!! Freedom, curious freedom, only exists for bolshevist financiers, pill-popping abortionists, suicidal physicists, pornographers, food and therapeutic chemists and, in general, for all circumcised polluters and the goys who follow them...

6. **FREUDISM**, whose physiological and particularly endocrinological realities demonstrate its falsity and perversity, attacks the family, abolishes, pornographs, deflowers our most sacred feelings, respect for parents, mothers, children and their innocence.

Because Freud was never able to understand that normal man is not free of his famous "libido", but that it is tightly framed within a set of rules of conduct and thought that do not allow it to invade the noble spheres of existence: the family, the spirit of sacrifice and love that drives it, knowledge, thought...

7.   **MARXISM** is spreading like the tentacles of an octopus across the entire planet. Education is now a breeding ground for consumer-voters who are often ignorant, sometimes illiterate or illiterate, drug addicts, disco customers, delinquents and decerebrate dress-cutters...

Under the sweet mask of neutrality and tolerance, secularism has long since barricaded all routes to the Spiritual. I've seen this vertical fall in forty years of secondary and higher education. Secularism has handed children over to zombism, revolutionary fanaticism and atheism. This is non-militant, indifferent atheism, the true atheism of the australopithecus or the chimpanzee. Militant atheism is a fanatical religion, a negative participation in the Sacred. You don't deny what doesn't exist, you don't express anything. The true atheist expresses nothing: the concept of God is foreign to him. The atheist is a rebel against God. Unfortunately, at the level of his intelligence, he has good reasons to justify himself. There is no neutrality at the international de-education, which produces thugs of all kinds, from drug addicts to mop-up politicians, and the teachers distil Karl Marx's Holy Gospel and Freudian fantasies.

Even the films we show children, including cartoons, are nothing but examples and encouragements of violence. Television inculcates the superiority of the criminal adorned with all the virtues, the victim of society (it's true that it mass-produces them).

The frenetic, hysterical sounds of Michael Jackson and Madona, which promote vandalism and murder, are being fed to a suicidal, zombified youth with no ideals and no hope...

The incitement to debauchery is now the work of circumcised ministers themselves. Through the insidious use of AIDS and condoms. Even in secondary schools. YOUNG PEOPLE ARE NEVER TOLD THAT LOVE IS THE ONLY WAY TO PREVENT

S.I.D.A. AND THE FIDELITY OF THE COUPLE. They are never told that the total absence of sexual preoccupations before the age of eighteen is an absolute rule. If not respected, it will lead to neuro-endocrine imbalances, often a state of leguminous amorphousness, degeneration, abulia, and of course the EASE OF BEING SUGGESTED ESPECIALLY BY THE MEDIA. In short, physical and psychological disintegration.

That won't stop one of these naturally mathematically gifted degenerates from graduating from Polytechnique and becoming... one of our ministers, a slave to all the Maastrichts...

Homosexuality has become a virtue and we don't hesitate to inculcate the idea that those who weren't lucky enough to be born inverted (i.e. glandularly ill!) are guilty!

Littering of clothing is encouraged. Our schoolchildren look like bags of colourful potatoes, often becoming sort of tramps, with jeans with holes in the knees, and they are taught to be ignorant or ashamed of elegance...

Everywhere, education becomes an alibi for spreading the message of drugs, thuggery, pederasty, pornography and terrorism.

School textbooks complete this despicable work of destruction: political manichaeism, anti-French racial masochism, condemnation of historians who try to examine the realities of history more closely.

Especially, of course, if we're talking about THE SACRO-HOLY MYTH OF 6 MILLION GAS CHAMBERS! So 85% of drug addicts are young people aged between 16 and 25. It is interesting to note in passing that 80% of crimes are perpetrated by non-Europeans, a very high percentage of whom are Africans.

Not the abolition of the death penalty, but THE GENERALISED DEATH PENALTY FOR INNOCENTS AND POLICE OFFICERS.

And yet 65% of French people rejected it!

The majority of rapists and murderers of little girls and boys are repeat offenders. In the USA, the recidivism of released murderers is a huge issue. In ONE state that does not have the death penalty, 72 police officers were murdered by gangsters in a single year!

THIS IS WHAT IS KNOWN AS ABOLISHING THE DEATH PENALTY! The death penalty does not act as a deterrent", the thurifers of the sacred system of democracy foolishly tell us. That's not the problem: it's about purging society of particularly dangerous people. The concepts of revenge and justice have nothing to do with it: you can't let people live who could rape and murder your child at any moment!

And how can it be said that the death penalty is not a deterrent?

How could anyone hijack a plane carrying 200 passengers with a small gun if the death penalty was not a deterrent?

We rely on the specious alibi of statistics, "this official art of lying" as Marc Blancpain used to say. But since when have statistics forbidden us to think?

Hitler would never have tolerated the shadow of a single one of these horrors. What a freedom to ban Professor Faurisson and allow pornography, the murderers of old ladies, the rapists and murderers of little girls, the ignorant and regressive singers who make 70,000 Judeo-Cartesian zombies take their pants off...!!

Pseudo-Jewish totalitarianism will take on tentacular proportions: all the Western countries under circumcision will pass a law forbidding anyone to express the slightest doubt about the *6 million people gassed* in Auschwitz, on pain of imprisonment. Huxley's *Brave New World* and George Orwell's 1984 will be outdated!

Tremble too, the octogenarian Germans who tried to pull your country out of the rot of Weimar and Europe out of the abject Judeo-Cartesian degeneration in which, frozen, we are surviving at the end of the 20th century. Tomorrow, "Jewish" hysteria will seek you out in the depths of South America, in some remote village, to judge you with the loud blast of a media trumpet...

8. The drugs are spreading freely, AS TELEVISION HAS REVEALED TO US, even though they are "Jewish" in essence, and they benefit and are managed by High Finance, whose identity is clear to no one.

I was told in a lodge, when I was a naive Freemason, that a European drug supplier was untouchable because he had ministerial rank! Demoncrassie is a fine thing!

I was thinking of the time when a Marshal of France, a companion of Joan of Arc that he was, was publicly hanged and burned for paedophilia and the murder of children.

Strange democratic justice where everyone is equal, but where, as Coluche said, "Jews are more equal than others"...

Armand Hammer Jr. and his associates (who have been financing Bolshevism since 1917, along with Warburg, Sasoon, Loeb, etc.), who created the Communist Party in the USA and was never questioned during the Macarthy era, will never be hanged for this supreme crime which caused the death of tens of millions of people. THE GREAT CRIMINALS ARE NOT IN PRISONS BUT IN LIBERAL SOCIETY, said Carrel.

We sometimes seize a little heroin to make it look like we're doing something, but the very essence of this pseudo-democracy makes it impossible to pursue an effective policy to eradicate the kingpins of drugs and drug production.

They are even arranging for countries to make a living from it, so as to make the death process irreversible.

Yet all it would take is for two international or even national drug suppliers to be publicly hanged on the Place de la Concorde in the NAME OF HUMAN AND CITIZEN RIGHTS, and the matter would be settled.

Old ladies could then go shopping without risking their lives, and mothers would no longer be worried about their little girls or boys.

Louis XVI was beheaded on the Place de la Concorde, but a major drug dealer won't hang there! In this short sentence lies the symbol of the mystification of the world mass, leading to two and probably three world wars, widespread pollution of souls and bodies, unprecedented degeneration drowned in socialpornographic sauce.

9. Delinquency is on the increase. How could it be otherwise among young people with no spiritual or moral foundations, fed on hysterical sounds that lead to crime, drugs or suicide. In such conditions, the break-up of couples and the misery of children can only increase in geometric progression.

In New York, the most 'circumcised' city in the world, there are 600,000 REVERTED drug addicts. Which means that this figure can be doubled.

Suicide is the second biggest killer of children and teenagers, after the mechanical goddess, to whom thousands of young people are offered as holocausts every year...

POINTS OF DETAIL THAN THAT.

Who would dare to claim that Hitler HAD TOLERATED ANY OF THESE CRIMES???

IT IS THERE, AND NOWHERE ELSE, THAT THEY ARE TO BE FOUND. THE IMMENSE CRIMES OF LÈSE-HUMANITÉ AND NOT IN THE HYSTERICAL AND PARANOID SEARCH FOR PSEUDO WAR CRIMINALS WHO DID EVERYTHING TO PREVENT THEM!!

THESE CRIMES ARE ALL CAUSED BY THE LIBERAL-SOCIALIST, SOROS-MARXIST SYSTEM.

10. A writer, Yann Moncomble, publishes a book entitled LES RESPONSABLES DE LA TROISIRE Guerre MONDIALE.

Indicted by those he accused (we can only guess who), HE WAS RELEASED AT FIRST TRIAL AND ON APPEAL!

Which proves that there is still a vestige of justice, which will eventually be destroyed.

11. Chemical medicine, with its iatrogenic and teratogenic effects, reigns over the entire planet, with very real progress in surgery, which is used for the most appalling abominations (theft of children's organs from Third World countries, appalling trafficking in transplants, etc., trafficking and experiments on "unborn" children (see "Bébés au feu"-Apostolat des éditions, rue du Four 75006 Paris).

Biological degeneration becomes abominable to contemplate, like uncontrolled overpopulation, which led COUSTEAU to wisely say that 300,000 people would have to disappear every day to restore balance to the planet.

THE WORLD'S POPULATION IS GROWING QUANTITATIVELY BUT HAS DISAPPEARED QUALITATIVELY.

"The concepts of health and medicine are radically alien to each other", said Dr Henri Pradal, an expert at the World Health Organisation. He won 17 lawsuits against the chemical drug manufacturing trusts, most of which cover the therapeutic field.

You only have to look at the VIDAL to see the niagara of "side effects", which are often "more serious than the disease they claim to treat", as many doctors themselves have said in specialist medical journals. For example, synthetic oestrogens administered for a benign prostate tumour inflict a fatal cancer and, before death, a stomach ulcer... This is just one example among many.

12. Anti-racism, which CREATES SYSTEMIC RACISM, reigns. It consists of imposing the mixing of very different ethnic groups, which is a CRIME PHYSIOLOGICAL AND PSYCHOLOGICAL. This is done for the sole benefit of ZIONIST RACISM, which doesn't really care about massacring the Arabs it imposes in Europe, in Dir Yassim, in Sabra, in Chatilla, in the Gaza Strip, in the West Bank and elsewhere if it suits them.

We know that the majority of drug dealers in the Paris region are North African or black, not to mention their astonishing level of delinquency, rape and theft...

A homosexual mulatto with AIDS confesses to 21 murders of old women. A Negro rapes 32 young girls.

France is turning into Lebanon and many Communists are voting... Le Pen!

13. The mass media and television spread "anti-racist racism", always anti-national, Marxism, Freudism, porn, ugliness, violence, immorality, pathogenic music...

AND ALL THIS WITHOUT THE SLIGHTEST INTERVENTION FROM SO-CALLED DEMOCRATIC GOVERNMENTS!

14. Since 1945, WITHOUT ANY RESPONSIBILITY FROM THE NAZIS OR VICHY, 150 WARS HAVE BEEN Waged IN THE BOLKISH LIBERAL ORBITON!!

Everyone knows about these horrors: India, Korea, Hungary, Cuba, Congo, Iraq, Indochina, Algeria, Biafra, Eritrea, Lebanon, etc. In one night, the world circumcisocracy was able to mobilise all the nations to DEFEND THEIR OIL IN KUWAIT...

A few days earlier we let the Christians in Lebanon be massacred without lifting a finger!!

Nations are only mobilised for money and oil.

As I write these lines, the former Yugoslavia is on fire. The idyllic Europe of the Maastricht Treaty is incapable of stopping this terrible massacre: IT MUST BE SAID THAT THERE IS NO OIL OR JEWISH OVER THERE...

Let's say a few words about the sweetness of decolonisation.

Vietnam is a hell from which millions of people can only dream of fleeing at the risk of their lives. Laos has sunk into indescribable anarchy, Cambodia has experienced the cruellest of genocides, UNENTITLED TO THERE, and is undergoing the Vietnamese occupation, which makes us regret our colonialism.

In Africa, the colonists have disappeared, but the unfortunate blacks have been deprived of all their rights and have been handed over to massacres and famine, and "liberated" South Africa will tomorrow experience inter-ethnic massacres and famine. Has colonialism on this continent ever been more atrocious than that of the Soviets and the Cubans? In the past, we may have stolen the natural wealth of these poor negroes who were incapable of exploiting it, but we brought calm and general ease.

Now a clique of local politicians and capitalist thugs are exploiting these people for their own profit, making them forget their hunger by stirring up fratricidal hatred.

There is talk of 200,000 deaths in Rwanda... What is the situation in Algeria today?

We saw it in autumn 1988, and in the years that followed. It was supposed to be a happy place if we left it. But alas! Revolt reigns there, as in all decolonised countries. When Algeria tries to recover its tradition through democratic elections, the elections are cancelled very democratically. Democracy is a crypto-dictatorship with no values, and accepts only itself.

WE NEVER HAVE THE RIGHT TO DEMOCRATICALLY CHOOSE A REGIME OTHER THAN SO-CALLED DEMOCRACY. THAT SHOULD BE PERFECTLY CLEAR TO EVERYONE.

IN A DEMOCRACY ELECTIONS ARE CANCELLED FOR YOUR OWN GOOD; IN THE URSS YOU WERE EXECUTED FOR YOUR OWN GOOD.

(6 to 8 million at once, as in Ukraine, if necessary)...

In Algeria we betrayed a million Europeans and nine million Muslims. We gave up prosperous agriculture, modern cities, enviable facilities and billions of francs worth of gas and oil that we had discovered but failed to exploit.

Marxist misery now reigns in Algeria as it will tomorrow in New Caledonia, and it will be the victims themselves who will be the driving force behind their suicide.

THE WHOLE OF AFRICA IS DYING CAUGHT CAPITALIST SPECULATION AND MURDEROUS MARXISM.

THERE IS NO HOPE FOR THESE COUNTRIES IN THE CURRENT HAMMER-MARXIST SITUATION...

When you know the responsibility of those circumcised on the 8th day (and not of the Jews, who are guilty only of the major sin of keeping silent, apart from a few honest Jews who, like Professor Henri Baruk, never cease to claim that "Freud and Marx are not Jews"), liberals and Marxists in the world massacre I have just described, you can then take a balance and weigh the putrescent world magma on one side and the 6-million-rooms-to-gas, supposedly true, on the other.

YOU'LL SEE WHICH WAY THE MAXIMUM HORROR LEANS.

This synthesis of maximum horrors can hardly be conceptualised at the level of the average human brain.

That's why all you have to do to convince the zombified masses is show them the film "Nuit et Brouillard" and all the other substitutes that periodically spring up, hammered and hypnotic.

Yet in these films, we don't see anyone gassed, nor any plausible gassing device, but prisoners who died of hunger, misery and typhus because, as I said, it was impossible to supply the camps as the ^{Third} Reich collapsed.

But the viewer, the unfortunate television viewer, WITHOUT REALIZING THAT ONLY JEWISH CAPITAL IS INVOLVED IN THESE OUTRECUDIANT PROPAGANDA FILMS, reacts like a dog that has been given a meatball to digest an arsenic tablet. I repeat that everyone is unaware, and one wonders why and how, that the same visions of horror were present in all the major German cities reduced to ashes by the Allies.

The dreadful synthesis set out in this book WOULD HAVE BEEN IMPOSSIBLE UNDER THE THIRD REICH, BECAUSE IT IS THE RADICAL AND ABSOLUTE ANTITHESIS OF THE THIRD REICH.

You only have to read MEIN KAMPF in the light of current events over the last half-century to be perfectly convinced.

This is no doubt why this book is so democratically banned.

Hitler's precise aim was to PREVENT all those who would carry out these deadly horrors and kill mankind and the planet.

WE BEGIN TO UNDERSTAND WHY HEIDEGGER WAS SILENT.

He had already begun to shut up in 1936. The advent of Hitler gave him back hope. Hope crushed, HE HAD TO BE SILENT.

As early as 1936, Heidegger foresaw the "ultimate bewitchment" of modernity in the "gigantic" of a "planning and calculating thought", oblivious to Being, which unfolds through technology, science and the modern economy, asserting its will to power based on the Cartesian concept of subjectivity which "centres knowledge on human reason considered as a universal and systematic measuring instrument. The rational animal becomes technicised, "the cancerous expansion of man and the machine economy" desertifies the planet, engenders massification, uprooting, boredom and monotony, and the Subject becomes the Object of its domination, seeking to overcome its anguish, to fill its inner void, through "lived experiences", in the cultural affair of the pursuit of speed, performance and all forms of DRUGS.

Including drugs themselves...

Let's summarise for a better understanding and repeat if necessary.

One wonders how human beings could have allowed themselves to be carried away to such a degree of stupidity.

IT'S ALL AS BRIGHT AS THE SUN. IT'S ALL PLAIN TO SEE.

All the evidence is there in front of us. A week in the press, on television, looking around, can convince even a fool.

Are humans now sub-imbeciles, barnyard animals? It's true that when you see that abject films such as LES VALSEUSES or ORANGE MÉCANIQUE can be successful with the masses, you think EVERYTHING IS LOST. Neither under Hitler, nor under Marshal Pétain ("I want to free the French from the most shameful guardianship, that of finance") would we have known the TOTAL SLAVERY OF MONEY, the arms sales to everything that exterminates itself, the growing unemployment which is increasing geometrically and which WILL NEVER STOP GROWING BECAUSE IT IS THE PRODUCT OF THE SYSTEM, the systematic chemisation of food and medicine, which affects man at the chromosomal level, young people who take drugs and kill themselves by the thousands, self-service abortion, the pathogenic and teratogenic pill (Pr Jamain), the trafficking in babies deemed to be unborn, used for vivisection and laboratory experiments, and discarded at 7 months "when they start to walk" in incinerators...

Not only is the pill pathogenic in general, it also causes ovarian blockages, stunted growth, sterility, frigidity and, of course, an exponential increase in venereal diseases, currently leading to AIDS, and other viral diseases which will kill without appeal, the disintegrating Freudian abulism, pornographism and navel-gazing, the Kahn-Nathan sexual encyclopaedia (assisted by a dozen circumcised people: Lwoff, Simon, Berge, etc.), terrorists who symbolically kill the Italian head of state, the head of German industry, the former viceroy of India, the Marxist hold that exterminates people for their own good, the mass production by secularism of physico-chemical amalgams who tomorrow will vote for singing gulags or any other imposture, under the pretext of 'change' preached by stupid politicians, a volcanic rise of demented, delinquent, homosexual, asexual, drugged by chemification, vitamin deficiencies, de-education, masturbation encouraged by TORDJMANN (whereas we know that schizophrenics are all masturbators and that masturbation irreversibly stupefies, which does not prevent some species from becoming polytechnicians), pregnant fifth form girls (6800 aged between 13 and 17 in 1978 alone), an 11 year old boy who raped and killed a little girl, and how many other similar cases which increase with the passing of time!

Exceptional cases? That is not the reality. They are symptoms of a global state: the lamentable state of the Judeo-Cartesian West.

Let us add that the famous contaminated blood affair would have been impossible under Nazism. (If it had happened, the world circumcisocracy would still be talking about it in 3,000 years' time!)

Firstly, because Hitler would have punished those responsible with the utmost rigour. Secondly, because the cleanliness of the regime would have prevented it from germinating. UNDER HITLER, TERRORISM AND THE PORNOGRAPHY OF SOCIETY THROUGH THE PILL AND CONDOMS WOULD NEVER HAVE BEEN POSSIBLE: HE HAD TOO GREAT A SENSE OF THE BEAUTY AND PURITY OF HIS YOUTH TO DEGRADE IT IN THIS WAY. Only those who are circumcised on the 8th day and the moronic Goys who follow them could implement such consummate immorality.

ALL THIS IS THE VERY EXPRESSION OF LIBERAL-BOLSHEVISM.

The 'quantitative' masses are going to sink into their household refuse, nuclear power, the psychological amalgam of the sexes and the death of motherhood (Gurgi-Eliachev, known as Françoise Giroud and Élisabeth Badinter), porn, media hypnosis, with its ocean of lies and permanent conditioning, all the 'HOLOCAUST' films, even all this destruction springs from Judeo-Cartesianism.

No more judgement, no more culture, a political and university system that can only recruit zombies because it is based on the farce of universal suffrage and mnemonics...

Alas, these unfortunate zombified peoples can no longer even understand what is destroying them, being totally deprived of the ability to synthesise. They will die of their S.I.D.A., on household rubbish, injecting themselves with chemicals or taking drugs, shouting "long live democracy"...

The national economy will be liquidated, all countries placed under the rule of high finance, which has wiped out small businesses, craftsmen and farmers...

OF COURSE, NONE OF THIS IS PART OF THE MEIN KAMPF PROGRAMME.

During your programme "Océaniques", a participant said: "to speak of spirituality within Nazism is of a rare unconsciousness".

I would say to the naive person who uttered this nonsense that he is of Mamouthesque unconsciousness if he does not find in this regime where cleanliness, family, honour, work and ideals were restored THE FUNDAMENTAL PREMISES OF A TRUE SPIRITUALITY TOTALLY ISOLATED FROM ALL THE MATERIALIST CONCEPTS WHICH HAVE ALREADY EXTERMINATED US.

No spirituality can germinate within the putrescent magma of liberal-socialist materialism, whose aberrant and suicidal synthesis I have just outlined.

Hitler knew that the GREAT DOGMATICS lay in respect for nature and not in cultish dogmas. He didn't eat meat because he knew that you don't talk to God with a mouth full of blood...

The Church itself has lost all lucidity, all moral sense. Canon Law, which is purely formal, is as suicidal as Public Law, and its pie-in-the-sky references to Human Rights, which are constantly trampled underfoot for everyone EXCEPT CIRCONCISES ON DAY 8, SERIOUSLY SHOWS THE STATE OF CARICATURAL FAILURE IN WHICH IT IS SURVIVING ITSELF...

WHO WAS HITLER?

If you ask anyone this question, whatever their social level, or what we call by semantic inflation their cultural level of official education, you will find that they have NEVER read "Mein Kampf", and a fortiori that they have never confronted its text with the current events of the last sixty years of the twentieth century.

What's more, you'll find that, just like a slot machine, it will give you exactly the same results as anyone else, and more often than not in THE SAME TERMS.

We are stunned to note that the effect of conditioning by publishing, the media and education IS OF UNUSUAL SUBLIMINAL EFFECT ON EVERYONE. This is a flagrant example of the total eradication of ALL FREEDOM.

IN FACT NOBODY KNOWS WHO HITLER IS.

We know that in 1917, the circumcised American bankers Warburg simultaneously financed the Allies, the Germans and the Bolshevik Revolution. They then arrived in Europe in 1919 as peace negotiators.

All the circumcised bankers Warburg, Schiff, Loeb, Sasoon and others financed the circumcised political teams that brought about the Bolshevik revolution. This process of financing, with capital and turnkey factories, has continued uninterrupted right up to the present day (see the articles in Le Point and L'Express on "LE MILLIARDAIRE ROUGE HAMMER"). We have also mentioned that under Stalinism, 50 Jewish prison and concentration camp executioners exterminated tens of millions of Goys, as Solzhenitsyn testifies in Volume II of *The Gulag Archipelago*.

In 1918, Germany was strangled by the TREATY OF VERSAILLES: it was from "this project of plunder", as the British minister Lloyd George put it, that HITLER's ABSOLUTELY SINCERE AND DISINTERESTED vocation emerged.

I am reminded of a very significant anecdote, told to me by one of my uncles, a Jewish doctor.

Before Hitler was imprisoned in Nuremberg, where he wrote *Mein Kampf*, during his trial a judge asked him: "What do you want, Mr Hitler, a ministerial post? To which Hitler replied: "I WOULD BE VERY MISPRISABLE, MR JUDGE, IF I WERE ONLY TO WANT A MINISTERIAL POSITION"...

He wanted to free his country and the world from the dictatorship of the dollar, which all the MAASTRICHTs have enslaved us to this day. He did NOT want Europe to be reduced to servitude, crumbling under the burden of monstrous debts. He did NOT want this dictatorship to destroy the national agricultures that are the fundamental wealth of these countries. Hitler was defeated by the circumcised Rothschildo-Marxist power which had openly declared war on him SINCE 1933 AS THE U.S. PRESS WITNESSES WITHOUT CONTEST.

In fact, since 1933, the American press has been reporting that the "Jews" were at war with Hitler, whose SELFISH system (the only valid system for any country that must always be able to live on what it produces itself. Moreover, only food that has grown in the place where an ethnic group lives has any physiological value, a guarantee of health, for that ethnic group. Another law of nature that Hitler understood perfectly well) was a nightmare for them. One well-known book even advocated the genocide of the Germans, to which Lech Walesa recently made a potential allusion, in the silence of the INTERNATIONAL HIGH CONSCIOUSNESS...

(If he had talked about the possibility of massacring the "evil" Jews instead of the "evil" Germans, we would have heard the so-called

INTERNATIONAL HIGH CONSCIOUSNESS screaming from the North Pole to the South Pole...

But not a word from BERNARD HENRY LEVY, that champion of humanity...

Who is familiar with this book? References to it can be found in the works of Faurisson and the Annales révisionnistes in particular.

We have already mentioned the fact that during the occupation of Europe in 1945, the Russians and Americans made rape and massacre an institution in German communities. We know that German troops made it an absolute rule not to rape in enemy territory, on pain of being shot on the spot, whether you were a soldier or an officer.

WAR WAS DECLARED ON HITLER BECAUSE HE WANTED TO ESTABLISH A NEW EUROPEAN ORDER FROM WHICH CIRCUMCISED PARASITIC SPECULATION WOULD BE RADICALLY BANNED.

The only value would be WORK, not MONEY.

THIS WAS THE ONLY REAL CAUSE OF THE 1939 WAR.

Officially, war was declared on him because he wanted Danzig, a German territory, Posnania, a German territory in Poland where Germans were mistreated and even murdered, and Austria, which wanted to be attached to the Reich and never hid the fact...

Germany no longer had any colonial empire, while the USA had long since imposed its world hegemony and England had a colonial empire "on which the sun never set", and the lands of German language and ethnicity were integrated into foreign countries. This was the case with the Sudetenland in Czechoslovakia, whose Masonic government was a real thorn in the side of the Third Reich. This was his crime, as analysed by any honest man, even a Jew. But when Stalin was in Eastern Poland and executed ALL THE POLISH OFFICERS with a

GERMAN (!) bullet in the back of the neck or ships purposely sunk in the Antarctic, the ticklish international conscience, THAT PRODIGIOUS BITCH, whom I have only ever seen whining about my fellow creatures, was snoring, probably so as not to hear the sound of the bullets.

I have NEVER seen a single president of the Ligue des Droits de l'Homme (Human Rights League) repeatedly speak out against this crime of lèse-humanité (and so many others over the last 50 years!), which does not allow the sacrosanct myth of *6-million-rooms-to-gas* to be challenged!

Moreover, the arithmetic of Human Rights is simple: 60 MILLION (UNCHallenged) EXTERMINALS BY KAGANOVITCH AND CONSORTS (JEWS) ARE LESS THAN 6 MILLION (CHallenged) JEWS BY HITLER.

This Ubuesque premise sums up the paranoid hysteria of the last 50 years in every field.

Henri Bergson, the "Jewish" philosopher, admonished the German Jews in 1921.

He told them that their numbers were out of proportion, that their amoral and asyncratic power was dangerous for them and that if they did not change their behaviour, they would unleash a terrible wave of anti-Semitism...

This was twelve years before the advent of Nazism.

Professor Baruk, the Jewish psychiatrist, often told me that "Hitler was God's instrument for punishing the Jews who were no longer Jews". How many times has he said to me: "FREUD AND MARX ARE NOT JEWS".

He rightly considered them to be extra-dimensional monsters, seriously mentally ill.

I'll always remember the Germans presenting arms to Henri Bergson, the 'Jewish' philosopher during the Occupation.

The Germans knew how to recognise values, even in Jews, and I have no doubt that my spirit of synthesis has earned me the title of honorary Aryan...!

UNDER THE WEIMAR REPUBLIC EVERYTHING WAS ROTTEN AND THE CIRCONCIS ON THE 8th DAY MANIPULATED EVERYTHING.

THAT'S A FACT.

TODAY, THE PHENOMENON IS IDENTICAL, BUT INFINITELY MORE SERIOUS, BECAUSE THE WEIMAR REPUBLIC IS THE SIZE OF THE PLANET.

I can't imagine that Louis Rougier, Gustave Thibon or myself would have been invited to this Océaniques programme. Even Maurice Bardèche would not have been invited, and yet there was no risk: he would have been crushed by the Pléven and Marchandeau laws, now consolidated by the totally dictatorial, radically RACIST and anti-democratic Fabius-Gayssot law.

This law also contains a serious VICE OF FORM (see letter to the President of the Senate, opposite). The Nuremberg Tribunal was never INTERNATIONAL but INTERALLIED, which is fundamentally different. A court of victors judging the vanquished!!! What can be the objective and moral value of such a tribunal?

Personally, I don't care about these laws: as far as I know, there is still no law that forbids a Jew or a Patagonian from saying what they think about their own people when faced with the staggering reality of FACTS.

So there were 6 million unemployed people in Germany, to whom Hitler gave bread, ideals and dignity.

When you see the horrible biotypological, bluejeanous degeneration in France, in the USA (in May 1994, an American woman writer "uttered this expostulation: 'do you know an American who has an orgasm?) in Italy, Germany, England and Spain, it's heartbreaking to see that the ONE person who almost succeeded in rooting out the rot in his country is being called a CRIMINAL, PROSECUTED 50 YEARS LATER IN THE PERSON OF THE OCTOGENARIANS WHO SERVED HIM, WHILE THOSE WHO REDUCED MANKIND TO THE STATE OF ATROCIOUS HOMUNCULI THROUGH A FUNDAMENTAL IGNORANCE OF THE LAWS OF NATURE AND OF ALL REALITIES, ARE PULLING ALL THE STRINGS IN FINANCE, GOVERNMENT, JUSTICE AND THE MEDIA...

This phrase from Nietzsche comes to mind:

"The history of Israel is invaluable and typical as far as the distortion of natural values is concerned. The Jews have a vital interest in making humanity sick, in turning the notion of good and evil, of truth and lies, on its head in a dangerous and slanderous way...".

The press, television, the media, teaching and publishing in their hands provide us every day with Niagara of examples of what Nietzsche tells us, as does Dostoyevsky. ("In a hundred years there will be nothing left but the Jewish bank and the desert")...

George Steiner, who was present at this ocean show, goes even further. That's why I find it hard to understand his solidarity with this programme. In his book "The Transport of A.H." (Adolphe Hitler) Steiner is absolutely lucid. Chapter XVII is a supreme summary of the Jewish tragedy and somewhere in the book we come across this dazzling formula:

"FOR 5000 YEARS WE HAVE BEEN TALKING TOO MUCH, WORDS OF DEATH FOR OURSELVES AND FOR OTHERS...".

***

In Germany, there was a parliament elected by the nation.

Referenda proved that millions of Germans were on Hitler's side. The 6 million unemployed regained their true freedom and human dignity happy work.

Before 1940, European workers NEVER had better living conditions (ask Germans of that generation, my generation) than those of the Third Reich: decent housing (not people's rubbish bins in council estates), outstanding libraries, ultra-modern health and safety facilities.

At the same time, millions of French and Belgian workers were rotting their lungs in industrial sheds and sheltering their families in insalubrious housing, if not slums. The factories of the Third Reich had their rest gardens, their swimming pools, their staff freed from the tyranny of politicians and trade unions. They had more social security and paid holidays than anywhere else.

THE GERMAN FAMILY BECAME A UNIT OF SOCIETY.

It is totally broken in the so-called "democratic" world at the end of this century. Women had the right to look after their homes and children. No drugs, no immoral secular Marxist education, no condoms, no S.I.D.A., no Madona, no Michael Jackson, no trashy clothes, no LEVIS blue jeans...

No stupid marriages, no stupid divorces, no children torn apart by pain, unemployment, drugs and suicide.

Today Professor Heuyer told us that all the children brought before the courts were the offspring of separated couples, either through divorce or the mother's intensive work outside the home.

Anyone can see this for themselves, even those who are not financially deprived.

THE CHILDREN WERE THEREFORE ENTIRELY SAVED FROM THE AByss of degeneracy into which they are plunging: drugs, pornography, terrorism, suicide, alcohol, unemployment and epistemology, in which they are incarcerated by the freedom of the human rights of the globalist circumcisionocracy.

I don't say "Judeocracy" because I can't repeat it often enough, all the ROTHSCHILDO-MARXO-FREUDO-EINSTEINO-PICASSIST speculation IS HERETIC AND CRIMINAL BEFORE THE THORA. I only reproach real Jews for NOT HURLING IT.

In Nazi Germany, being the mother of many children was an honour, not a painful burden. They often rape and steal and sell drugs around schools, while our teenage girls have abortions and take pills that are pathogenic in general and carcinogenic and teratogenic in particular.

The German birth rate reached 1,800,000, while the French birth rate was 600,000. Hitler designed the Volkswagen Beetle, which became the most popular car in Europe. We still see it everywhere today, and it even became the star of American films!

The worker felt respected and the 6 million German communists became supporters of the Führer. The social and moral reform that Hitler achieved in just a few years by freeing his people from all the liberal-Bolshevik conditioning is staggering.

Anyone of good faith who has studied the problem will agree with me. Only the deliberate denial of the truth, only the conditioning of minds incapable of probity, can fail to recognise this obvious fact.

To understand fully, you need to study what Hitler wanted to do and what he did against all the odds. You need to have read MEIN KAMPF, which today leaves you stunned as to its lucidity in the face of national and international realities. You also need to have read Rosenberg's MYTH OF THE XXTH CENTURY, to see the global putrescence of the 50 years that followed the war...

This brings to mind the words of Hitler's minister, who committed suicide with his wife and children: "We must not allow our children to live in the horrible world that the Jews will prepare for them from now on"...

Without this knowledge, NO DIALOGUE about Nazism is possible.

To this elementary synthesis of information, which nothing but probity prepared me to receive, must be added the essentials of the work of revisionist historians. What is revealing about these works is not even the works themselves, BUT THE INCREDIBLE HYSTERIA WHICH THE SIMPLE NEGATION OF THE GAS CHAMBERS AND THE BOURSOUFLYED FIGURE OF 6 MILLION DISCLOSES. BAD FAITH, HYSTERIA AND A CATEGORICAL REFUSAL TO TALK ARE FAR MORE CONVINCING THAN THE TECHNICAL AND ARITHMETICAL FACTS, WHICH LEAVE NO ROOM FOR DOUBT.

Since Hitler's essentials are unique in the history of a recovery (as the President of the Bundestag, Jenninger, who paid for them by offering his post immediately to a Jewess, has expressed), and since all the parameters of the circumcisionocracy of these 50 years demonstrate that Hitler was right in everything that is essential, it remains for the media and publishers in the circumcisionist boot to accuse Hitler of Satanism and to trombone the pseudo-Holocaust in the most diverse and overbearing forms. If only the "Jews" would do the same for the 60 million Russians exterminated by Frenkel, Yagoda, Firine, Jejoff and the fifty or so "Jews" in the Soviet prison and concentration camp system, there would be a balance and we could put up with these obscene "monumental", televisual, cinematographic, "celebratory" etc. clamourings?

But this is not the case.

In the flood of the first accusation, in a rationalist context, nothing can be demonstrated. As for the second, the force of the clamour acts hypnotically and subliminally, and the conditioning of the masses is perfect...

But it's starting to crack badly...

For the time being, Hitler will be to the man of the masses, including academics and politicians, what pork is to the Muslim.

I remember that before the war, in Germany, you could leave your bicycle against a wall, without a lock, and pick it up again in the evening: you'd find it intact. Nowadays, people try to leave their cars even locked in certain towns, in Italy for example, but also elsewhere, and we'll see what happens!

***

The Pope condemned Nazism in the encyclical MIT BRENNENDER SORGE. What are the charges for this condemnation?

The proud apostasy of Jesus Christ, the denial of his doctrine and his redemptive work, the worship of strength, the idolatry of race and blood, the oppression of freedom and human dignity.

What is the reality of these accusations BEFORE THE FACTS?

Admittedly, Hitler did not believe in the doctrine of Christ, which always seemed to him to be an aborted and perverted Platonism. Eternal morality seemed to him to have been distorted by the doctrine of the Gospel, which would distort the notion of charity and honour, handing men over to atheistic Jewish speculation, to the pampering of morons, to the nipping in the bud of genuine geniuses (minds of synthesis and moral sense).

Redemption seemed to him the most absurd of beliefs, especially as man has never been so wicked and regressive as he has been for 2000 years. How could the fact that the wicked had committed the worst of crimes, that is, CRUCIFYING GOD, redeem them???

In the name of Christ, the worst exterminations were committed that Paganism had ignored, just as it totally ignored the racist notion bequeathed to us precisely by the Jews, who belong to no ethnic group and even less to no race, since these do not exist, as endocrinology has demonstrated to me without appeal.

Hitler worshipped moral and spiritual strength, not brute force, which he abhorred. His notion of strength was of a spiritual nature, and it was not he who said, referring to the Vatican, "how many divisions", it was Stalin!

He wanted to EXACERBER the concept of ethnic protection of the white "race" (this word can be used for the 4 different skin colours but must not have any other meaning). It's easy to see why this is the case today, when miscegenation is institutionalised. It is this miscegenation that will give rise to the most appalling forms of racism, created by pseudo-antiracists.

His racialism was a defensive reflex against the prodigious Jewish racism that has relentlessly invested us for 5000 years and is now forcing on us the mass immigration of Muslims, Blacks, Asians etc.

As for freedom and dignity, he gave them back to an entire people that was grateful to him. The documentaries of the time show the clear vision of young Germans who have rediscovered their ideals, their dignity and their purpose.

Look at our unisex, lousy, frizzy, collapsed, disco, drug-addled bluejeaners, YOU CAN'T SEE THE DIFFERENCE????

IN REALITY, EVERYTHING IN THE ENCYCLICAL MIT BRENNENDER SORGE RELATES PERFECTLY TO BOLSHEVISM AND NOT TO NAZISM. HITLER SAID: "IT WAS THE CHURCH AND THE PRINCES WHO HANDED THE PEOPLE OVER TO THE JEWS".

He was not an atheist like the Bolshevik leaders and ideologues.

What a lot of detail!

Pius XII was perfectly aware of all this when he said: "Only Germany and the Vatican can save civilisation, the former militarily, the latter spiritually". And later: "Germany fights for its friends AND FOR ITS ENEMIES, because if the Eastern Front collapses, the fate of the world is sealed".

It collapsed and look what a Liberal-Marxist cesspool we are in... As for the Church, it did not survive Pius XII and collapsed in 1945.

It burst like a rotten apple. NOT A WORD to save from the firing squad the last Knights of Europe who had joined the L.V.F. and the Marshal's Militia to fight against Bolshevism and preserve essential human values. From now on, this phantom of the Church will take up the mantle of politicians and drape Israel in the mantle of innocence.

The Pope will be kissing the gums of the Chief Rabbi while Rothschildo-Marxo-Freudo-Einsteino-Picassism finishes exterminating all Christian values, with the Vatican's blessing...

Only a mentally retarded person would claim that Hitler was not essentially right. It is true that JUDÉOCARTÉSIANISM HAS MANUFACTURED A WORLD OF DEFECTS...

The Nazis in no way dishonoured humanity. I'M SURE THAT ANYONE OF GOOD FAITH WHO IS AWARE OF THE WORLDWIDE ACTIVITIES OF THE "JEWS", PARTICULARLY SINCE THE FRENCH REVOLUTION, WILL AGREE WITH ME.

Those who lie about Hitler, relying on the mental inadequacy of the great majority of human beings - that diabolical keyboard on which the "Jews" play as astounding virtuosos - are dishonourable.

They are the cause of millions of deaths, degeneration and collapses.

The current death of French farmers, and American farmers for that matter, is directly linked to Judeo-U.S. policy.

What's more, they have to rehash their endless, disgusting auschwitzian jeremiads through the media in order to continue extorting huge sums from the FRG, sums that the country has never paid, by establishing their hegemony on the dogma of institutionalised miscegenation, with their omnipresent anti-racist whining, WHICH DOESN'T HIDE THEIR MEGALOMANIAQUE RACISM.

No doubt thousands of Jews died in the camps (70% were Germans in Dachau) and between Poland and Russia, exterminated by the German army and the UKRAINIANS.

We're not told how many times the Germans on their march against Russia were welcomed as liberators!

As for the *6-million-gas-chambers*, cyclone B, it will remain the most fantastic historical lie in history.

Let's add that if these "6 million" were true, they would only be a "small point" compared to the extra-dimensional crimes of lèse-humanité that I have just briefly outlined.

These crimes will reach their peak: multiform global pollution, civil wars, multiple wars, inter-ethnic massacres, exponential unemployment, not excluding a 3rd world war that situations like the one in ex-Yugoslavia could generate.

POINT OF DETAIL, CERTAINLY

TRUE democracy would be an agreement, a perfect symbiosis between the leaders and the nation.

AS THE FACTS PROVE, Nazism was a true democracy in this respect. Hitler was elected in a perfectly legal and constitutional manner.

Did such a situation exist in 1984 and the years that followed? ALL socio-professional categories were on the streets.

Farmers, teachers, air traffic controllers, nurses, students, etc.

Apart from the financiers and the politicians whose pockets they line by mystifying the ballot paper, no one is satisfied.

And let's not even mention the essential majority of young people: they are as content as can be: unemployment, drugs, suicide, all bathed in the frenetic rhythms of stupid, regressive, pathogenic and criminogenic "music"...

LONG LIVE DEMOCRACY!

If Heidegger remained silent, it was because he knew that in the suicidal path humanity was embarking on, THERE WAS NOTHING MORE TO SAY.

Nor was he unaware of the ARITHMETICO TECHNICAL INEPTIA of the *6-million-gas-chambers.*

He knew that SCIENCE DOES NOT THINK and, as I added, that "FINANCE DOES NOT THINK either"...

Without a true spiritual elite, finance becomes an instrument of death for humanity as a whole.

He knew that Nazism had been mankind's last chance, the ultimate effort to resurrect a traditional society in accordance with the order of nature, but that the brains rotted by Judeo-Cartesianism would understand nothing despite the obvious... In the worldwide agony that would follow 1945, Brazillach would be shot and the 'Jews' would refuse to understand.

But didn't Hitler say:

"The aim of international Jewish finance is to dissolve national economies and bring them under its hegemony, and then, through pseudo-democracies, to push all countries towards Marxism".

And again:

"If the Jews, with their Marxist profession of faith, take over the reins of humanity, there will soon be no human beings left on the planet, which will resume its course through the ether as it did millions of years ago"...

As I approach my conclusion on all these 'loose ends' that perpetrate the 'circumcised' extermination of humanity as a whole, it is mind-boggling to note the despicable and radically anti-democratic way in which Professor Faurisson and all those who, perfectly well-founded arguments, seek to revise an imposed truth that in no way corresponds to the truth, are treated.

What the hell! If the Revisionists are lying, let's contradict them on concrete problems that are strictly a matter of arithmetic, physics and chemistry!

But it's their BEHAVIOUR that proves they're right, and it's above all their PSYCHOLOGY that's typical: if THEY WERE WRONG WE WOULD NOT BE ATTENDING THE INCREDIBLE CIRCUS BEHIND US WITH THE ATTEMPTED ASSASSINATION OF PROFESSOR FAURISSON!!!! (and systematic persecution of all Revisionists...)

Once again, we must remember that Professor Faurisson wants as large an audience as possible and an unlimited number of opponents!

They're being refused! So who's right and who's wrong? Haven't we already been convinced of the beginnings of this problem?

It reminds me of a boy who punched one of his friends: "Why did you hit him? "He was beginning to be right!"

The trouble with Faurisson is that he immediately began to think he was right! Unforgivable!

The New World Order is in fact the NEW WORLD CHAOS, totally divorced from all reality. But isn't the main thing to keep up the propaganda with films presented as documents when in fact they are nothing but fiction (Spielberg and co. have been proliferating since 1988, the date of the "Oceanique" programme which gave rise to this book).

Nature is Nazi and CERTAINLY NOT LIBERAL OR SOCIALIST. WE ARE BEGINNING TO SEE THAT IT NEVER FORGIVES.

Who are the criminals? The Nazis who put their enemies in camps where many died of misery and typhus, or the Jews who invented 6 million IMPOSSIBLE, and TECHNICALLY INCEPTED gas chambers????

Let it be known that when, in 1950, numerous communist figures denied the existence of the SOVIET GULAGS and their tens of millions of victims, THEY WERE NOT TRIED IN JUSTICE!!

But in 1988, when I started this book, GULAGS AND PSYCHIATRIC HOSPITALS STILL EXIST!

I don't hear historians or moralists from the INTERNATIONAL HIGH CONSCIOUSNESS shouting on television and in the press on a daily basis about a regime that has been dead for 50 years!

But the old survivors of this regime, who had the misfortune to understand the evil of our fellow creatures, and had an ideal that Hitler had realised to the full in a minimum of time - see the testimony of the great Lindbergh - are hunted down relentlessly, without honour...

But it gets worse: Monsieur Marchais tells us that "COMMUNISM IS GENERALLY POSITIVE"...

This would have been true of Nazism had it not been crushed by the Judeo-Anglican war machine. There was INCONTESTABLY in Nazism a return TO THE LAWS OF NATURE.

In this case, this sentence by MARCHAIS IS UNLIKELY BELIEVED BY EVERYONE, INCLUDING HISTORIANS AS OFFICIAL AS MADAME CARERRE D'ENCAUSSE, WHO SAID ON BERNARD PIVOT'S "APOSTROPHES" PROGRAM:

"EVEN IF COMMUNISM HAD SUCCEEDED, WHICH IT DIDN'T, IT WOULDN'T HAVE JUSTIFIED SO MANY TENS OF MILLIONS OF CORPSES"...

Everyone knows that Ukraine has seen its inhabitants massacred to the tune of 6 to 8 million and that this country was the granary of the world in the days of the Tsars. Under communism, IT CANNOT EVEN PRODUCE ENOUGH WHEAT FOR ITS CONSUMPTION.

It is also clear that Mr Marchais, like Mr Le Pen, considers these to be "points of detail":

THE STALINIST PURGES

THE TENS OF MILLIONS OF VICTIMS OF BERIA, KAGANOVICH, FRENKEL, YAGODA AND 50 OTHER CIRCUMCISERS

BUDAPEST PRAGUE LE K.G.B

THE BOAT PEOPLE AFGHANISTAN

Unfortunately, this is not exhaustive, and we'll come back to that later. POINTS OF DETAIL.

***

As a Jew, I legitimately have the right to attack my own people, given that their suicidal dynamic is predominant and that we cannot, if we are conscious, ALLOW THE PLANET AND MAN TO DISAPPEAR.

I wrote somewhere that "there was no Jewish question, BUT ABOVE ALL A QUESTION OF GOY SOTTISE"...

I'm always amazed, for example, at the most basic aesthetic level, to see how easily, how delightfully, the Goys wear that hideous uniform of international bullshit, the LEVIS bluejeans. To tell the truth, if we're not in a theocratic regime where the leaders are spiritually-minded synthesists, WHY SHOULD JEWS AVOID SELLING SHIT TO THOSE WHO ASK?

The problem is the same for those who produce socialism and pornography or synthetic chemistry ingested by organisms from the earth up to teratogenic therapeutics...

He's a Goy who should do for his people what I do for mine.

He will tell us how the Goys provide their share of the disastrous Jewish activity. Without the complicit collaboration of the Goys, how could the Jews do what they do?

THE GOYS PASSIVELY ACCEPT THE FATAL CONSEQUENCES OF JEWISH INFLUENCE, and we will come back to this.

There is, of course, and I've talked about this, the mental inadequacy of the unconscious followers I've met by the hundred in Masonic lodges.

There are the Germans, for example, some congenitally naive, others consciously complicit, which makes them MORE EXECUTIVE THAN MY CONGENERATES. Just look at the establishment of the

R.F.A., headed by its president, who devote themselves with fanatical zeal to perpetuating the spiritual and moral servitude of their people.

The statement made by Jenninger, President of the Bundestag, is undoubtedly a real miracle, and also a heroic one.

Behold again, in all its GROTESQUERIE, the circus of the American elections, where the 2 candidates, hand-picked by the financial world for their insignificance, have nothing to do but attest to their unconditional subservience to the Zionist cause, which will subsidise at least 60% of their election, and vie with each other in servitude, the better to win the election!

This world of perverts and morons in distress is truly painful to contemplate...

I will conclude by saying that this Jewish tragedy, which comes at the end of a traditional cycle, the Dark Ages, gives the Jews a speculative, analytical, involutive, atheistic superiority, which is the exclusive result of the psycho-hormonal consequences of the 8th day, 1st day of the 21 days of the first puberty.

Doctors are hardly aware of this, as they have not yet understood THE FUNCTIONAL PREFERENCE OF THE HORMONAL SYSTEM ON THE NERVOUS SYSTEM AND THE BEING IN GENERAL.

I don't expect these obvious facts to be accepted until we are all gone. If they were, EVERYTHING I HAVE JUST WRITTEN WOULD BE VOID.

We live in an age of reversals. Justice serves crime. I've just learned that fraud is now protected by law. If someone sells you something and you realise it's been stolen, if you didn't ask for an invoice in good faith, you can't stop payment on the cheque or lodge a complaint. Your complaint, which could at least prevent the perpetuation of this practice by prosecuting this type of thief, is no longer admissible. It was only a few years ago. There is no limit to the descent into degeneracy.

But I had to respond to this programme, and in particular to the naive conclusion of Glucksman, whose intellectual probity will never exceed that permitted by the effects of circumcision on the 8th day, which establish what some call, not without reason, "the curse of Israel", which has become infrangible and irrefragable since Moses consolidated this misunderstood sexual mutilation, whose psychohormonal effect is clear to those who have perceived the scientific reality of the anteriority of the hormonal system over the nervous system.

The panorama of history and current events offers us a hymalaya of laboratory evidence and proof by nine.

I want to distinguish myself from my fellow human beings, of whom SIMONE WEIL said, not without reason:

THEY NEVER HAVE THAT MODEST ATTENTION THAT IS PROPER TO TRUE INTELLIGENCE...

THIS FAKE THAT TELLS THE TRUTH

I hadn't read THE PROTOCOLS OF THE WISE MEN OF ZION for 25 years. At the time, they seemed obvious to me, but they didn't traumatise me. Which goes to show that there is an age and a maturity for reading a book.

If you don't have enough maturity and information, you can completely miss out cultural masterpieces.

A few days after the 'Océaniques' programme that gave birth to this book, I received the first few pages. I was stunned. In those few pages there was EVERYTHING.

Anyone can see that, because I have reproduced them here in their essentials. Three points need to be made first:

This text is INCONTESTABLY a forgery. It was written by a remarkable genius. If the circumcised on the 8th had written it, they would have been aware, and if they were aware, they would have done everything to prevent this suicidal plan for humanity from coming to fruition.

They are too deprived of THE SPIRIT OF SYNTHESIS AND MORAL SENSE, (parameters of composition of the brilliant concept, of which we will speak in a final chapter) to have written it. Everything I have read is rigorously accurate, and continues as I write. In May 1994, 6 Jews presented a list for the European elections. Six 'Jews', virulent, holocaustic preachers who have never allowed Professor Faurisson a free democratic speech...

While the political-financial system is denounced, THE IMPLICATIONS OF THE ATROCITIES are not: general pollution of the planet, of souls and bodies, bestial regression and aberrant conception of freedom, music that kills, drugs, national ruin, globalist dictatorship, mapping of humanity, iatrogenism and teratogenism, overpopulation, pornography, S.I.D.A., 2$^{(nd)}$ (and 3$^{(rd)}$)) world wars, tentacular Marxism, ethnic tearing in the name of anti-racism exclusively in the service of Jewish racism, etc. We'll have the opportunity to talk about this again, both pedagogically and didactically, in the rest of the book, since it's a question of nothing less than our immediate survival.

This means that the PROTOCOLS OF THE WISE MEN OF ZION (democratically forbidden!), are rose water compared to the reality already denounced and which I will specify again by replying to Simone Veil (not to be confused with my illustrious congener Simone WEIL), who had the audacity, taking human beings for morons to declare to us: "Nazism must not be trivialised"...

Finally, a general remark of cosmic importance: everything disintegrates. But people have so little sense of synthesis that they fail to see that the aetiology of disintegration is precisely THE PSEUDO DEMOCRACY and the erroneous conception of SCIENCE and PROGRESS.

So we're always talking about 'reforms'. I've seen the CNE, for example, change its name several times to become the CNED (Lycée et Université d'Enseignement à Distance). This derisory 'change' has changed nothing. In 40 years of teaching, I've seen HUNDREDS OF CHANGES. They have never changed anything and have only made things worse in the direction of a vertical fall. All the pseudo changes are mere trifles that will not prevent young people from remaining barred from the Spiritual and the Moral Sense, and youth unemployment and suicide from growing exponentially. It's the SYSTEM that has to change, otherwise nothing will change anything.

And yet everyone continues to dig their own little termite hole in the pseudo-democratic framework. The naivety and vanity of women and children is put to good use. RIGHT to everything, except to be really informed, except to have access to the elementary truth.

THE WOMAN WHO IS PROMOTED DISINTEGRATES INTO A KIND OF PRETENTIOUS HULK AND THE CHILD COMMITS SUICIDE...

Here are a few quotations from the beginning of the book that will leave any reader with a knowledge of history and the national and international situation stunned, especially after MAASTRICHT.

"These days, the power of money - our own power - has replaced the power of liberal governments.

The idea of freedom is unattainable because no one knows how to use it in the right measure: it is enough to let the people govern themselves for a while for this freedom to be transformed into licence. All that is needed is for the people to govern themselves for a while, and that freedom is transformed into licence. From then on, dissensions arise which soon degenerate into social wars in which states are consumed and their greatness reduced to ashes. Whether a state is exhausted in its internal convulsions or civil wars place it at the mercy of external enemies, it can in either case be considered irretrievably lost: it is in our power.

THE DESPOTISM OF OUR CAPITAL OFFERS IT A LIFELINE TO WHICH IT IS FORCED TO CLING IF IT IS NOT TO SINK.

Crowds are guided exclusively by petty passions, superstitions, customs, traditions and sentimental theories. THEY ARE SLAVES TO THE DIVISION OF PARTIES WHICH WILL ALWAYS OPPOSE ANY REASONABLE AGREEMENT.

He who is to rule must resort to cunning and hypocrisy. The great popular qualities of honesty and frankness are vices in politics. They dethrone rulers better than the most skilful enemy. These qualities must be the attributes of the Goyim governments, which we must in no way take as our guides...

Compared to the current fragility of all powers, ours is INVINCIBLE BECAUSE IT IS INVISIBLE and will remain so until it has acquired such a degree of power that no ruse can threaten it.

A PEOPLE LEFT TO ITS OWN DEVICES, THAT IS TO SAY, TO PARVENUS FROM ITS OWN MILIEU, WORKS TO ITS OWN RUIN AS A RESULT OF THE PARTY QUARRELS THAT ARISE FROM THE THIRST FOR POWER AND THE HONOURS AND DISORDER THAT FLOW FROM IT.

Is it possible for the popular masses to reason calmly and without disputes and to direct the affairs of state, which must never be confused with PERSONAL INTERESTS.

This is RADICALLY IMPOSSIBLE: A VAST AND CLEAR PLAN CAN ONLY BE DEVELOPED BY A SINGLE SUPERIOR MAN.

He coordinates all the cogs in the machinery of government. The conclusion to be drawn is that it is preferable for the well-being of a country that power be concentrated in the hands of ONE RESPONSIBLE INDIVIDUAL.

CIVILISATION CANNOT EXIST WITHOUT ABSOLUTE DESPOTISM BECAUSE IT IS NEVER THE WORK OF THE MASSES BUT OF THEIR LEADERS, WHOEVER THEY MAY BE.

THE MOB IS BARBARIC AND PROVES IT AT EVERY OPPORTUNITY. AS SOON AS THEY SEIZE UPON THE PSEUDO IDEA OF LIBERTY, THEY IMMEDIATELY TRANSFORM IT INTO ANARCHY, WHICH IS THE HIGHEST DEGREE OF BARBARISM.

Look at these alcoholic beings, stupefied, stupefied by drink, which they have the democratic right to consume without limit, a right conferred on the Goys at the same time as FREEDOM.

We cannot allow our people to fall to this level.

The Goy peoples are stupefied by alcohol: their youth is deranged by classical studies and the precocious debauchery to which our agents push them.[2]

That is why we must not be afraid to use corruption, deceit and treachery when they can serve our purpose. In politics, we must know how to seize the property of others without hesitation, in order to gain submission and power by this means.

From the time of the flowering of Ancient Greece, we were the first to cry out the word "liberty", so often repeated since then by unconscious parrots who, attracted from all sides by this bait, have used it only to destroy the prosperity of the world AND THE TRUE INDIVIDUAL FREEDOM SO WELL GUARANTEED AGAINST THE CONSTRAINTS OF THE CROWD... Men who thought they were intelligent did not know how to distinguish. THEY DID NOT EVEN NOTICE THAT THERE IS NO EQUALITY IN NATURE AND THAT THERE CAN BE NO FREEDOM EXCEPT THAT WHICH NATURE ITSELF HAS ESTABLISHED.

NATURE HAS FIXED THE INEQUALITY OF MINDS, CHARACTERS AND INTELLIGENCES BY SUBJECTING EVERYTHING TO ITS LAWS.

These fanatics of freedom and equality, which do not exist, have not seen that OUR POLITICS HAVE KICKED THEM OUT OF LIFE IN THE WAY THAT ABOUTS OUR HEGEMONY.

---

[2] I remember hearing the sexologist TORDJMAN on television saying that masturbation was not dangerous, and that children should not be prevented from masturbating: this practice is however an endocrino-neuro-psychic and physiological cataclysm. It's true that you can masturbate and become a polytechnician or an Énarque: it's not a reference point.

Our call, LIBERTÉ, ÉGALITÉ, FRATERNITÉ, brought to our ranks from the four corners of the world and thanks to our blind agents, whole legions who carry our banners with enthusiasm.

However, these words were worms that gnawed away at the prosperity of the Goys, destroying peace, tranquillity and solidarity everywhere, all through obedience to our laws that undermined the foundations of their States.

You will see later that this is what contributed to the triumph of our system of peaceful conquest of the world. We were then able to obtain the abolition of privileges, the very essence of the aristocracy of the Goys, an aristocracy which was the natural bulwark of peoples and nations against our action.

ON THESE RUINS WE HAVE BUILT OUR ARISTOCRACY, THE ARISTOCRACY OF FINANCE AND SCIENCE.

Our triumph was made easier by the fact that in our dealings with the men we needed, we were always able to strike at the heartstrings of human nature: calculating greed, insatiable material needs. Each of these human weaknesses taken on its own capable of destroying all personal initiative, by placing men at the disposal of whoever buys their activity.

THE ABSTRAIN NOTION OF FREEDOM, never defined, allowed the masses to be convinced that their government was merely the manager of the owner of the country, i.e. the people, and that the manager could be changed like worn gloves.

THE REMOVABILITY OF THE PEOPLE'S REPRESENTATIVES PUTS THEM ENTIRELY AT OUR DISPOSAL.

It makes them dependent on OUR choice.

People have a deep respect for those who embody strength.

Every time there's an act of violence, they exclaim: "That's obviously very scoundrelish, and what a masterly trick it was played with!

We intend gradually to draw all nations into the construction of a new work, the plan of which we have in mind and which involves the DISCOMPOSITION OF THE EXISTING ORDER, which we will replace with our order and our laws.

That's why we need to enlist the help of our agents, the modern leaders of the world, who are a force to be reckoned with. It is this force that will destroy all the obstacles in our path.

When we have carried out our coup d'état, we will say to the people:

"Everything was going very badly for you, and you're all exhausted with suffering. We're going to remove the cause of all your torments: NATIONALITIES, BORDERS, DIFFERENT CURRENCIES. Admittedly you do not understand our motives, so you are free not to swear obedience to us, but can you do so justly before you have examined what we are proposing to you?"

Then they will carry us triumphantly on their shoulders, in a unanimous wave of hope.

THE VOTE, WHICH WE WILL MAKE THE INSTRUMENT OF OUR ADVANCEMENT, by accustoming even the humblest among men to it (by organising, wherever possible, groups and associations) will play its part in helping us to confirm our laws.

BUT WE MUST USE UNIVERSAL SUFFRAGE WITHOUT DISTINCTION OF CLASS OR WEALTH IN ORDER TO OBTAIN THE ABSOLUTE MAJORITY THAT WOULD BE LESS EASILY OBTAINED FROM THE WEALTHY INTELLECTUAL CLASSES ALONE.

THIS IS HOW, AFTER HAVING PENETRATED EVERYONE WITH THE IDEA OF THEIR OWN IMPORTANCE, WE WILL

BREAK THE BONDS OF THE FAMILY AMONG THE GOYIM, WE WILL PREVENT MEN OF VALUE FROM BREAKING THROUGH BECAUSE, BEING DIRECTED BY US, THE MASSES WILL NEVER ALLOW THEM TO REVEAL THEMSELVES. THEY WILL GET INTO THE HABIT OF LISTENING ONLY TO US, WHO PAY THEIR ATTENTION AND OBEY THEM.

This means will put in our hands a force so blind that it will not be able to move in any direction if it is not guided by our agents, judiciously placed to direct the crowds who will know that, on these agents, depends their livelihood, their rewards and all sorts of advantages.

When we are in power, we will replace the terms of the liberal appeal: "liberty, equality, fraternity" with formulas expressing the idea contained in these words. We will say, "the right to liberty", "the duty of equality", "the ideal of fraternity", and in this way we will once again grab the same thing by the horns.

In fact, OUR POWER HAS ALREADY BEGUN ALL OTHERS. In fact, our super-government no longer faces any obstacles in the government of the Goys.

It is in an ABSOLUTELY LEGAL SITUATION OF DICTATORSHIP. I CAN TELL YOU QUITE FRANKLY THAT AT THE MOMENT WE ARE THE LEGISLATORS.

We are also the judges. We are like a commander-in-chief riding at the head of all our armies of LIBERALS.

Our unconscious agents include men of all opinions: MONARCHY RESTORERS, DEMAGOGUES, SOCIALISTS, ANARCHISTS, COMMUNISTS and all sorts of utopians. We've got them all doing the same thing: each one is undermining the other and striving to REVOLVE EVERYTHING THAT IS STILL STANDING. All the States are fed up with these manoeuvres. They are looking for peace and are ready to make any sacrifice to obtain it.

BUT WE WILL NOT GRANT THEM PEACE OR TRUST UNTIL THEY OBSERVINGLY RECOGNIZE OUR INTERNATIONAL SUPERGOVERNMENT and submit to it.

THE PEOPLES ARE CRYING OUT THAT IT IS NECESSARY TO RESOLVE THE SOCIAL QUESTION BY MEANS OF INTERNATIONALISM. THE DIVISION OF THE PARTIES HAS HANDED THEM ALL OVER TO US, BECAUSE TO WAGE A PARTY STRUGGLE YOU NEED MONEY, AND WE HAVE THE MONEY.

WE WILL DIRECT IT TOWARDS OUR GOAL, WHICH IS WHY OUR AGENTS ARE INFILTRATING THE VERY HEART OF THE PEOPLE.

In order not to destroy the institutions of the Goyim prematurely, we have touched the main springs of their mechanism with a cautious, experienced and masterful hand. These springs used to operate in a severe but rigorous order, which we have skilfully substituted for a STUPID AND ARBITRARY LIBERAL DISORDER.

In this way, we have influenced the courts, electoral laws, the press, individual freedom and, most importantly, INSTRUCTION AND EDUCATION, THOSE CORNERSTONES OF SOCIAL LIFE.

AS FAR AS EDUCATION IS CONCERNED, WE HAVE STULTIFIED, DUMBED DOWN AND CORRUPTED GOYIM CHILDHOOD AND YOUTH.

As for the Goyim, whom we have accustomed to seeing only the apparent side of the things we present to them, they take us for the benefactors and saviours of the human race. We are ready to respond immediately to any opposition that arises against us in any country, by starting a war between it and its neighbours, and if several countries were planning to join forces against us, we would start a WORLD WAR and push them to take part in it.

We have already forced the Goyim governments to wage war on many occasions by means of so-called public opinion, having ourselves prepared this opinion in secret.

It is essential that wars do not bring any territorial advantage: ANY WAR WILL BE TRANSPORTED TO THE ECONOMIC TERRAIN.

Then the nations will recognise that ON THIS GROUND, SUPREMACY DEPENDS ON OUR COMPETITION. This situation will leave our adversaries at the mercy of our international agency with its millions of eyes that no nation can stop, and our international rights will sweep away all the rights of nations and GOVERN THIS ONE. In order to gain more control over the institutions, we have promised many administrators the right to govern the country together, unchecked, on condition that they actively help us to create pretexts for discontent over the CONSTITUTIONS themselves, thus preparing for the advent of the Republic in their country.

THE REPUBLICS WILL GIVE US THE THRONE OF THE WORLD.

SO FAR, ALL WE HAVE DONE IS REPLACE THE INFLUENCE OF LIBERAL GOVERNMENTS WITH OUR OWN POWER, WHICH IS THAT OF FINANCE.

THESE DAYS, NO MINISTER CAN HOLD ON TO POWER WITHOUT US BACKING HIM UP WITH OUR SUPPORT OR A SEMBLANCE OF POPULAR APPROVAL THAT WE ARE PREPARING BEHIND THE SCENES.

It's all mind-boggling: as I was reading it, I could see in my head ALL THE POLITICS OF THIS CENTURY. Nothing was missing! And that's just quoting from a few opening pages of the! All the events and all the press of this century are summed up in it!

Who doesn't understand Maastricht, G.A.T.T.[3] and all the rest, after reading these lines? Who doesn't understand THE NEW WORLD ORDER, i.e. the NEW GLOBAL CHAOS, where enslaved peoples will be handed over to cretinism, drugs, pornography, socialism and unemployment?

In what follows, we will see the reality synthesised from the press and publications entirely controlled by the circumcised on the 8th day.

Add to this the dazzling revelations of the Revisionists, who reveal the arithmetical and technical ineptitude of the 6 million gas chambers, as well as the extreme clumsiness of the "Jews" in this ultra-scabrous affair.

What is written in these pages has long since been realised. Unfortunately, the global horror far exceeds anything that can be read in this book, which does not express the COROLLAIRS OF THE DESTRUCTION OF MAN AND NATURE.

WHAT WE HAVE JUST READ FALLS FAR SHORT OF THE TRUTH IN ITS IMPLACABLE ANAESTHETISED HORROR...

"We manipulate morons who lead the masses we have driven mad" says an oil and finance tycoon in a METRO GOLDWIN MAYER film...

Perfect formula, perfectly obvious...

---

[3] Later to become the World Trade Organisation

NAZISM MUST NOT BE TRIVIALIZED, SIMONE VEIL?

BUT WE'VE MADE IT COMMONPLACE...

"Freud and Marx are not Jews" (Professor Henri Baruk)

A speculative, agnostic and atheistic sect is in the process of wiping out mankind and the planet, with the flaccid complicity of other human beings...

Haven't we trivialised money, separated from spirituality and moral sense?

Didn't we trivialise ROTHSCHILD, the kings of Europe, who channelled raw materials through Switzerland to Germany in 1914-1918?

Haven't we trivialised the SCHIFFs, LŒBs, SASOONs, HAMMERs, et al. who, at the same time, financed the Allies, Germany and the Bolshevik revolution and then, in 1919, came to Europe as negotiators of the peace that was to lead to the iniquitous Treaty of Versailles, a second world war and the abandonment of Yalta?

Hasn't Bazille ZAHAROFF, who earned 30 billion selling arms to the whole world (Europe, Middle East, Africa, America), become one of the largest shareholders in the Banque de France, the press and the benefactors of all the political parties?

Hasn't BLOCH, known as Dassault, been trivialised by decree, allowing himself to sell arms to Sadat and Gaddafi under government regulations, without being prosecuted by Mrs KLARSFELD AS AN ANTI-SEMITIC WAR CRIMINAL?

Haven't we trivialised France, disfigured by the "people's dustbins" where all forms of delinquency and criminality flourish?

Haven't we trivialised a materialistic, chemical medicine, based on Judeo-Cartesianism, served by a majority of circumcised mandarins who ignore the Torah, which affects man on a chromosomal level, culminating in a monstrous iatrogenism and teratogenism?

Have teams of circumcisers and blinded followers not trivialised the trafficking of genes and chromosomes for the sake of miraculous medical progress, while the degeneration of young people is dramatically on the rise, with delinquency, crime, homosexuality, suicide, drug addiction and widespread deaths from cancer and cardiovascular disease increasing exponentially despite the development of research?

Hasn't FREUDISM become commonplace? It invades, pornographises, abolishes, attacks the family, deflowers our most sacred feelings, respect for the mother, the child and their innocence, and prepares us for the Marxist mentality? Haven't we made the LEVIS blue jeans commonplace, this uniform of international bullshit in which are dragged wrecks with ambiguous sex, smokers, or drug addicts, perfectly enslaved by the MARX MERDIA, in the hands of this sect as well as by a secular FREUDO MARXIST teaching EMPTY OF EVERYTHING ESSENTIAL TO MAN.

Didn't you, coming out of Auschwitz, trivialise self-service abortion (WHEN PURE EUGENISTIC ABORTION WAS DECLARED A CRIME OF HUMANITY AGAINST NAZISM AT THE NUREMBERG TRIAL!), the pathogenic and teratogenic pill which, according to Professor Jamain, President of the French National Syndicate of Obstetricians and Gynaecologists, induces ovarian blockages, stunted growth and sterility in adolescent girls?

Hasn't sexual education and even masturbation become commonplace?V programme, which only featured people who had been circumcised on the 8th day, flanked by a few freaks who called themselves exhibitionists), which reduce children to nothingness through irreversible hormononeuropsychic imbalance, will produce mass characters and criminals, like the 11-year-old boy who raped and killed a 4-year-old girl (we've seen other cases of this atrocious type since), a symbol of world pathology... Did ANY of these cases exist under Nazism? And all this under the masterly aegis of FREUD, KAHN-NATHAN, TORDJMAN, COHEN, LWOFF, SIMON and others BERGE, assisted by a few fags in cassocks, or rather turtlenecks...

Haven't we trivialised MARXISM, which flourishes in the form of various forms of communism and socialism, despite all the gulags, the 200,000,000 physical victims officially counted in communist countries since 1917, the psychiatric hospitals where you are socialised by chemical drug injections, and which reduces man to the state of an elementary matriculatory statistical unit??

Has it not been trivialised that, despite the anti-Semitism of Marxist countries, the entire Bolshevik revolutionary team was made up of people circumcised on the 8th day, like the leaders of the prison and concentration camp system, and that these people exterminated around 120 million Goys in the USSR?

For the latter (FRENKEL, YAGODA, ABRAMOVICI, FIRINE, APETTER, OURITSKI, SORENSON, JEJOFF, DAVIDOVITCH, BERMAN, RAPPOPORT) there is no Nuremberg super-trial, even posthumous, any more than for the financial backers, LŒB, WARBURG, HAMMER, SCHIFF, SASOON, KISSINGER, who subsidise this ideal regime of freedom and human development...?

Hasn't Communism been trivialised as the "defender of the worker", when everyone knows that in Prague, Budapest, East Berlin, Gdansk and Warsaw, the rebels were only workers and students? Despite these obvious facts, have we not trivialised the Himalayan error of communism as the "defender of the little guy", WHEN COMMUNISM TAKES EVERYTHING FROM EVERYONE??

Have we not trivialised the atomic frolics of the circumcised Einstein and Oppenheimer, even though everyone knows the terrible dangers of radioactive waste, the threat of genetic damage, the dangers of cataclysmic accidents at nuclear power stations (CHERNOBYL HAPPENED AFTER THIS WAS WRITTEN), which can carcinogenise vast areas for centuries to come?And yet, didn't OPPENHEIMER say: "I did the devil's work"?

That hasn't stopped SAMUEL T.COHEN from putting the finishing touches to the neutron bomb, which the U.S. bank of WARBURG AND CO. is talking about selling to China (T.V. news broadcast)...

This devil's work would not have been allowed in a theocracy run by conscious leaders endowed with a moral sense and a spirit of synthesis.

Hasn't Mrs GURGY-ELIACHEV trivialised the psychological amalgam of the sexes since nursery school?

Haven't we trivialised the charnel house art of PICASSO, who himself said to Papini: "I'm just a public clown who has understood his time and exhausts the vanity and greed of his contemporaries as best he can"??

Haven't we trivialised this vomit from the POMPIDOU centre, who some nasty tongues claim to be the natural son of a ROTHSCHILD and who was nevertheless a director of his bank?

Haven't we made commonplace a press that is entirely subservient to those circumcised on the 8th day, like publishing and television, that enslaves and stultifies the masses, trapping them between the uniform of international bullshit that is LEVIS blue jeans, Rothschildian production-consumption, Marxism and Freudian sex, AND THAT MAKES THEM TAKE ALL THE FORMS OF THEIR ASSERTION FOR FREEDOM?

Haven't we trivialised the ROTHSCHILDO-MARXIST economic process, which has totally destroyed small businesses, murdered agriculture and will soon leave us with over a billion unemployed and irreversible multiform pollution (Club of Rome, Carter Report)?

In this way, the complicit and bloody antagonism of Rothschildomarxism will have achieved its goal: the destruction of mankind and the planet PERFECTLY FORECASTED BY HITLER IN MEIN KAMPF...

Haven't we trivialised a university and political system THAT PROHIBITS ANY RECRUITMENT OTHER THAN THAT OF THE MEDIOCRES, because no thinking person would take these masquerades seriously: the mnemonics of official competitive examinations and "universal suffrage" have never made it possible to recruit genuine elites - quite the contrary.

Memory has never been the only parameter of intelligence, and the people are PERFECTLY UNABLE to access the concepts that would enable them to elect an elite endowed with MORAL SENSE AND THE SPIRIT OF SYNTHESIS. Thus the elected, the polytechniciens, the agrégés, the énarques, necessarily Freemasons at least in spirit, immersed in SPECIALIST MINUSCULARITY, will be manipulated unconsciously like puppets and fetuses by Rothschildomarxism until they are enslaved, until they are transformed into PHYSICOCHEMICAL AMALGAMOUS DOCILES (billionaire or drug addict, it doesn't matter), CANCEROUS, CARDIOPATHIC, REGULATED BY THE PROFIT AND LOSS CAISSE OF "DEMONCRASSIA"...

HAVEN'T WE TRIVIALISED THE INTEGRATION OF THE JEWISH QUESTION INTO THE MYTH OF RACISM? And yet these people are circumcised on the 8th day, NOT JEWS.

BEING JEWISH IMPLIES FIDELITY TO THE TORAH, TO THE PRINCIPLE OF TZEDEK. Now these people circumcised on the 8th day are speculative atheists or agnostics:

WARBURG, MARX, FREUD, OPPENHEIMER, BENEZAREFF, KAGANOVITCH, SOROS ET AL ARE CRIMINALS AND HERETICS BEFORE THE TORAH.

SPINOZA, who separated mysticism from philosophy and paved the way for rationalism and modern science ("the lie of progress is Israel" Simone Weil), was excommunicated by the Synagogue of Holland. In the name of criminal "anti-racism", they are trivialising the mixing of different ethnic groups ("race" is an empty concept: there are only ETHNICS, WHICH ARE THE RESULT OF HORMONAL ADAPTATION TO A FIXED PLURISECULAR ENVIRONMENT) which are in no way made to be mixed, many of whom become delinquents, thieves, rapists, drug suppliers, alcoholics, tuberculosis sufferers, who provoke inevitable racism and all the more interesting because those circumcised on the 8th day benefit from advertising, They also exploit a sub-proletariat that is a disgrace to France and often a horror in South Africa, where gold and diamonds are in the hands of circumcised people (OPPENHEIMER, the world's largest diamond merchant, spends a whopping 150 million old francs on a single evening reception)...

Didn't Professor David's department trivialise artificial insemination after masturbation by idiots paid for the purpose? (How deep does one have to be to be able to trivialise such a practice, whether it's the masturbator or the doctor?)

Have we not trivialised voting at the age of eighteen, whereas a great politician in a theocracy will think long and hard before taking a decision? These cohorts of unconscious bluejeaners who will be made to believe that they have valid opinions, when in fact they are totally conditioned and can only modulate in insignificance, embroiled in the pseudodifferences of all the political parties, anarchists included, will vote while RothschildSoros, Marx, Freud, Bloch-Dassault, Warburg, Rockefeller and consorts will continue to enslave them, manipulate them, degenerate them, BY CONDITIONING THEM SO THAT THEY WILL *FREELY* CHOOSE ALL THE FORMS OF THEIR ENSLAYMENT.

Have we not trivialised the working mother, so that she loses her identity as mother and wife once and for all, so that, like 18-year-old voters, she can be transformed into a "circumcised" customer for the supermarkets and department stores advertised by BLUSTEIN BLANCHET? WHEREAS PROFESSOR HEUYER REVEALED A FEW YEARS AGO THAT ALL THE CHILDREN COMING BEFORE THE COURTS WERE SOURCED FROM DISASSOCIATED OR FANTOMATIC COUPLES (divorce, and intensive work by the mother outside the home)...?

THIS IS PREPARING GENERATIONS OF SERIOUS CHARACTERISTS, DISLINQUERS, CRIMINALSDRUGS, SUICIDALS, HOMOSEXUALS (absence of the father, vitamin E deficiency, early masturbation encouraged as fundamental factors of homosexualisation), And all this by making women love a form of subjugation that is all the crueler because it is chosen FREELY BY CONDITIONING, so that they sincerely believe that it is an evolution when in fact it is THE MOST BARBARIC INVOLUTION.

They will not understand that they have become chemotherapists, leading to iatrogenism and teratogenism, lawyers or judges, totally deprived of any moral sense and devoting their fees to the disintegration of couples and the misery of children, ministers, promulgating a pathogenic and carcinogenic pill, like the butchery of healthy new-born babies, that they are AT THE ANTIPODES OF CULTURE. They can no longer even suspect the IMMENSE AUTHENTIC CULTURE THAT A WOMAN MUST HAVE IN THE HOME TO MAKE HER CHILDREN REAL MEN AND REAL WOMEN...

HASN'T IT BEEN BANALISED TO TAX THE DECLARATION OF THESE CLEAR FACTS AS RACISM AND ANTISEMITISM (empty words). EVEN IF IT IS CLAIMED THAT THE RACIST MYTH HAS NO SCIENTIFIC FOUNDATION AND THAT THESE TRICKY SPECULATIONS ARE ONLY HORMONAL PATHOLOGY INDICATED BY CIRCUMCISION ON DAY 8,

WHICH SUSPECTS A REGIME PRIVATE OF ANY PROVIDENTIAL ELITE. PROVIDENTIAL ELITE, THE HEGEMONY OF SPECULATORS DEPRIVED OF ANY MORAL SENSE OR SPIRIT OF SYNTHESIS, CULMINATING IN A VERITABLE INTELLECTUALIST TERRORISM IN WHICH ALL TRUTH IS FORBIDDEN BY LAW (THE HEIGHT OF "DEMOCRATIC" MYSTIFICATION)...?

Any true elite would know, for example, that laboratory chemistry can in no way be a principle of health, even if it allows spectacular symptomatic repression in patients who have had a deplorable diet and hygiene for years. Hasn't the SACRO-SAINT MYTH OF 6 MILLION GAS CHAMBERS BEEN trivialised, when the verifications made by historians such as Rassinier, who weighed thirty kilos when he left DACHAU, and Professor Faurisson, a democrat and anti-Nazi, who studied the problem for 20 years, have demonstrated the inflation of more than 5 million, and the technical impossibility of B cyclon gas chambers for 1,000 or 2,000 people at a time. This can be verified by anyone familiar with the technical standards for gassing, and will one day be confirmed by serious expert reports (LEUCHTER report) and counter-expertise. It should be noted that a gas chamber has never been seen, while the crematoria are all present and in good condition.

They were essential in concentration camps to prevent typhus and plague epidemics.

This unheard-of jeremiad has been trivialised, while since the Second World War tens of millions of dead have known nothing but silence, just like the tens of millions exterminated by the Bolshevik "Jews".

It is commonplace that these people are of no interest to anyone, belonging to "that vile seed of cattle", they are not Jews!

Hasn't the silence surrounding the Red Cross report of 1944 been trivialised? After a meticulous examination of the German camps, the

Red Cross declared that "DESPITE THE RUMOURS, NOT A SLIGHT TRACE OF A GAS CHAMBER EXISTS ANYWHERE".

Has it not been trivialised that at the trial of DEGESH, the manufacturer of Cyclon B, the Director and chemists stated that gas chambers, as claimed by the propaganda, were technically IMPOSSIBLE AND IMPENSABLE?

Hasn't it been trivialised that the famous GERSTEIN REPORT, which revolves around this problem, WAS REJECUTED AT THE NUREMBERG TRIAL, because it was so silly and caricatural...?

WASN'T THE SILENCE SURROUNDING THE FACT THAT HITLER, THREE YEARS BEFORE THE WAR, HAD SUBMITTED TO GOVERNMENTS AN AGREEMENT UNDER WHICH, IN THE EVENT OF A CONFLICT, CIVILIAN POPULATIONS WOULD NOT BE BOMBED, AND ABOVE ALL THE REFUSAL OF THIS AGREEMENT BY THE GOVERNMENTS WHOSE TRUE MASTERS WE ALL KNOW?!!!

And yet, the bombing of Dresden alone claimed 125,000 victims in one night, and that of Tokyo 195,000, i.e. more than Mr Oppenheimer's bomb on Hiroshima...

NOW, MADAME VEIL, IF YOU HAVE READ MEIN KAMPF EVEN DIAGONALLY AND OBSERVED HITLER'S POLICIES IN HIS COUNTRY, YOU WILL KNOW THAT IT IS PRECISELY ALL THESE HORRORS THAT HITLER WANTED TO AVOID FOR HIS COUNTRY AND "EVEN FOR HIS ENEMIES", TO QUOTE POPE XII...

Anyone who knows the facts and has read Mein *Kampf*, especially in the light of the events of the last 50 years, WILL BE PERFECTLY CONVINCED.

This is undoubtedly why this book is banned, while the EXPRESS by GOLDSMIDT, ARON, MENDES-FRANCE, SCHREIBER,

ABITTAN, GRUMBACH, PISAR, LAZLICH, KANTERS, GALLO, OTTENHEIMER etc., advertises a novel which narrates the venal homosexual adventures of a 13-year-old boy WITH A RECOMMENDATION TO YOUNG PEOPLE OF THIS AGE TO READ IT.

I was driving down the road when I heard this advert: emotion forced me to stop...

GIVE THE POLICE AND JUSTICE TO MR LEVY HE WILL NO LONGER BE RIDICULOUS OR ABJECT AND THERE WILL BE THE 20th CENTURY...

Given these obvious facts, can we not see that the Nazi regime was "A SOCIOLOGICAL REACTION OF LEGITIMATE DEFENCE", or as Carrel put it, "the normal reaction of a people who do not want to die..."?

In the German camps were all those who, consciously or unconsciously, promoted all these horrors "circumcised on the 8th day": Freemasons, Communists, priests who were never supported by Pius XII who said: "Germany fights not only for its friends but also for its enemies, because if the Eastern Front collapses, the fate of the world is sealed".

He also said: "Only Nazi Germany and the Vatican are capable of opposing the Bolshevik danger, the former politically, the latter spiritually"...

WHO CAN CONTRADICT YOUR NAMESAKE SIMONE WEIL WHEN SHE SAID:

"THE JEWS, THIS HANDFUL OF UPROOTED PEOPLE, HAVE CAUSED THE UPROOTING OF THE ENTIRE GLOBE...".

Why not trivialize a regime, admittedly transitional, which has successfully tried to give back to its country its traditional dimension that ROTHSCHILD, MARX, FREUD, EINSTEIN, PICASSO AND CONSORTS have totally destroyed?

Didn't Solzhenitsyn tell us: THE NAZI REGIME WAS THE ONLY POLITICAL FORCE CAPABLE OF COMBATING THE GLOBAL MARXIST SUICIDE...

In this global Rothschild-Marxist game, which rules the world in the most totalitarian way, no account is taken of the real needs of mankind:

Biological: the damaging effects of chemising the earth, food and medicines.

Ecological: destruction of nature and universal pollution (50 years of chemical fertilisers have totally sterilised the soil) Sociological: monstrous unemployment, which in the current situation, wrongly called "democratic", can only grow exponentially.
(Return of the woman to the home, and to the value of "work" and not money). The system is stupid and its "progress" aberrant.

Moral and spiritual: the evils of secularism, Marxism and Freudianism, disseminated by zombified teachers.

So, Mme Simone Veil, are you a criminal or just unconscious? Couldn't you read your HOMONYM Simone Weil?

I'm afraid you're unconscious, because no one would want to wish for the holocaust of others as well as their own.

CAN'T YOU UNDERSTAND THAT IN A FINITE WORLD THERE CAN BE NO INDEFINITE GROWTH?

Especially when the processes used are anti-biological, artificial, pathogenic and destructive to humans and the planet, as Hitler saw so clearly in Mein Kampf.

This despiritualising anti-insect campaign, with its hypertrophied intellect shaping a monstrous, homicidal and suicidal mind, has only two strategic parameters: RADICAL SUPPRESSION OF CIRCUMCISION ON DAY 8, DAY 1 OF THE 21 DAYS OF THE FIRST PUBERTY. [4]

A RETURN TO SMALL, AUTHENTICALLY RELIGIOUS COMMUNITIES, I.E. IN ACCORDANCE WITH THE LAWS OF NATURE.

---

[4] Basic note: (see next page)

FUNDAMENTAL NOTE

The radical abolition of circumcision on the 8th day of the first puberty, which lasts 21 days, would have the immediate effect of restoring the internal genitalia in all its integrity.

Religious minds would say that the conversion of Israel requires the abolition of misunderstood circumcision. (I use the word 'conversion' not as a 'return to the Catholic religion', which has shown its weaknesses enough 'and its ignorance of the laws of life', but as a return to the laws of life and respect for nature.

In addition, over-stimulation of the organic endocrines (pituitary, thyroid, adrenal, reproductive genital) would remain hereditary for several generations. This means that Jewish children would become pituitary and thyroid INTERSTITUTES like the Pharaohs of Egypt.

They would thus constitute a veritable elite, moving from an analytical to a synthetic mindset, from the quantitative to the qualitative, from a lack of moral sense to a great moral sense.

Ideas like Marxism, or that "motherhood doesn't exist" would be impossible. The Warburgs, the Marxes, the Freuds, the Oppenheimers, the S.T. Cohen, the Bénézareffs, the Simone Veils, the Gurgi-Eliachefs, the Gurgi-Lazarus, the Soros etc. would be impossible.

As DOMINIQUE AUBIER says about the rite of circumcision in a book she sent me:

Circumcision "would not risk destroying everything on the borders of nations"...

BEYOND ANTI-SEMITISM

THE KEY TO JEWISH TRAGEDY: CIRCUMCISION ON THE 8TH DAY AND THE DARK AGES.

> "Who would have thought that a rite could go so far and risk destroying everything on the frontier between nations"
> (Dominique Aubier)

One historical fact is undeniable: anti-Semitism (a misnomer, moreover, as many true Semites have never experienced anti-Semitism) against the Jews has manifested itself at all times and on all continents where Jews have been present. It is therefore, as Bernard LAZARE says in his book on ANTISEMITISM, in permanent gestation in the Jew himself and NOT in the anti-Semite.

Not all eras and not all latitudes have joined forces to persecute the Jews. The Church's warning against Jewish perversity only affected Catholics, a small fraction of all peoples and places who did not need Rome to practise bloody anti-Semitism, even when the Jews possessed maximum political and financial power.

This ANTI-SEMITISM (a word made all the more absurd by the fact that a Jew whose ancestry has lived in Poland for centuries is in no way Semitic) IS DUE TO THEIR CONSTANT PARTICULARISM IN TIME AND SPACE.

The 'Jews' (a misnomer, as we shall see) have considerable speculative powers, but to the detriment of MORAL SENSE, which should not be confused with their often rigorous morality, and of the SPIRIT OF SYNTHESIS. Their modern speculations, JUDÉO CARTESIENNES, offer us a deadly niagara of proofs by 9 of this phenomenon. This particularism owes nothing to the THORA, THE

JEWISH HOLY BOOK, for the pseudo-Jews who rule the world have hardly received any religious instruction and are, in their speculations as in their lives, radically atheistic.

The spirit of synthesis and the moral sense THAT CHARACTERISE THE TRUE ELITES are totally absent from political officialdom.

The pseudo-democracy will thus be transformed into a globalist Judeocracy which imposes its Caesarism through the unconscious vote of the disintegrated masses. The dialectic of the freedom of man, woman and child is at the strategic epicentre of this demagogic destruction, which plays on the naivety and vanity of the masses. The "Michael Jackson" and "Madona" phenomena are dazzling symptoms of the physiological and psychic collapse of the masses.

The word "Jew" has a strictly religious meaning. A Jew is someone who follows the precepts of the THORA, the only orthodox Jewish holy book," says specialist Alexandre Weil.

WARBURG, who in 1914-1918 simultaneously subsidised the Allies, the Germans and the Bolshevik revolution, only to come to Europe in 1919 as a peace negotiator (we know what the VERSAILLES TREATY was and where it led), HAMMER, who in 1940 alone possessed as much oil as the 3 Axis powers, MARX, KAGANOVITCH, AND 50 JEWISH CARCETAL AND CONCENTRATIONARY BOURREAUX WHO EXTERMINATED DZINES OF MILLIONS OF GOYS IN THE U.R.S.S. (FRENKEL, YAGODA, JEJOFF, FIRINE, APPETER, ABROMOVICI ETC), FREUD, abuliant and pornographer with his smoky pansexualist theory based on nothing, SIMONE VEIL, piluloavorteuse, (the pill is pathogenic and teratogenic),BENEZAREFF, king of the pornographic film, with many others of the same origin in the U.S.BENEZAREFF, king of the pornographic film, with many others of the same origin in the U.S.A., and in Europe, such other "Jew" king of world alcohol, of meat, of the monopolization of wheat, of mind-numbing soap operas of systematic propaganda, of violence and sex, NOT ONLY ARE NOT JEWS BUT ARE MAJOR CRIMINALS OF HUMANITY, AS ARE THE

KINGS OF THE MAXWELL AND GOLDSCHMIDT PRESS, who manipulate the masses on a sea of low-level anti-traditional propaganda, lies, errors and horrors.

The only criticism that can be made of the TRUE JEWS is that they keep quiet about these major criminals who, what's more, usurp the title of "Jew"...

Once we have perfectly understood the ASYNTHETIC AND AMORAL speculative particularism of this atheistic sect which has its origins in Judaism, once we realise that a Jew in Poland and a Jew in South America are somatically very different, often sharing only their caricatured facial features and their speculative powers, WE HAVE TO LOOK FOR THE COMMON DENOMINATOR WHICH CAN ACCOUNT SUCH PARTICULARISM.

THERE IS ONLY CIRCULATION ON THE 8th DAY AFTER BIRTH.

This becomes clear when we understand the FUNCTIONAL PRIORITY OF THE HORMONAL SYSTEM OVER THE NERVOUS SYSTEM AND BEING IN GENERAL (work by endocrinologist Dr Jean Gautier). In other words, it is our glandular system that directs us, the nervous system being only a bridge, ensuring our automatisms, between our glandular nature and our actions.

In my doctoral thesis, I showed that the romantic dandies (Chopin, Lamartine, Musset, Liszt, Goethe, Byron etc.) were 'thyroid' with a 'hyper' tendency. This explains their lanky form, their aestheticism, their intuition and their imagination.

When you also know about the first puberty, which begins on the 8th day and lasts 21 days, you're in for a real treat.

Moreover, it can be done before by pure intelligence, because circumcision on the 8th day is the ONLY CONSTANT PARAMETER that can justify such particularism, especially since there is a complete absence of ethnicity, since the Jews have always been practically spread across the planet, never having been able to settle for more than a few centuries, which does not allow them to obvious ethnic characteristics. Moreover, no ethnic justification could justify such speculative powers, which are devoid of any moral sense or spirit of synthesis.

If the Jews had any sense of synthesis, they would have discovered long ago that circumcision was the source of ALL THEIR EVILS and they would have done away with it. Their fate, it seems, is precisely that they SHOULD NOT have discovered it...

Circumcision was performed on the 8th day, i.e. the first day of puberty, which lasted 21 days and was to be considerably disrupted. It will determine the very particular mentality of those who undergo this mutilation permanently.

On the 8th day, all our endocrines are in turmoil. For 21 days, this will be the FIRST PUBERTY. It manifests itself through genital signs and mammary gland activity. The importance of this puberty is considerable for our general glandular functioning and for all our vital possibilities. The pituitary gland is very active and acts on all our other glands to adapt them to the new life. It can thus maintain the organic environment of the young child and enable it to resist external influences.

IF, DURING THIS HORMONAL EFFECTIVENESS, AN INSOLUTE TRAUMATISM HITS THE PLACE WHERE THE PREPUCE IS LOCATED, close to our internal genitalia, a fundamentally important endocrine system, it is obvious that the GLANDULAR BALANCE WHICH MUST BE ESTABLISHED AT FIRST PUBERTY WILL BE PERTURBED.

There is no doubt that this mutilation will divert to its own benefit the circulatory and metabolic activities that should apply to the internal (or interstitial) genitalia. It is therefore this endocrine system, which we have known for 40 years to be atrophied in dementia patients, which will be damaged, frustrated and affected.

This will not be the REPRODUCTIVE genitalia, which is not yet formed and will only evolve later. This trauma will therefore result in HYPOFUNCTION OF THE INTERNAL GENITAL.

But it is the gland of the will, of intellectuality (which has nothing in common with the INTELLECTUALISM of modern science, finance and murderous ideologies such as Marxism, Freudism and anarchism, not in its real sense, but in the sense of 'chaos') and of the moral sense.

This hypotrophy of the internal genitalia will be to the benefit of the reproductive genitalia and the other endocrines, ESPECIALLY HYPOPHYSIS. These endocrines will become seven to ten times more efficient than those of other humans; THE RESULT IS THAT IN A PSEUDO DEMOCRACY PRIVATE TO ANY SPIRITUAL ELITE, THE CIRCONCIS ON DAY 8th WILL TAKE ALL THE POWER.

They will take them all the more easily because they are TOTALLY DELETED OF MORAL SENSE AND MIND OF SYNTHESIS.

They will therefore be able to use any process they like without any qualms.

It is therefore these endocrines, to the exclusion of the internal genital gland, which will ensure the development of genitality. As a result, the brain, made up of an over-powerful endocrine concert BUT WITHOUT ANY EFFECTIVENESS FROM THE INTERNAL GENITAL, will free the individual from all the opposing, sentimental and authentically intellectual forces. (Moral sense, synthesis), which may, for example, oppose the use of sexuality, as well as developing systems or discoveries which will turn against man (Freudism, Marxism, atomic bomb, neutron bomb, "liberation" of men, women and children etc.).

What's more, this pre-pucial trauma, recorded automatically, will divert all the genitalia's efforts on the reproductive organs during the other 2 puberty periods (between the ages of 13 and 18). Circumcision also causes scarring, which requires special activity on the part of the hypophysis. THIS ENDOCRINE SYSTEM IS THEREFORE CALLED UPON TO FUNCTION AS SOON AS THE CHILD IS BORN.

IT WILL THEREFORE CONTINUE TO DOMINATE THE GENERAL HORMONAL ECONOMY. It will remain persistent in its activity. It will act on the somatic and the psychic.

NORMALLY THE PITUITARY'S REASONING PERSPECTIVES ARE TEMPERED BY THE INTERNAL GENITALIA.

But in this case, as Jacques Bergier quite rightly says, speaking of the speculative circumcisionists he wrongly calls "Jews", "THERE IS A SICKNESS OF ULTRA REASONING"; THIS IS FATAL BECAUSE IT IS HYPOPHYSIS THAT ALONE ENSURES INTELLECTUAL ELABORATIONS.

The thinking of those circumcised on the 8th day (an exceptional circumcision will not have all these consequences) will therefore be exclusively materialistic, calculating, abstract, ANALYTICAL; so the being hormonally marked in this way will elaborate analyses, calculations, in which NO MORAL CONSIDERATIONS OR CONCERN ABOUT THE HUMAN SYNTHETIC GLOBALITY IN TIME AND SPACE CAN ENTER. THE EXCLUSIVITY OF THIS TYPE OF HEGEMONIC SPECULATION WILL MEAN THE SUICIDE OF EVERYTHING AND EVERYONE.

Science will become black magic because it will be exclusively ANALYTICAL, MICROSCOPIC, QUANTITATIVE, WHILE KNOWLEDGE, white magic, is SYNTHETIC, MACROSCOPIC, QUALITATIVE.

The person circumcised on the 8th day is therefore responsible, as a cosmic agent, for the global collapse: HE IS NOT GUILTY.

He is no more guilty than the Colorado beetle is of the potato. He did not choose the repercussions of circumcision on the 8th day, which he is not even capable of conceiving. He is unaware of the mentality it confers on him. A victim of anti-Semitism, he does not understand that his amoral and immoral speculations are the cause.

If he had such an awareness, HE WOULD HAVE REMOVED THE CIRCUMSTANCES A LONG TIME AGO, especially as, curiously enough, he only retains this misunderstood RELIGIOUS rite and ignores the Torah.

Moses was less familiar with the glandular question than the priests of Horus. So he inflicted this misunderstood circumcision on an entire people, turning them into glandular freaks and inflicting on them, in addition, THE IDEA OF WORLD HEGEMONY.

They achieved this on the putrescent and bloody ruins of degenerate nations. So there is no such thing as a Jewish race (because they don't exist) or ethnicity.

(Ethnicity being the result of hormonal adaptation to a fixed environment for at least a millennium). ONLY the 8th circumcision gives an account of the speculative, amoral and synthetic mentality of the circumcised, WHO ARE ENTERING THE ULTIMATE PHASE OF THE AGE OF THE TENEBRIES ANNOUNCED BY THE WISE FOR THOUSANDS OF YEARS.

Today, the expropriation of all human beings by circumcised vagrant finance has become institutionalised. Usury, the all-encompassing crime denounced by all civilisations, has taken on the very official mantle of credit, which, along with alcohol, is the source of all our ills.

All this can only be supported by the mass disintegration of individuals whose biotypical appearance and clothing, for example in the Paris metro, is something atrocious and repulsive.

The parahuman being enslaved by credit, food and therapeutic chemification, Freudism, Marxism, pathogenic and criminogenic music, has become a sort of physico-chemical amalgam in Levis blue jeans, governed by the profit and loss account of pseudo-democracies, which are in fact nothing more than the dictatorships of banking and Marxism.

Drugs spread freely, MANAGED BY HIGH FINANCE, putting the final touch to this degeneration, while the young, defenceless, unemployed, in a pitiless "circumcised" world, commit suicide en masse, while the real elites, who no longer have any dialogue with anyone, look on in tears at this distressing spectacle. Today, the circumcised own what remains of the States. Only the Apocalypse will bring about an irreversible change in their fate and ours.

Their pituitary combinations can be found in religious reforms, revolutions such as those of 1989 and 1917, wars, zombifying mindlessness and pornography. Civilisation has disappeared under the effect of their disintegrating pituitary glands. This is a natural tendency for them, since the 4 organic endocrines (thyroid, pituitary, adrenal, reproductive genital), which are much more powerful than in other humans, are permanently opposed to the synthetic, moral, divine and altruistic values conferred by an internal genital system in perfect working order.

The circumcised financiers Warburg, Hammer, Rothschild, Lœb, Kuhn, etc., like Freud and Marx, Einstein, Oppenheimer, S.T. Cohen, are exemplary in this respect. SPINOZA, excommunicated by the Synagogue of Holland, and therefore NOT a Jew, represents the first materialist conception of modern times. He separated mysticism from philosophy and paved the way for RATIONALISM and MODERN SCIENCE, which has almost finished exterminating us.

FREUD makes our intellectual possibilities depend on our sublimated sexual tendencies. It reduces us to the level of a bestial unconscious and, thanks to pseudo-democracy, has imposed its neurosis on the ENTIRE WORLD.

In fact, this glandular anarchy, barely kept in check by a deficient interstitial, leads the circumcised on the 8th day to psychologies of upheaval, destruction and annihilation, in order to establish the general direction of the world. They ignore the Torah and retain only circumcision and the Mosaic announcement of their world hegemony. At the end of the twentieth century, they enslaved governments and the judiciary entirely to their devotion. The courts now apply their racist and dictatorial laws, disguised as "anti-racist and democratic". In this way, the circumcised ensure their hegemony over the decomposed masses.

Only those who form small communities organised along ethnic lines, where spiritual and moral values are restored, will be able to escape the globalist suicide which, as I write, will manifest itself in economic ruin and inter-tribal butchery in South Africa, for example. It is absolutely certain that after global suicide, the 21st century will only regain its hierarchical coherence through that which LINKS, i.e. religion. Today everything is reversed and only TRUE RELIGION will put things back in their providential order.[5]

The global hegemony of the circumcised on the 8th day only fulfils the Dark Ages on the empire of ruins. Ultimately it will also be their own

---

[5] According to Dr Alexis Carrel, appointed by Pius XII as a member of the Vatican's Scientific Institute, the Church should be criticised for **its doctrinaire formalism and ignorance of the laws of life (dietetics, controlled breathing, genuine prayer, which alone can unite us with the transcendent).**
It is also absolutely essential to eliminate toxic substances which cause serious deficiencies and damage, and which disrupt the thyroid gland, the GLAND OF TENTATION: coffee, tobacco, alcohol, chemical foodstuffs, meat.
You can't talk to God with a mouth full of blood.
It's hard to imagine slaughterhouses in the vicinity of the Temple of Luxor or the Acropolis...

suicide and the end of the misunderstood practice of circumcision. The Judeo-Cartesian psychosis is integrated into the absolute determinism of those circumcised on the 8th day, who are in no way Jewish.

Their cosmic mission is to assume a higher involutive intellectualism (Analyticism).

Perfect understanding of this text implies a thyroid and internal genitalia in good condition.

A TYPICAL EXAMPLE FROM THE 90S OF THE EFFECTS OF CIRCUMCISION ON THE 8TH DAY: THE FINANCIER SOROS.

Who is Soros?

A speculator and philanthropist (it is fashionable, after making ten billion on speculation permitted only by democracy, to donate a few million to good causes), Soros is a Hungarian Jewish émigré. He became an American billionaire by sleeping...

Its fortunes are so recent that it does not feature in Henri Coston's famous book "Le veau d'or est toujours debout" (The Golden Calf is Still Standing), published in 1987.

According to Le Monde on 16 September 1992, his fortune increased overnight by one billion dollars, or 5 billion francs, or 500 billion centimes. As everyone knows, such fortunes in a monarchical or theocratic regime were commonplace!

History tells us, rightly or wrongly, that the superintendent Fouquet, of whom King Louis XIV was jealous, was a beggar next to Soros!

It took democracy to finally achieve perfect Equality (+ Equality and Fraternity!) between SOROS and ONE BILLION UNEMPLOYED PEOPLE WORLDWIDE...

It has worked against European currencies, particularly the British currency.

Le MONDE tells us that in Great Britain, he is known as "the man who broke the pound"...

After the storm that deepened the recession in Europe, Soros raked in two billion dollars. (Seven months later Soros was back in the news on the gold market. He bought a stake in one of the biggest gold mines in the US, NEWMONT MINING, for 400 million dollars, and drove up the price.

He is the very type of cunning, mysterious businessman, neurotically stimulated by an over-stimulation of the pituitary gland due to circumcision. Like Rothschild, he acts alone. But he has a tool at his disposal that the winner of the dishonest Waterloo swindle did not have: the telephone. He likes to say that the telephone is enough to keep him informed.

The telephone is also all he needs to place his stock market orders in Wall Street, the City, Paris, Tokyo and Frankfurt.

He is just over sixty as I write this book, and he holds the strings of a network that encompasses banks and trusts that are obliged to do his bidding and obey his instructions.

You don't need to be intelligent to understand the power that such a man can have over all the politicians of any country and over all the masses. It's people like that who can globalise Freudism overnight, make the whole world wear blue jeans, start a war that favours them and tomorrow, if the mental degradation has been well dosed, make everyone wear a feathered cap up the backside... This grotesque example is healthier than the global advent of pornography in the name of freedom!

Since the collapse of the communist system in Eastern Europe, financier Soros has "embarked on a new life". A great speculator, he is a philanthropist in the East, says Le MONDE without laughing:

"Through a network of foundations set up in 18 excommunist countries, he is helping to build democracy by trying to encourage the emergence of open companies (i.e. trusts or financial groups dependent on him and his accomplices).

He devotes the best part of his time to his foundations, to the tune of 50 million dollars a year. In 1992, he also donated 100 million dollars to help scientific research in Russia, 50 million dollars in humanitarian aid to Bosnia and a 25 million dollar loan to Macedonia.

According to LE MONDE, George Soros' foundations have had varying fortunes in different countries. In China he gave up fairly quickly after being infiltrated by the security services. In Poland he made a first attempt with intellectuals from SOLIDARITÉ, but without success...

The story of his foundation in Moscow, which closely parallels the evolution of Russian society, begins in 1987, when Sakharov turned down Soros' offer to collaborate, convinced that his foundation would be infiltrated by the KGB. "We started out as a Soviet organisation," says Soros, "it took us two putsches within the foundation to correct the trajectory and five years to get up and running.

Have the poor Russians escaped the Red Rule to fall under the golden rule of a Hungarian cousin of the Gulag chiefs?

Soros came up against the Bolshevik clique and had to change the way he worked on the ground:

"The director arrived at the meeting as director and left as ex-director. Then the person who had arranged the putsch, the foundation's legal adviser, took over. He was "politically correct", but he turned out to be a worse dictator than his predecessors. So after a year, I had to organise another putsch while he was in America"...

Ex-Soviets whose necks are too stiff are broken without scruple. The new Moscow government "gives him little hope". He is counting on it:

"Help the Ministry of Education to replace all Marxist-Leninist teaching with that of the humanities" (i.e. that of capitalism)."

Much depends, as LE MONDE always observes, on the choice of people for whom Soros can make up his mind in five minutes, on instinct, impulse, intuition:

Sometimes we haven't found the contact," says Soros, "for example in Lithuania we did a very good job, but not in Latvia. When I say 'we', it's really me: you need a personal contact to start with".

Once they have made their choice, they have complete confidence in the foundations, including the money. The use of the funds is decided locally by each of the foundations, and a copy of the accounts is sent to New York.

"He's empowering people in Eastern Europe," says Sandra Pralong, who runs the Soros Foundation in Romania.

In Warsaw he had to operate differently. The Poles were more wary and resisted (Soros admits as much). They had a different conception. In the end, the financier triumphed. Le MONDE says: "The Stefan Balory Foundation is now the flagship of the Soros foundations"...

Clear-sighted Americans have spotted the "exploitative philanthropist" who "plays the foundation" "like an umbrella-shaped shotgun".

This "philanthropist", who started out as a financial analyst, "took the plunge" in 1969 by setting up his own fund.

His story can be summed up as follows: From Hungary, where George Soros lived in semi-landestinity during the war to escape the control of Regent Horthy's police, he went to London in 1947, where he lived from hand to mouth. He managed to obtain a scholarship and study at the LONDON SCHOOL OF ECONOMICS. He did not return to Budapest, where the Soviet tanks had brought the country under Communist rule. It was on Wall Street that he made his career, first as a financial analyst and then, from 1969 onwards, as 'boss' of his own business, the QUANTUM FUND, which he took the precaution of registering in Curaçao, the well-known tax haven.

Since then, he's piled up billions without making any waves. He's a smart guy and he knows that "to live happily, let's live hidden"...

It's not him who, like the wretched Tapie on whom the television cameras and courts of justice are focused, is going to be waving around like a pathetic puppet in the media. Tapie is a pauper compared to Soros.

The government uses him to amuse the masses and focus their attention on something other than growing unemployment. And yet Soros' actions amount to the most serious of delinquencies in a NORMAL political system. These crimes are so great that in a traditional regime THEY COULD NOT EVEN BE PERPETRATED...

As for Soros, lurking in the shadows, he's taking on big politics.

In his expatriate country, Hungary, his game has been guessed and several leaders of the Magyar right have pilloried him in their writings. In Slovakia and Romania, he is violently denounced. The ferocious speculator will never become a Saint Bernard. He is an astute and greedy "democratic" financier (what a mockery!!). Recently, when Soros bought 10% of the shares of his friend Jimmy GOLDSMITH of NEWMONT MINING, he caused a surge in the gold market.

In "democracy" we haven't heard the last of him.

Mr Emmanuelli, the Socialist President of the National Assembly, refused to take his seat because King Juan Carlos of Spain was coming to make a presentation. A king from a socialist country even more rotten than ours!

Let's bet that if SOROS comes to speak at the Assembly, he will be there to applaud this manipulative multi-billionaire sprung from nothing...

These political puppets are so grotesque that we can't find the words to describe them...

Goys, wake up or die!

"And the world will be ruled by monsters" (Apocalypse)

"The truth, that old witch" (Oscar Wilde)

"The Jews, that handful of uprooted people, caused the uprooting of the entire globe" (Simone Weil).

"The advent of Jewish Caesarism is only a matter of time. World domination belongs to Judaism. The twilight of the gods has already reached us. If I may address a prayer to my readers, it is this: that they keep this book and pass it on to their descendants. I do not claim to be a prophet, but I am deeply convinced of what I am saying here: WITHIN FOUR GENERATIONS THERE WILL BE ABSOLUTELY NOT A SINGLE OFFICE IN THE STATE, NOT EXCEPTING THE HIGHEST, THAT IS NOT IN THE POSSESSION OF THE JEWS."

This quotation is taken from WILHELM MARR's book LE MIROIR DU JUDAÏSME.

It was written a hundred years ago!!!

The rejection of religion has led to unjust economic structures.

For 2 centuries we have been doing everything to uproot and debase the people, to strip them of all ideals, all love of their craft, all religion. The proletariat is born and crushed.

The world's cattle handed over to slaughter, the wars of 14-18, 39-45 and the 150 wars of this half-century between the liberal system and Marxist ideology...

They bring in huge fortunes for the "financiers who run the world", the Bazile Zaharoffs, the Bloch-Dassaults...

There is no example in the history of humanity of a more profound dehumanisation. The fall of the Roman Empire was only a small detail compared with this global collapse, in which man, isolated from all natural and supernatural ties, has been handed over to universal madness like a wreck that can be made profitable and pornographed at will.

Man has lost all power to adapt to reality.

The domination of the circumcised on the 8th day is definitive: we will have the New World Order, i.e. universal chaos.

They are not Jews, because all the materialistic speculations that dissolve humanity are heretical and criminal before the THORA.

They are speculative brains deprived of a moral sense and a spirit of synthesis by the fact of their circumcision. It is not a question of race, because races do not exist, it is not a question of people or ethnic group, because the pseudo-Jews have not been constituted by a multi secular belonging to a fixed environment. It is a sect of glandular patients suffering from chronic speculationism whose murderous "talents" are given free rein the farce of "demoncrassie".

A curious "chosen race" (the most racist in the world) who, through finance and Marxism, are reducing the earth and its naive inhabitants to ashes.

They have every right. They are above international law, not only in Israel where they can massacre Palestinians and take their land with impunity, but in every country where they are a tiny minority.

What's more, they get the laws passed by the LICRAsseuses and politicos on all sides. If the UN has been able to stigmatise Zionism as racism, it is only a blunder that will soon be reversed. The important thing is also not to let a heroic professor talk about historical studies that they don't like, especially as they are incapable of contradicting the facts, and the certainty that there were never any gas chambers or 6 million Jews gassed in the German camps IS BAD NEWS TO BE IMPITOYABLY SANCTIONED BY A JUSTICE SERVILY APPLYING INICIOUS AND DESIRABLE LAWS...

Their "democracy" has instituted totalitarian thoughtcrime, as in George Orwell's 1984... Anti-Semitism, i.e. lucidity towards them, is the inexpiable crime of crimes. It is being pursued dictatorially and without appeal 50 years after the crushing of Germany. And this against octogenarians who tried to save Europe from the absolute horror into which it is plunged!!

As for anti-Germanism, it is not only tolerated, but recommended as a virtue... HITLER AND NATIONAL SOCIALISM ARE ABSOLUTE EVIL!!

What does it matter if we have never seen a single drug-addicted or alcoholic child, a single unemployed person, a single unfortunate worker on the territory of the Reich! Their non-existent crime, because everyone knows today that the myth of "six million gas chambers" is an arithmetic-technical nonsense, is greater in horror than the hundred million or so exterminated in the USSR by the Warburg-Lenin revolution and the 50 Jewish prison and concentration camp executioners (Frenkel, Jagoda, Firine, Apetter, Jejoff, Rappoport, Abramovici, and KAGANOVITCH, Stalin's brother-in-law. On the other hand, democracy, a screen for the absolute and worldwide circumcised dictatorship over a decomposed world, is the absolute good!

What does it matter if the world dissolves into a foul putrescence, what does it matter if the international chaos, the destroyed family, the chemically sterile soils, the 5,000 biologically dead lakes in Canada, the 2,000 dead lakes in Sweden, the reigning pornography, the perversion of our children, through the sexual permissiveness taught from the earliest age, like the refusal of the authority of parents and teachers, the iatrogenism, the teratogenism, the massive suicides of our children, the unemployment, the amnestied political scandals?..

It's all a blunder of the ideal political regime: CIRCUMSTANT DEMONCRASSIA.

The ethnic pride of whites is a crime, the ethnic pride of people of colour, of Muslims (except in Palestine) is the greatest of virtues.

Equality is the absolute revealed truth. Warburg or Soros, whose power has never been equalled by any potentate in history, or Hammer, who owned as much oil as the 3 Axis powers in 1941, are the equals of the unemployed. The village idiot and Landru are as good as Pericles or Goethe. They all have the right to vote: criminal or professor, drug dealer or scientist, all equal before the ballot box!

Undesirable minorities, unless they have had the misfortune, like the Harkis, to fight for France, and degenerates of all kinds, must be given special support and special rights. Women's rights must be widely propagated, so that through work and perversion they lose their feminine identity and their purpose as mothers and wives. Women are better than men. As matrimonial judges, for example, they will be able to complete the total abolition of paternal authority and support psychopathic and delinquent mothers against Law and Justice.

Separate ethnic groups are the nightmare of circumcisocrassia: they all need to be mixed together (except for the circumcised, who only mix with the upper middle classes and the goy nobility) that circumcisocrassia can rule over a zombified world of physico-chemical amalgams governed by the profit and loss account of globalist democracy. God created differentiated ethnic groups, and this cannot go on: let's rectify creation: the concept of Nation must be abolished. On the other hand, the artificial borders imposed by colonialism and democracy are untouchable: it doesn't matter if their artificiality makes them permanent tragedies and causes of wars, possibly world wars.

THE CONSTITUTION IS MORE IMPORTANT THAN THE NATION

The economy is far more important than ecology! It doesn't matter if universal famine is just around the corner. Economic liberalism and indefinite production are intangible dogmas. We must transport food around the world for the benefit of soulless financiers, who ignore the fact that only food grown in a specific place has any real nutritional value for those who live there. So SELF-CARE MUST BE BANNED (Hitler's great crime) WHEN IT IS THE FUNDAMENTAL RULE OF PEOPLE'S HEALTH.

CONSUMPTION FOR CONSUMPTION'S SAKE IS A VALUE IN ITSELF

It must grow indefinitely in a finite world. Economic growth, the cannibalisation of nature and the disappearance of species through the poisoning of the environment are absolute imperatives: no matter how suicidally aberrant they are...

The aim of production is not to satisfy needs, but to constantly create new ones. Frugality is to be discouraged, hedonism is to be recommended (cardiovascular diseases, cancers, AIDS, small demoncrassic burrs...) The rich nations must help the poor nations even if the latter refuse to work and are responsible for their misery. Anyone can kill a healthy baby in its mother's womb, but if it is born a degenerate, a mental or physical cripple, we must make it survive at all costs, while we let nations massacre each other by the hundreds of thousands in Europe or Africa, and mobilise the whole world for a matter of oil, in one night! (Yugoslavia, Rwanda etc. and Kuwait)...

THE ONLY REIGNING VALUE IS THAT OF MONEY

Drugs are spreading everywhere with the complicity of international finance (T.V. programme: "Le nouveau désordre mondial" - 1994). It expresses the biological and psychological misery of those who choose this suicidal palliative.

IF YOU ARE A FIRM BELIEVER IN THE PERPETUAL ADORATION OF ALL THIS DEMONCRASSIC MADNESS YOU WILL SUCCEED IN LIFE. If one day or other, for example, you sell arms to everything that's being exterminated on the planet like Bloch dit Dassault, you'll be decorated with the Legion of Honour along with some whore or invert from the film.

In this beautiful democracy, by far the worst of all regimes, since it is the only one to achieve INTEGRAL POLLUTION OF PEOPLE AND THE PLANET, the big American cities are hell on earth. They murder, rape, steal, pillage, blackmail and take drugs: don't worry, French Goys, morons, look at the state of the suburbs in 1994. Paradise will soon be here as it is in the USA.

How can the zombies of the planet react, dressed in their Levis blue jeans and zoomorphic ornaments? Are they now no more than the humus on which to germinate the rebirth, after the almost total extermination of the planet by polluting finance from Rothschild to Soros, of exterminating Marxism, of socialism which ruins without appeal, of abultifying and pornographizing Freudism, of nuclear power and its instockable waste from Einstein, of Oppenheimer's atomic bomb, of S.T.'s neutron bomb? Cohen's neutron bomb.

This globalist herd of homunculi is now crawling under the totalitarian rule of the globalist, racist, megalomaniac, MACRO CRIMINAL OF HUMANITY circumcisocracy, which will posthumously appear before a Nuremberg super-tribunal that will be genuinely INTERNATIONAL AND NOT INTERALLIED...

THE TRUTH ABOUT RACE AND RACISM

THE RACISM OF PSEUDO-ANTI-RACISM

We have been lied to for decades. We have been deliberately misled on the issue of racism and race.

It is vital to know the truth about this fundamental issue. First of all, it is possible to merge similar ethnic groups such as the French, Germans, Russians, Spanish, etc., but it is CRIMINAL to attempt to mix very different ethnic groups such as the French, Black Africans or North Africans. In the latter case, the result is beings who are internally torn, unstable and neurotic, and who can make up ideal revolutionary masses because of the anarchic factors that make them up.

The first thing to remember is that RACES DO NOT EXIST.

THE ONLY ETHNIC GROUPS THAT EXIST ARE THOSE THAT ARE THE RESULT OF HORMONAL ADAPTATION TO A FIXED ENVIRONMENT WITH NO CONTINUITY, OVER A MILLENNIUM OR SO.

This means, for example, that a pair of Eskimos determined by the cold and polar food will not retain their "hypothyroid" biotype if they go and generate for centuries in a geographical position other than their own. Similarly, a black man from the Equator will only retain his "pituitary with acromegalic manifestations" characteristics if he remains in his constitutive environment, which allows the powerful action of the sun's rays on the median lobe of the pituitary gland.

A thyroid CHOPIN will never be born in an equatorial country. The particular aspect of Indians is and will remain only in the specificity of India, which is both climatic and nutritional.

Pygmies, who are also "hypothyroid", have certain deficiencies related to a particular climate and environment.

This reality is spectacularly demonstrated in extreme cases such as certain human groups suffering from dwarfism, where iodine deficiency prevents normal thyroid function.

The only real anti-racism, and there is no other kind, is to support and help deserving, hard-working ethnic groups in the geographical place where they were formed. Institutionalised miscegenation is therefore a grave crime of lèse-humanité.

A breeder of pedigree dogs and horses knows perfectly well that their animals must have a specific diet and that cross-breeding is only possible in small doses and according to rigorous standards.

WHY should animals be denied preferential treatment to humans in the name of so-called anti-racism, which is nothing more than the orchestration of the degeneration and suicide of the human race?

What we do for animals must be done even more rigorously for humans. Ethnic mixing automatically generates all kinds of racism.

Ethnic groups were never created to be mixed. The sacred books of all religions make it clear that "man must not mix what God has separated". The most elementary empiricism proves how wise this rule is, and becomes a simple statement of common sense. The psychology and physiology of different ethnic groups are different, and it is normal for them to react to each other like foreign bodies that must be forcibly rejected if necessary. THIS IS WHAT THE PSEUDO-ANTI-RACISTS ARE PREPARING FOR US WORLDWIDE.

Two different ethnic groups can only coexist if they have reached an advanced degree of deculturisation and degeneration. This will manifest itself in general vulgarity, the absence of moral rules, physical slouching and dress, facial asymmetry, disproportions and a taste for regressive and bestial music.

At this level of collapse, miscegenation is no longer important: with the ethnic group gone, there's nothing left to preserve.

As far as the "Jews" are concerned, the problem is radically different.

THE TERM "JEW" HAS NO MEANING OTHER THAN RELIGIOUS. It implies fidelity to the teachings of the THORA AND TO A THEOCRATIC TRADITION UNDER WHICH ARE HERETIC AND CRIMINAL ALL AMORAL AND ASYNTHETIC SPECULATIONS ATHED AT THE SAME TIME AS THOSE OF WARBURG, HAMMER, ROTHSCHILD, MARX, FREUD, EINSTEIN, OPPENHEIMER, S.T.COHEN, PICASSO, MEYER-LANSKI, FLATO-SHARON, KAGANOVITCH, FRENKEL, YAGODA and others who rule over a planet deprived of providential spiritual elites.

There is therefore NO JEWISH RACE OR ETHNIC. On the one hand because races do not exist and on the other because NO JEWISH PEOPLE HAS BEEN CONSTITUTED BY A BELONGING TO A FIXED ENVIRONMENT FOR AT LEAST A THOUSAND YEARS.

The Nazi teaching that Jews come from Negro mixtures or other combinations is an absurdity stemming from the fact that Nazi scientists could not have thought of circumcision because they knew nothing about hormonal man and in particular the functional anteriority of the hormonal system over the nervous system and the human being in general.

Moreover, a "Jew" from Poland and a "Jew" from South America have completely different somatic characteristics.

They may share caricatural traits that are the subject of historical derision, as well as unparalleled speculative possibilities, such as those of stateless finance, physics, allopathic medicine, Freudism and materialistic Marxism, but this is EXCLUSIVELY due to a hormonal disturbance brought about by circumcision on the 8th day, the 1st day of the 21 days of the 1st puberty.

IT IS VERY EASY TO UNDERSTAND that the misdeeds of Rothschild-Soros finance, which enslaves the whole world and pollutes the earth, of Marx and the 50 prison and concentration camp executioners who exterminated some 100 million Goys in the USSR, of Oppenheimer's atomic bomb, of S.T. Cohen's neutron bomb, of Picasso's normalisation of ugliness, and of Meyer Lanski's and Flato-Sharon's gangsterism, ARE AT THE ANTIPODES OF THE TEACHINGS OF THORA. Cohen's neutron bomb, Picasso's normalisation of ugliness, and the gangsterism of Meyer Lanski and Flato-Sharon, ARE AT THE ANTIPODES OF THE TEACHINGS OF THE THORA.

What we have here is an INTERNATIONAL SECTOR which, by means of a pseudo-democracy FROM WHICH THEY HAVE TAKEN ALL THE FICKS, has succeeded in making all the major forms of crime enshrined in liberal-socialism normative.

Liberal financial and Marxist apocalyptic speculation dominates the whole world in a perfect symbiosis that is not hidden by the supposedly murderous antagonism between liberal capitalism, dominated by the Warburgs and Hammers, and the State Capitalism that has just collapsed in the USSR, financed and dominated by Marx-Warburg-Hammer.

It is remarkable to note that this sect of people circumcised on the 8th day, which orchestrates all our collapses, which is in no way Jewish, but macrocriminal of lèse-humanité, is megalomaniacally racist on the one hand and ON THE OTHER STIMULATES ALL RACISMS IN THE NAME OF ANTI-RACISM, BY IMPOSING AND DEFENDING THE INSTITUTIONALISED MISM THAT DESTROYS ALL CULTURE.

All these clear facts make it possible to understand perfectly, on the one hand, the non-existence of races, and on the other, the widespread racism IN THE NAME OF ANTI-RACISM, which will soon turn countries like France and Germany into Lebanon.

It's worth noting in passing that South Africa's famous struggle against apartheid led to economic misery, appalling inter-ethnic massacres and the disappearance of the white population.

What needed to be done in South Africa was quite simply to improve the condition of black people. It seems that it was no longer so bad, since all the blacks in Africa, including those from Mozambique who jumped on mines at the border, were trying to join their ethnic brothers in South Africa, whose condition they envied...

It is therefore essential that ALL SEXUAL MUTILATION BE REMOVED AS PROVIDED FOR UNDER THE NEW PENAL CODE, PARTICULARLY WITHIN THE FIRST DAYS OF BIRTH.

This measure and a natural return to theocracy will make it possible to avoid the liberal reign of suicidal speculation for mankind and the planet, which has no chance of escaping the enduring JUDÉO CARTÉSIANISM.

The only way to achieve a return to vital standards is through dictatorships based on Tradition, because as Dr Alexis Carrel, who cannot be in the odour of sanctity in the political rot in which we live, said: "DICTATURE IS THE NORMAL REACTION OF A PEOPLE WHO DO NOT WANT TO DIE"...

Just as I'm finishing this part of my book, my cleaning lady tells me that a twenty-year-old boy has committed suicide...

He had said to his mother a few days earlier: "There's no hope, there's no work"...

THE MARSHAL IN "1984"

This essay was written 10 years ago, at the time of writing in 1994. The truths set out in this essay have been brought into sharper focus by another 10 years of accelerating suicide. 10 years ago, the suicide of children and young people, of which I have just had another example among my acquaintances, did not occupy the front page of the news, any more than the cataclysms of Maastricht and the G.A.T.T.,[6] Yugoslavia Rwanda, the explosive expansion of the Maffia, drugs, Marxism...

"I WANT TO FREE THE FRENCH FROM THE MOST SHAMEFUL GUARDIANSHIP, THAT OF FINANCE".

This sentence, which sums up ALL the Marshal's policies, would be enough to absolve him if necessary.

In 1984, aren't we in a far worse situation than that predicted by Orwell in his novel "1984"? "Selected lies became the permanent truth". "Thoughtcrime" came to the fore in the Faurisson affair, which denounced the arithmetical-technical ineptitude of the sacrosanct dogma of *6 million gas chambers*. In the same breath and for the first time in the history of humanity, a doctoral thesis, which a Socialist Minister, historian and French Academician had spoken very highly of and attested to the seriousness of, was annulled (Roques affair).

A colonel, head of the army's historical services, was dismissed solely because he had expressed himself badly on the subject of the Dreyfus affair!

---

[6] Later to become **the World Trade Organisation**

There was ambiguity in what he said! He had not expressed clearly enough the certainty of Dreyfus's innocence!

UBU CIRCUMCISED KING!

There is no freedom of thought, and even less freedom to PROVE, outside the hypnotic twilight world carefully concocted for us by the madmen who rule us.

Let's quote a few passages from "1984" which are a description of our current liberal-Bolshevik situation: "History was scraped away as often as necessary. There was a whole series of special departments for proletarians, dedicated to recreation. They produced stupid newspapers about sport, crime and violence, and mechanically composed songs. There was a sub-section called "pornosex", dedicated to producing the lowest kind of pornography.

"The reality is worse: regressive, bestial rock and later music, where people hurt, kill and trample, as in Vancouver, Melbourne, Altamont, Cincinnati and Los Angeles, where 650 young people died at a rock festival. These regressive sounds, with their repeated beats and multiple pathogenic effects on the body and mind, stimulate the physiological production of adrenalin abnormally, creating a criminogenic aggressive state, as well as the level of endorphins in the brain, which determines a state of stupefaction by anaesthetic effect, and hundreds of people are also killed at football matches. 1984 is over!

So we can "accept the most flagrant violations of reality because no one grasps the enormity of what is being asked" as a result of GENERAL SUBLIMINATION. In Orwell's 1984, the people vented their hatred on the television screens in front of a head that symbolised the "fascist enemy", the foul beast. We will have our symbol, probably on television, with the farce of the Barbie trial, while the executioners will never say a word about the 150 million physical victims of Bolshevism, financed by the Jewish bank USA. And meanwhile, the Iraq-Iran war, with a million dead, is rebalancing the budgets of the USA, France and

Israel, which are supplying arms to all the belligerents to the great benefit of Our Lady of Finance and our father Marxism...

150 totally CAPITALOMARXIST wars over the last 50 years have done nothing to change people's confidence in all the political parties. They will swallow anything, of course, except the truth if anyone has the bright idea of serving it to them. With calculated cynicism, the truth is handed out in bits and pieces. This diabolical concession may give the impression of a certain freedom: it is not dangerous and does not call the system into question. At the beginning of 1994, television informed us that "High Finance was profiting from and managing drugs"...

Has this enormity woken the consumer-producer-voter out of his coma? No! " Freedom could be granted to the people because they were totally deprived of intelligence: newspapers and television were enough for them"...

Isn't ATHELEVYSION enough for zombified populations? "The governing mental condition must be directed madness"...

"They had been inculcated with the ability NOT TO UNDERSTAND AN ANALOGY, not to be able to see the errors of the most elementary logic, not to understand the simplest arguments. They had been trained by the audiovisual media to feel boredom and disgust FOR ANYTHING THAT WAS NOT IN THE LINE OF OFFICIAL ORTHODOXY.

But 1984 is less tragic than 1994. Nowhere are pathogenic music and global drugs predicted. If pornography is foreseen, it is not displayed in the streets like the placards in Bénézareff's films between Montparnasse and the Gare de l'Est in Paris: "Salopes à enfiler" and "Plein le cul"...

If there are two antagonistic blocs, they are diverse. The first bloc does not have its red billionaires, Hammer, Oppenheimer, Rockefeller and consorts, to subsidise the worst form of tyranny that history has ever known. Nor is about the massive breakdown of couples, which is increasing in geometric progression, on the paranoid futility and death of love. A woman who has been legitimately corrected leaves her husband, who will henceforth live on the brink of suicide, and marries the first man who comes along; a sixty-two-year-old man leaves his sixty-year-old wife, who commits suicide... Examples like these abound internationally...

In "1984", Orwell did not foresee the death of the Rhine, Chernobyl, 6 million immigrants from Africa and Asia, monstrous unemployment, which according to the Club of Rome will soon exceed one billion. The incredible increase in venereal diseases and the appearance of AIDS. Nor did "1984" foresee the advent of iatrogenism and teratogenism (diseases caused by chemical drugs, systematic vaccinations and genetic damage). Nor did it foresee the trafficking in genes and chromosomes, or the monstrosity of "surrogate mothers", which have become the norm in brains totally deprived of any sense of morality or aesthetics. In 1984 "THE MOST INTELLIGENT IS THE LEAST NORMAL"...

That sums it up, and Orwell's novel is a sob story CLOSED TO FRENCH AND GLOBAL FACTUALITY...

As for education, that breeding ground for consumer-voters, illiterates, illiterates, disco-customers, delinquents, colourful sacks of potatoes and total decerebrates, it has nothing to envy to "1984".

Under the imperturbable mask of neutrality (this fanaticism of nothingness), it has long since barricaded all the exits towards the Spiritual, delivered the dreams of childhood to zombism, to revolutionary messianic fanaticism...

There is NO NEUTRALITY in Teachers who, like docile robots, distil the holy gospel of Karl Marx, including free education.

AND ALL THE ZOMBIFIED POLITICAL PARTIES MANIPULATED BY WARBURG-MARX ARE RESPONSIBLE FOR THIS PLANNED AND CONSENSUAL COLLAPSE.

All the so-called democratic constitutions do not allow any freedoms other THAN THAT OF WORLD SUICIDE COATED WITH THE ORIPS OF THE GREAT COUTURER LIBERTÉ-EGALITÉ-FRATERNITÉ; Nice freedom that granted to FAURISSON, to NOTIN, to ROQUES, to ZUNDEL, to COLONEL GAUJAC and so on.

What equality between the red billionaire Hammer and the financier Soros, and the unemployed! What fraternity we have today in Rwanda and Yugoslavia, in the capitalist hunger of the Third World, and now of the Fourth World, which will continue to grow, and in the 150 capitalist-Marxist wars of this half-century!

AND THE MARSHAL? What did he DO, what did he WANT to do?

DID HIS POLICIES LEAD US TO THESE HORRORS?

For him, the work of the French was the supreme resource of the country. It had to be sacred. Capitalism and international socialism, which had exploited and degraded it, were part of the pre-war period. They were all the more disastrous in that, while seemingly opposed to each other, they were secretly at one with each other.

"WE WILL NO LONGER SUFFER THEIR TENEROUS ALLIANCE", he said. We will do away with dissension in the city, we will not allow it inside our factories and farms. We will not give up the powerful engine of profit, nor the reserves that savings accumulate, but profit will remain the reward for hard work and risk.

MONEY WILL ONLY BE THE REWARD FOR EFFORT. A RACE OF MASTERS MUST NOT TURN THOSE WHO WORK INTO A RACE OF SLAVES.

We will have to restore the tradition of craftsmanship and re-root the Frenchman in the land of France.

THE CLASS STRUGGLE, SEEN AS THE GREAT ENGINE UNIVERSAL PROGRESS, IS AN ABSURD CONCEPT WHICH LEADS PEOPLES TO DISINTEGRATION AND DEATH...

A new status was to prelude the relationship between capital and labour that would ensure dignity and justice for all. Never in the history of France had the State been more enslaved than in the pre-war decades, enslaved simultaneously by coalitions of economic interests and by political and trade union teams falsely claiming to represent the working class. The Marshal's regime was to be a social hierarchy, no longer based on the false idea of the natural equality of men but on the necessary equality of opportunity given to all Frenchmen to prove their aptitude for service. The pre-war economic system had the same defects as the political system: the appearance of liberalism, but in fact total subservience to the moneyed powers.

Free competition was the mainspring and regulator of the liberal regime; the day the coalitions and trusts broke this essential mechanism, production and prices were left defenceless to speculation.

Then there was the spectacle of millions of people lacking the necessities of life in the face of unsold stocks and even, supreme crime, destroyed WITH THE SOLE PURPOSE OF SUPPORTING THE PRICE OF RAW MATERIALS.

"I will take up again", said the Marshal, "against selfish and blind capitalism, the struggle that the sovereigns of France began and won against feudalism. I INTEND THAT MY COUNTRY SHOULD NOT BE EXTERMINATED BY MARXISM AND ECONOMIC LIBERALISM".

Since all the political parties, without exception, are accomplices of both, how can we hope that the Marshall could be rehabilitated by ROTHSCHILDO-MARXO-FREUDO-EINSTEINO-PICASSISM?

For those who think that the Marshal does not need to be rehabilitated.

As for the others, we don't ask the executioners to rehabilitate their victims!

All this is blatantly topical. We're in a mess that's infinitely worse than the one described by the Marshal, because while it's the same qualitatively (with its aggravations: women totally destroyed as wives and mothers), quantitatively it's taken on bloated proportions, accelerating exponentially towards the worst.

The remedies? THOSE OF THE MARKET, in other words, GOOD SENSE. The dilemma is simple: it's either that or death...

AFTER THE ATTEMPTED ASSASSINATION OF PROFESSOR FAURISSON

THE *6-MILLION-GAS-CHAMBERS* MYTH AND DOGMA OR REALITY? PR FAURISSON PUBLIC ENEMY N°1 OR INTERNATIONAL HERO OF THE XXTH CENTURY?

MAJOR PSYCHOLOGICAL ARGUMENTS

The *6-million-gas-chambers* dogma is as set in stone as the Redemption dogma. Who would quarrel with a professor who revealed that Pol Pot (who was never tried for crimes of lèse-humanité!!) murdered 2 million human beings instead of 4 million, according to official information? Who would be indignant if we learned that the Jewish prison and concentration camp executioners (Kaganovitch, Frenkel, Yagoda, Firine, Rappaport, Abramovici etc.) massacred 30 million people in the USSR instead of the 60 million they are credited with? NO ONE.

Why on earth would announcing the EXCELLENT NEWS that there were no 6 million Jewish victims and no gas chambers to exterminate 1,000 people at a time BE BAD NEWS TO BE SANCTIONED BY THE JUSTICE????

In 5000 years of history, this case is unique: it is a dazzling illustration of well-known Jewish phenomenon of jeremiad. PAUL RASSINIER, a Socialist MP and history teacher who was interned for years in the German camps, came out weighing 30kg, died as a result of his internment and was prosecuted for the books he wrote to expose the truth. Since his death, his publications have been shrouded in a conspiracy of silence, no doubt in the name of democratic freedom of expression...

PROFESSOR FAURISSON, who studied the problem for 20 years, was convicted even though the jury "DID NOT OBJECT TO THE SERIOUSNESS OF HIS WORK IN DEBATING WITH SPECIALISTS AND THE PUBLIC"... (recitals of the judgment).

HENRI ROQUES, whose thesis on the Gerstein report was annulled for the first time in history, even though the most important media historian, Alain Decaux, now a Socialist minister, publicly attested to the excellence of this thesis. In fact, this thesis should have been useless, since it was challenged at the Nuremberg trial!

ERNST ZUNDEL, in Canada, whose trial caused quite a stir. Not only did it destroy the myth of the Holocaust, but the engineer specialising in gassing in the USA, F. LEUCHTER, demonstrated that there could not have been ANY GASPING OF HUMANS WITH CYCLON B at Auschwitz. Furthermore, the trial established without the slightest ambiguity, AN INTERNATIONAL CONJURATION OF ZIONIST BANKERS AND BOLCHEVISM...

Despite the considerable publicity this trial generated in Canada, NO INFORMATION WAS RELEASED IN THE MEDIA, WHICH HAD A TOTAL HANDLING.

At the colloquium held in 1980 against Faurisson (AND WHICH HE WAS NOT VERY DEMOCRATICALLY INVITED TO: "WE SPEAK ABOUT THE REVISIONISTS BUT NOT WITH THEM", said, without shame, an Exterminationist CONFIDENT IN INTELLECTUAL PROBITY AND DEMOCRATIC FREEDOM OF EXPRESSION!!),

Raymond Aron admitted that there was no concrete evidence of any kind, no written document establishing the indisputable existence of homicidal gas chambers...

ANNALES RÉVISIONNISTES is seized, again in the name of democratic freedom of expression. No right of reply for Professor Faurisson, rudely insulted on Polac's programme. On the same day

70,000 zombified youngsters take off their knickers to imitate a little bleating girl chanting ignorant texts. Pornography and drugs are spreading very democratically, as is regressive and pathogenic music.

Since when does democracy not allow FREE EXPRESSION AND THE RESPONSE AND EVIDENCE THAT WOULD ANNOY A POSSIBLE LIE???

Faurisson implores, begs to be put face to face with multiple contradictors in front of as large an audience as possible!!

SHOW ME ONE SINGLE LIAR IN 5000 YEARS OF JUDEO-CHRISTIANITY WHO HAS DONE AS MUCH!

The bad faith, the general huffing and puffing, the tear gas, the assault and battery, the assassination attempts PROVE UNAPPEARABLY THAT FAURISSON IS RIGHT BEFORE EVEN STUDYING THE ARITHMETIC AND TECHNICAL RELATIONSHIPS CONCERNING THIS ISSUE...

What's more, he is called a "Nazi", as are all those who raise this sacrosanct issue of PERPETUAL ADORATION.

Yet everyone knows that Faurisson is a democrat, anti-Nazi and a member of the League of Atheists. Let us note in passing that this league which shouts its democratic epicentrism did not want to keep Faurisson among its members BECAUSE OF THE NATURE OF HIS RESEARCH AND DISCOVERIES. If Mr Lévy is no longer ridiculous in the twentieth century, neither is Mr Homais!

There's no doubt about it.

The nineteen-fourty-fourths absoluteness conferred on the *6-million-chambers-to-gas* dogma is the flagrant psychological proof of its imposture.

If Faurisson was wrong, he would have been proved wrong a long time ago in front of as large an audience as possible, which was very easy for the ruling Jewry...

ARITHMETIC AND TECHNICAL PROOF

6 million, or even 4 million (assuming that 2 million died as a result of the war, which is inaccurate), represent a country like Switzerland. They were exterminated in 7 concentration camps in 1943-44.

We know the exact number of crematoria and the individual and total duration of cremation. IN FACT, THE PERFECTIONISED CREMATORY OVENS WERE INSTALLED ONLY AT THE END OF 1943 (Georges Wellers himself confirms this in his book in favour of the gas chambers). This means that cremation only became technically perfect once these ovens were installed. Earlier mass cremations could not have been exhaustive. They would have triggered typhus epidemics throughout Europe.

IF WE OPERATE THE CREMATORIA ACCORDING TO THE KNOWN DURATION OF HOLOCAUST CREMATION (LESS THAN 2 YEARS) AND THE KNOWN INDIVIDUAL DURATION, THE RESULT IS THAT THE CREMATORIA WILL CONTINUE TO OPERATE UNTIL THE YEAR 2020!!!

ALL the crematoria, which were absolutely necessary to prevent typhus, were in working order. We know exactly how they work.

ON THE OTHER HAND, THERE IS NO SUCH THING AS A CYCLON B GAS CHAMBER. This product has been used in Germany by the hygiene services since 1921.

In this respect, it is amusing to visit the Struthoff gas chamber in Alsace, where hydrocyanic acid is said to have escaped through a chimney, after gassing, FIFTY METRES FROM THE COMMANDER'S RESIDENCE....!!!

"After the gassing, we opened the door: the victims, still throbbing, fell into our arms. Five minutes later, we cleared away the corpses.

This is nonsense, because you need 20 hours of ventilation and gas masks to carry out such an operation...

Anyone can find out more about the gas chamber used in the USA for ONE (maximum 2) people sentenced to death. ITS UNBELIEVABLE COMPLEXITY CLEARLY SHOWS THAT GASSING 2000 PEOPLE AT A TIME WITH HYDROCYANIC ACID IS A TECHNICAL NONSENSE.

The fact that the tiny Struthof camp was mistaken for a gas chamber for 40 years will go down in history as a memorable example of the naivety of the masses. The same is true of this whole affair, which does not stand up to a few minutes of arithmetic-technical reflection at primary school level. It is certain that if a CM2 pupil were given the *6-million-rooms-to-gas* problem and solved it according to the official propaganda assertions, he would get a zero on his paper.

In 1949, at the trial of DEGESH, the manufacturer of Cyclon B, the CEO of the company, Dr Héli, and the inventor of Cyclon B, Dr Ra, stated that gassing under the conditions described was impossible and ESSENTIAL. NO ONE TELLS US ABOUT THIS TRIAL, JUST AS NO ONE TELLS US THAT THE GERSTEIN REPORT, WHICH THE JUDEOCRACY HAS BEEN EXALTING FOR 50 YEARS, WAS CHALLENGED AT THE NUREMBERG TRIAL!

A famous American newspaper, the AMERICAN JEWISH YEAR BOOK, tells us in n° 43 page 666, THAT IN EUROPE OCCUPIED BY THE GERMANS IN 1941, THERE WERE 3,300,000 JEWS!

We can admire the conscience, logic and good faith of the exterminationists in this extract from Le Monde dated 21 NOVEMBER 1979: "Everyone is free to imagine or dream that these monstrous events did not take place. Unfortunately, they did happen, and no one can deny their existence without offending the truth. We must not ask ourselves how such a mass murder was technically possible: IT WAS TECHNICALLY POSSIBLE BECAUSE IT HAPPENED.

THIS IS THE STARTING POINT FOR ANY HISTORICAL INVESTIGATION INTO THE SUBJECT.

It is up to us to simply reiterate: there is no, THERE CAN BE NO DEBATE ON GAS FIREPLACES"...

The unfortunate thing is that it was precisely on the basis of the above-mentioned and underlined starting point that FAURISSON STARTED HIS WORK TO DEMONSTRATE TO HIS STUDENTS THE RELATIONSHIP BETWEEN GAS FIREPLACES AND THE 6 MILLION. The unfortunate thing is that it was this "reality" that led him to discover the greatest deception in history.

In any case, to the stupefying paranoid and dogmatic assertion that precedes it, the insanity of which is obvious to anyone (what mark could we give to a student who would write an essay according to such logic?!). A Swiss teacher and journalist, Ms Paschoud, (who has since suffered THE WORST PERSECUTIONS), tells us: "The gas chambers existed, so be it! I would like someone to explain to me why, for more than 20 years, Revisionists have been targeted in their professional and private lives, when it would be a simple matter, IN ORDER TO SHUT THEM DOWN DEFINITELY, TO PRODUCE ONE AND ONLY ONE OF THESE INNOMBRABLE IRREFUTABLE EVIDENCE THAT THEY PRETEND TO BE ABLE TO BRAND OUT WITHOUT STOP"...?

Who could say that these two sentences are not a definitive response to the insane text that precedes them?

But here is the nail in the Soviet coffin: "THE PUBLICATION OF THE RUSSIAN AUSCHWITZ ARCHIVES BRINGS THE

NUMBER OF AUSCHWITZ VICTIMS TO 75,000 DURING THE PERIOD OF HITLERISM...

FAURISSON PUTS THE TOTAL NUMBER OF VICTIMS AT AUSCHWITZ AT AROUND 150,000.

THE CONCLUSION IS CLEAR: WHICHEVER WAY YOU LOOK AT THE PROBLEM, THE DOGMA OF 6 MILLIONGASROOMS IS NONSENSE:

PSYCHOLOGICAL ARITHMETIC TECHNICAL

FAURISSON IS THEREFORE A HERO WHO RISKS HIS LIFE AGAINST BIGGEST, MOST UNIQUE, MOST UNUSUAL AND MOST USELESS LIE IN HISTORY.[7]

The Stalinist, Orwellian, unconstitutional laws on "thoughtcrime" are now the ninth proof of the imposture: everyone has understood...

We don't need dictatorial laws to impose the TRUTH...

---

[7] When we say "useless", we're not talking about the crass and shameful political and financial exploitation of this jeremiad.
It should also be noted that the unconstitutional Stalinist "thought crime" laws are now NINETEEN PROOF of the imposture: you don't need dictatorial laws to impose the truth.

THE MYTH OF INDEFINITE PRODUCTION AND THE CANNIBALISATION OF NATURE

Humanism has made man the navel of the universe, and the result is the agony of man and nature: humanism is therefore repudiated.

Despite a slight halt in economic growth, the myth remains entrenched and absolute. We persist in poeting higher than we have lute. Some, like Cousteau, realise that we are looking after nature's deathbed. Our planet is 10,000 km in diameter. It is 3/4 water and 2/5 land. If we remove the polar regions, the deserts and other inhospitable places, we find that our viable space is reduced to a narrow strip around the 50th parallel. A thin, narrow strip indeed.

However, the industrial countries that lie precisely in this viable space have gradually invested a lot of fertile land that consequently no longer produces anything, because they need this treasure for streets, houses and, above all, INDUSTRIAL COMPLEXES. Like all neurotics, we firmly believe that this is indispensable to our economic growth, vital to our well-being, AND A SINE QUA NON CONDITION FOR PROGRESS.

We have become accustomed to the good life. We run to the drugstore or to the allopathic practitioner for the slightest thing, believing that modern medicine, which, alas, is highly qualified, pathogenic and teratogenic - but who knows? - will cure us and reassure us, and that we will live a long life in comfort, of course. We are allowing ourselves freedoms that no previous generation has ever dreamed of. Thanks to the marvels of technical achievement, time and space have shrunk. We can see the big picture and distinguish the small one. We use this hyper-analytical perspective of the mind not only to promote what we mistakenly call "education", but also to keep the wheels of industrialisation and mass production turning. The result of this frenetic production is a form of hysteria characterised by one symptom: PRODUCTION CEASES TO SATISFY OUR NEEDS TO FALL INTO THE VESANIA OF PRODUCTION FOR PRODUCTION, CONSUMPTION FOR CONSUMPTION.

Our knowledge and resources are now used for a single purpose: THE EXCLUSIVE PROCESS OF KILLING NATURE. In liberal economics, this is called "economic growth", and the communist economy has only relentlessly reproduced the capitalist crime of irreversibly mutilating our earthly environment. THINKING AND ACTING ECOLOGICALLY MAKES SENSE.

Unfortunately, if those who are known as "Peasants" (a word meaning "peasants") were aware of this meaning, those who call themselves "ecologists" are VERY CLOSE TO KNOWING what it means.

It's clear.

We have to understand that the profound reality of everything is that: everything in this world is interdependent and you can't make fun of nature because *IT NEVER GIVES UP.*

Consequently, our entire civilisation must adopt a different direction to the suicidal Judeo-Cartesian strategy: it must be REASONABLE, not profitable in the short term, and PARALOGICAL.

Our economy is using up infinitely precious energy and raw materials THAT HAVE BEEN BUILT UP FOR THOUSANDS OF YEARS.

It's a consumption process that we have no reason to be proud of, despite all the little gadgets it provides, which we admire, wide-eyed, with the naivety of a five-year-old who has just been given an electric train. As we know, our society produces objects that have no chance of being used in 100 years' time.

THE MOST TERRIFYING THING IS THE EXPONENTIAL RATE AT WHICH WE ARE CONSUMING RAW MATERIALS AND ENERGY:

IT DOUBLES EVERY 40 YEARS. We can therefore estimate how much time we have left to use up iron, aluminium, copper, coal, petroleum, uranium, etc.

Big business is feverishly racking its brains to find ways of staving off the inevitable before we have exploited the last drop of the planet's precious oil. It is quite absurd to think that new discoveries of reserves will allow us to prolong our plundering of nature.

THE TIME OF THE END OF EVERYTHING CAN BE EXTENDED BY A TINY LITTLE CHOUYA. That's all we can hope for.

In the meantime, we continue to stammer like robots, uttering idiotic slogans in honour of "marvellous progress".

THEORETICALLY we could cure this psychosis of endless exploitation for profit without honour and return to an "economy of nature". For ages we have used regenerative energy sources such as water and wood.

Unfortunately, the reality is that this is almost impossible.

It's hard to see how we can reduce the consumption of raw materials and energy, because on our little planet, MORE THAN 4 BILLION human beings have to live, 3 billion of them in countries referred to by some black comedian as "developing"... These countries are RADICALLY incapable of feeding their citizens and reject the effort needed to limit the birth rate of their starving citizens.

From time to time we receive visual, written and spoken documents depicting the shocking horror of children suffering from malnutrition and asking for our help. It's true that the gigantic sums invested in arming the world's nations would, for a time, relieve their suffering and clean up the environment somewhat, since the industry, which pollutes by definition, would no longer be producing weapons. This charitable view would only be a very temporary palliative. THE AID WOULD ALSO SERVE TO INCREASE THE RATE OF BIRTHS GOING TO FAMILIES and, as a result, the demand for aid WOULD INCREASE EXPONENTIALLY...

We know that most of the children in these countries will die of hunger.

However, the birth rate and the cycle of impoverishment are concentrated in ever tighter knots.

Nevertheless, our businessmen continue to regard these countries as markets for their mass-produced goods, which are so over-produced that there are no outlets for them in the countries where they were manufactured. It is true that when these countries are insolvent, finance, unable to exercise its hidden totalitarianism of the Multinationals, hands over the appropriate countries, in the name of the right of peoples to self-determination, to EXTERMINATE MARXISM. We are constantly told that, by helping these poor countries, we are securing our jobs and raising our standard of living. Is it worth it for 4 billion people on an overpopulated planet to buy televisions, fridges, cars and holiday trips?

It's not worth it because it will take 40 years, if we still have raw materials, to give this pleasure to 4 billion people, who will be seven billion by the end of those 40 years.

What's more, the items supplied will have long since worn out or expired.

WE ARE THEREFORE LEADED BY PARALOGICAL GRIBBS WITH WHOM ANY SYNTHETIC DIALOGUE IS IMPOSSIBLE and who, moreover, even lucid, COULD DO NOTHING BECAUSE OF THE ABSOLUTE TOTALITARISM OF SO-CALLED "JEWISH" FINANCE...

Overpopulation in the Third World is a Disaster

It would have been better to promote a reduction in the population of the Third World, but many politicians in the countries concerned regard birth control as a euphemism concealing a desire to exterminate non-whites. They have even instituted a birth programme...

It is therefore certain that aid to underdeveloped countries, and not "developing" countries, is for us AN ADDITIONAL FORM OF SUICIDE AND NOT AUTHENTIC CHARITY.

Any help we get will come back like a boomerang in the form of a gigantic, starving army that will demand more and more help.

Helping pregnant women will mean starving children in the future. There are no illusions about this.

They will be niagaras of miserable refugees streaming towards us day after day. And all of this in an Ubuesque context, because WHAT HELP CAN WE OFFER WHEN OUR RAW MATERIALS WILL BE VIRTUALLY DEPLETED?

I recently read in the "CARTER REPORT", among a sea of dead ends, that, for example, Catalonia will be a desert by the end of the 21st century...

In 60 years' time, there will be 12 billion people on the planet if our Judeo-Cartesian civilisation, the logical conclusion of Judeo-Christianity, has not totally collapsed.

VERY FEW of us understand that the process of extermination known as economic growth is exponentially linked to the increase in the population of the Third World. The rate at which we are consuming the planet's raw materials and energy is doubling at the same time as the population, and this despite the fact that WHITE POPULATIONS ARE DECREASING IN INCREASING PROPORTIONS.

Led by incompetent demagogues who owe their allowances to the "democratic dictatorship of finance", and who, LIKE THEIR MASTERS, are COMPLETELY LACKING IN THE SPIRIT OF SYNTHESIS.

We are forced to believe that economic growth is more important than our children's future.

So GROWTH is the all-purpose fetish of these demagogues.

One obvious fact is that politicians, priests, various pastors and other puppets and clowns (THINK THAT ABBÉ PIERRE VOTED FOR MAASTRICHT!!!!) are pushing us to the perpetual adoration of ECONOMIC GROWTH, a dogma as sacrosanct as that of the HOLOCAUST.

We will pay with our lives and the lives of our children.

Economic growth is a splendid water lily that we watch adoringly as it grows and grows and grows until it covers the entire surface of the lake, smothering it in the very mirage that dazzles us.

After all, we get the masters and myths we deserve...

UN STATISTICS

The figures are frightening: one and a half billion people living in absolute poverty. One billion people on the brink of poverty.

800 million undernourished. One billion illiterates.

And every day everyone wonders what the 21st century will be like. Humanity is in retreat, material progress is a general regression and poverty for the majority...

THE MYTH OF PROGRESS

"The lie of progress is Israel" (Simone Weil)

"Your essay on progress is perfect" (Gustave Thibon).

No term is more overused than that: "Vive le progrès", "on n'arrête pas le progrès", and other slogans that popular frivolity unselfconsciously utters.

This ambiguous word covers only one aspect of progress: MATERIAL, TECHNICAL progress and its unexpected corollaries.

Of course we know that man has created machines, cars, aeroplanes, rockets, computers, refrigerators, radios, televisions, thermonuclear power stations with their Chernobyls and the potential to transform the places where they are installed into radioactive deserts for millennia...

But is this progress a profound reality or is it part of the tragic chimera that Eastern metaphysics calls "MAYA", which means "illusion"?

There are many distressing reverse sides to the progress coin: the destruction of ecological balances, the disappearance of animal and plant species at an exponential rate, the spiritual, moral and biological collapse of mankind through chemically-treated industrial food that is RADICALLY NON-SPECIFIC TO THE HUMAN BIOTYPE, a pathogenic and teratogenic therapeutic method, the existence of practically indestructible and unstockable radioactive waste, the influence of monstrous inversions such as Marxism and Freudism, in short, THE UNIVERSAL POLLUTION OF THE PLANET, SOULS AND BODIES...

Such is the dismal price of progress.

TRUE PROGRESS MUST BE THE PERFECT SYMBIOSIS OF FOUR PERSPECTIVES:

Equipment:

But without negative consequences. In Ancient Egypt, when a scientist made a discovery that could one day harm synthetic man, i.e. man considered in his entirety within nature, THE SACERDOTAL CAST REQUIRED HIM TO SYMBOLICALLY SWALLOW THE PAPYRUS ON WHICH IT WAS EXPOSED. An instrument or a system that improves the work of a craftsman should never be rejected. But as Simone Weil said, "all material progress that leads to the concentrationary system of factories must be banned". This "progress" can only lead to the dictatorship of finance, overproduction, overconsumption, toxic and soulless products, the reign of usury (official credit), economic and international wars and all forms of concrete and abstract pollution.

That's why the pre-war German attempt (1939) to return to the AUTARCHIC tradition was doomed to failure by the very fact of the absolute dictatorship of finance, which will one day lead to globalism, a polluted and degenerate world.

The alienated proletariat, exploited by Capitalism, easy prey to suicidal ideologies of extreme robotisation, and which destroys tens of millions of people "for their own good", is also the product of this fraudulent and polluting progress...

Spiritual:

And this is FUNDAMENTALLY before even being material. But spirituality has disappeared to such an extent that the majority of sub-humans left on the planet don't even know the meaning of the word. People have become 'unconscious' atheists, like the most primitive man. Curiously, militant atheism still marks a vestige of spirituality. People hate or ignore each other, nations and individuals fight each other for derisory reasons, because the psyche no longer has a basic sense of rigour, truth, justice or love. All forms of mental abnormality or delinquency flourish, increase, become commonplace and become normative, like homosexuality for example. Spirituality is so little the prerogative of today's statesmen that atheism reigns in politics as elsewhere in almost the entire dying world, and this for the first time in the history of conscious humanity.

Morale:

It involves an increasingly acute awareness of right and wrong.

This awareness is given to beings by their soul and not by abstract intellectualist definitions. TODAY WE ARE WITNESSING THE LIQUEFACTION OF THE MORAL SENSE...

The consequences are obvious: wars and revolutions based on cortical demands driven by finance rather than on the only legitimate demand for the advent of a genuine elite body worthy of the name.

In a world ENTIRELY LACKING THE SPIRIT OF SYNTHESIS, pathogenic and criminogenic regressive music, drugs and homosexuality (the aetiology of which is particularly based on vitamin deficiency and precocious masturbation encouraged by the

TORDJMANs and Co), are growing geometrically, as are all forms of delinquency, of which juvenile delinquency is the most tragic.

In 1991, even though the death penalty had been practically abolished, more than 20,000 people died violently in the United States!

Aesthetics:

It implies the blossoming of a sense of beauty.

And not abstract paintings created by a donkey's tail or a bird's legs...

These days, ugliness dilutes humanity: IT IS LIKE MADNESS, BEASTNESS, ATHEISM, HOMOSEXUALITY THAT HAS BECOME NORMATIVE. Subhumans in their sexual ambiguity, wrapped up in their unisex Lévis blue jeans, no longer have anything in common in their biotypological appearance with a craftsman of the Middle Ages or a nobleman of the

Renaissance. Pictorial art is lost in the horror, in the words of Picasso himself, who confessed to the writer Papini, of "exploiting human stupidity and greed as best he could"...

The architecture ranges from the hideousness of skyscrapers and the Pompidou Centre to the "people's dustbins" of modern housing estates, which have a lot to do with the aetiology of juvenile delinquency.

THE PENALTY IS NON-EXISTENT OR PUNISHABLE BY LAW. It can land anyone with the audacity to express it in prison if it thwarts the cryptodictatorship (less and less crypto) that rules us.

Literature is lost and drowns in insignificance, in infantile formalisms that are nothing more than a cloak of total emptiness. Psychology disappears and is replaced by Freudian libidinous hells, which have no basis in scientific reality.

This pansexualism, this demony of the Marxist economy, combine to destroy man FROM THE INSIDE AND THE OUTSIDE.

SO THERE'S NO REAL PROGRESS.

If progress had been real, it would not have reduced the Third World to famine, the Western world to the Fourth World, to political scheming, and to all forms of crime and pollution.

Progress as we know it is an illusion, because it leads to the destruction of the human species and its environment. The Mediterranean and the Rhine are dying from the dumping of industrial waste. 2000 lakes are biologically dead in Sweden, and 5000 in Canada. Forests are disappearing not only because of the over-consumption of paper, but also because of the toxic gases emanating from factories and cars, such as sulphuric acid.

This pseudo-progress only implies an advance in the mathematical-analytical approach to the mind.

IT IGNORES REALITY.

So he has the same pathology as the mental illnesses that display this symptom: he destroys himself and everything he touches.

We are tragically moving backwards, not forwards. This regression could lead to collective suicide, not true progress.

A maths-savvy primate with a bathroom, a machine-gun, the lottery, a pathogenic and teratogenic pill for his partner, the Express, and infantile and subliminal television is no more advanced than his ancestor who only had a slingshot and a river to swim in.

HE DID NOT RISK DESTROYING HIS FELLOWS AND NATURE OR KILLING HIMSELF AFTER HAVING BEEN DISAGGRAVED BY WARBURG, MARX, FREUD, AND EXTERMINATED IN THE END BY OPPENHEIMER'S

ATOMIC BOMB, PERFECTED BY MR S.T.COHEN'S NEUTRON BOMB...

GLOBAL SUICIDE JUDEO-CARTESIAN

In this analytical and speculative world, which is entirely devoid of intelligence, i.e. of a spirit of synthesis and moral sense, we have realised:

The chemification of the soil, making it sterile. (50 years of chemical fertilisers make the soil permanently unproductive)

Food chemification (colourings, preservatives) and therapeutic chemification cause degeneration of the human race, and diseases such as hereditary chromosomal damage (teratogenism).

The disappearance of QUALITATIVE humanity, the moral sense, the spirit of synthesis and the aesthetic sense. Any kind of chanted music or shapeless painting will be appreciated by the zombified masses.

The exponential growth of a purely quantitative population.

Viral diseases will grow in geometric progression. A.I.D.S. WILL ONLY INCREASE IN ENORMOUS PROPORTIONS AS LONG AS THE FIDELITY OF THE COUPLE IS NOT CONCERNED. Although the S.I.D.A. is still in its infancy, this elementary truth no longer needs to be proved: it is self-evident...

Atomic bombs, nuclear power stations and sunken atomic submarines can all generate Chernobyls.

Instockable nuclear waste that cannot be neutralised can be a veritable cataclysm.

Household waste, produced exponentially without enough time to destroy it, can invade us with typhus, plague and cholera...

The disappearance of forests for advertising and the ballot paper, in particular, will have cataclysmic ecological consequences.

Animal and plant species are disappearing at an alarming rate, completing an irreversible ecological imbalance.

THE DISAPPEARANCE OF THE PEASANT CLASS, WHICH IS THE ONLY WAY OF ENSURING A SELF-SUFFICIENT NATIONAL LIFE, CAN REDUCE A COUNTRY TO FAMINE OVERNIGHT THROUGH A SIMPLE POLITICO-FINANCIAL DISORDER ORGANISED BY FINANCE.

Institutionalised miscegenation, which is a real CRIME AGAINST HUMANITY, is creating PERMANENT AND INEVITABLE racism. It will degenerate into the LIBANISATION OF COUNTRIES AND CIVIL WAR.

THE PSEUDO FREEDOM OF WOMEN masculinises them and deprives them of their qualities as mothers and wives, which are absolutely necessary for THE BALANCE OF CHILDREN. Divorces and a lack of mothers will produce worldwide juvenile delinquency, youth suicides, and a convergence towards Michael Jackson, Madona and drugs... HUMANITY IS THUS VIRTUALLY DEPRIVED OF BECOMING.

MONSTROUS UNEMPLOYMENT will soon reach 2 billion people. Of these, the older generation will be skilled, but there will be a shapeless mass who are uneducated, illiterate or illiterate.

Megalopolises will be saturated with cars and noxious gases. Refuelling will become impossible. Forests that have already been destroyed will be corroded by car exhaust fumes, as is the case in Germany.

The ozone layer will disappear imperceptibly, leaving humans exposed to deadly radiation.

It should be noted that even if we were to cancel out the damaging effects of some of the above-mentioned parameters, it would only take ONE of them to ensure our destruction (atomic waste, global overpopulation, disappearance of mothers, etc.).

What would a king, i.e. someone born providentially with a spirit of synthesis, do in such a situation?

NOTHING.

The first step would be to eliminate all humans unfit for life by allowing natural selection work. We would have to abolish all forms of food and therapeutic chimification, including systematic vaccination, which destroys immune systems. We should totally abolish the rule of money and replace it with the value of work. We should allow the human hierarchy to be reconstituted according to the spiritual density of each individual, which is OUR SUPREME INEQUALITY (but our equality before God!).

It was the ancient reality of the Castes that the degenerate West no longer understands.

Despite the social abolition of the caste system, IT CANNOT BE ABOLISHED PSYCHOLOGICALLY: WE HAVE FRIENDS AND DEEP RELATIONSHIPS ONLY WITH THOSE OF OUR Caste.

A BRAHMIN TODAY IS DOOMED TO TOTAL INCOMPREHENSION AND SOLITUDE.

MARXISM, WHICH HAS KILLED AND WILL KILL AGAIN

In George Orwell's 1984, the socialist society has its dogmas in every perspective and it is forbidden, on pain of the most severe penalties, to question them.

That's where we are at the end of the 20th century. NOBODY would dare to question democracy, even though it is the worst of regimes, since it is progressively bringing about radical concrete and abstract destruction, abulising and "liberating" Freudism, medicine and chemical fertilisers, systematic vaccinations which disintegrate the immune system, etc...

This totalitarian dogmatism manifested itself spectacularly in the Faurisson affair we mentioned earlier.

He was never allowed to express himself freely in official newspapers and publishers. He was fined 300,000,000 centimes, which he could never pay. However, it was ruled that the seriousness of his work was not in question. He demanded stricter controls than those imposed by KATYN (!!!), but NEVER got them!

THE LICRA SEIZES THE PROFESSOR'S TREATMENT TO PUBLISH THE JUDGEMENT AND _TOTALLY OMITS THE PASSAGE CONCERNING THE SERIOUSNESS OF HIS WORK TO BE DISCUSSED WITH SPECIALISTS AND THE PUBLIC!!_

Jewish honesty!

But not a day goes by without capitalist-Marxist "Big Brother" inflicting on us the subliminal, hypnotic *"6-million-rooms-to-gas"* hype that makes everyone so nauseous...

The absolute and atrocious ban on discussing dogma has appeared. The imprudent were promised the stake, just as witches were burned at the stake in the Middle Ages!

And yet the objective study of this problem leaves no room for doubt.

Let's look objectively at Communist realities...

These realities were denounced by Solzhenitsyn, Pascalini and Khrushchev himself. We can talk about 150,000,000 deaths...

It is true that they were not Jews, that they were exterminated by Jews, and that in this case 150 million true are much less than 6 million false! Such is the accounting for "this vile seed of cattle"...

The Communist regime imposed the following measures in the most totalitarian way: it dispersed the Constituent Assembly and introduced the practice of summary executions. It crushed strikes and when the dispossessed peasants revolted, it crushed them in the most ferocious way. He broke up the Church and reduced 20 provinces to famine.

Then came the terrible Volga famine of 1921. Finally, having ruined Russia through civil war, he called on America for help. America, which had already financed the revolution through its Jewish financiers, Warburg, Loeb, Schiff, Sasoon, Hammer etc., came to the rescue. But the memory of the people has been erased of the saving of millions of lives by the AMERICAN RELIEF ADMINISTRATION.

It should be noted that socialist regimes of any hue live only through Capitalism, of which they are both the enemy and the offshoot...

The first concentration camps where huge numbers of people were herded together were set up by the Bolshevik regime (the British also set up atrocious camps in South Africa for the Boers, but although they were murderous, they were never on the scale of these slaughterhouses of millions of people).

In the 80 years leading up to the Bolshevik Revolution, there were 17 executions a year, DESPITE THE REPEATED ATTACKS ON THE LIVES OF THE TSARS.

But the Cheka executed more than 1,000 people a month, and in 1937, under the Stalinist terror, there were 40,000 executions a month...

SINCE 1941, IT HAS BEEN PERFECTLY CLEAR THAT LIBERAL CAPITALISM HAS CONSTANTLY HELPED RUSSIA TO STRENGTHEN ITS HYPERTOTALITARIAN REGIME.

(No doubt in the name of basic human and civil rights!)

At YALTA, for no apparent reason, the liberal democracies recognised the Soviet occupation of Mongolia, Estonia, Latvia and Lithuania, and 7 or 8 European countries were handed over to the USSR.

Over the next 3 decades, the site was abandoned one after the other.

In Africa, more and more satellite countries are in a distressing situation... Almost all of Asia is in Communist hands.

Portugal and Spain, despite a few convulsive rejections, have fallen into the Marxist precipice.

FOR 30 YEARS THE WEST HAS GIVEN IN TO TOTALITARIAN COMMUNISM MORE THAN ANY DEFEATED NATION HAS GIVEN IN TO ITS VICTOR.

Vietnam and North Korea have been ceded, and tomorrow it will be Japan, Formosa, Malaysia, the Philippines, Thailand and 10 African countries and more...

Why not, since a Western politician, Willie Brand, said: "I would accept détente even with Stalin"...

EVEN WHEN HE WAS EXECUTING 40,000 PEOPLE A MONTH, NO DOUBT...

And they dare to talk to us about Hitler, who did nothing more than put in camps ("no more painful than the Soviet camps", as Bloch-Dassault himself told us) his long-standing enemies who were preventing the rebirth of Germany...

What did détente mean in the USSR?

Those who tried to cross the Wall of Shame to take refuge in the West and escape the Soviet paradise WERE MURDERED WITHOUT PITY IN THE NAME OF DEMOCRATIC FREEDOM.

Despite the known risks they were running, SOME PREFERRED TO DIE IN THIS HEROIC FLIGHT.

How did this relaxation manifest itself? The mere fact of dining with an American was an offence punishable by 10 years' imprisonment.

The headlines read: "Bloodthirsty American imperialists want to enslave the world".

This is true, even of Communism, because the major billionaires who financed Bolshevism were Communist circumcisionists (Hammer founded the American Communist Party and was never bothered during Macarthyism!). BUT IS THAT A NICE RELAXING TITLE?

Only the party governs AND IN A WAY THAT WAS INFINITELY MORE TOTALIST THAN THE TZARS.

In 40 years there have only been derisory sham elections. The people have ABSOLUTELY NO INFLUENCE. Neither the press nor the judiciary have the slightest independence or freedom. ANY THOUGHT THAT IS NOT THAT OF THE STATE IS NIPPED IN THE BUD.

Since the Faurisson affair, we have been on this path...

Under this terrible regime, the MOLOTOVs and other butchers who murdered millions of people were never brought before a court and retired with comfortable pensions.

THE CONSTITUTION HAS NOT BEEN APPLIED FOR A SINGLE DAY.

All decisions are made in secret by a small group of irresponsible people and then struck down like lightning on the people.

Thousands of people are put on 'special diets' in psychiatric hospitals, and injections of chemicals destroy part of their brain cells.

There are thousands and thousands of political prisoners.

When the regime has condemned a man, he finds neither housing nor work. Young people no longer believe in Higher Education, which is totally reductionist and propagandist. They prefer not to go to university.

Solzhenitsyn does not understand why democracies used a regime so much worse than Nazism, when Nazism was the only political force capable of defeating Bolshevism...

(He hasn't read Mein Kampf, which would explain it all very well!)

"We would have seen afterwards", says Solzhenitsyn.

"We have killed the wrong pig" said Churchill...

Wouldn't the ultimate goal of the dollar's hegemony be an Americanomarxist condominium, like the one announced by George Orwell in "1984", a condominium of which Yalta would be the first step?

The delights of Chinese Communism are no better: 60 MILLION CHINESE PEASANTS EXTERMINATED BECAUSE THEY DIDN'T WANT TO LIE DOWN ON THE BOLCHEVIAN BED OF PROcUSTE.

YET EVERYONE KNOWS THAT CHANKAITCHEK AND MAC ARTHUR WERE READY TO PREVENT CHINA FROM SINKING INTO COMMUNISM AND THAT THEY WERE BOTH PREVENTED FROM DOING SO BY THE IMPLACABLE INTERVENTION OF THE U.S.A. GOVERNMENT...

It's worth noting in passing that the leaders of Communist China were trained by the Americans and the Jesuits... (lecture by Marc Blancpain).

In the USSR, not to mention the millions of victims who perished during the revolution financed by American Jewish bankers, 60 million were exterminated between 1932 and 1939. This fact denounced BY THE COMMUNISTS THEMSELVES ON BERNARD PIVOT'S "APOSTROPHES" PROGRAM.

As we have said, the vast majority of the executioners were people circumcised on the 8th day, like FRENKEL and YAGODA, who ARE ALONE RESPONSIBLE FOR MILLIONS OF DEATHS.

There is absolute silence about this truth, but the 6-million-rooms-to-gas figure is bandied about and hammered home every day in the media, despite the arithmetical and technical impossibility denounced by RASSINIER and FAURISSON. One wonders if there is a SINGLE ETHNY in the world that would bring to trial, followed by implacable condemnations, on the sole grounds of minimising, rightly or wrongly, the number of its victims in a war that took place 50 years ago, and whose enemy was totally defeated...

THIS PSYCHOLOGICAL FACT ALONE PROVES THE IMPOSTURE OF THE HOLOCAUST. This is why only

TOTALITARIAN MEASURES CAN ARTIFICIALLY MAINTAIN THE MYTH.

One historical fact is well established: as soon as the Bolshevik regime was established in 1918, i.e. 15 years before Hitler's K.Z., concentration camps were set up for the regime's enemies: monarchists, social democrats and anarchists. The camps were run by Jewish executioners. The People's Commissariat for Internal Affairs was responsible for the Guepeu, the militia and the administration of the concentration camps.

The sinister YAGODA was head of the N.K.V.D. OURITSKI, SORENSON, JEJOFF were his collaborators.

It was under their control that the main management of the camps functioned: DAVIDOVITCH, BERMAN, were heads, and KOGAN, SEMEN, FIRINE, APETTER, were in charge of various regions or sectors. APETTER was in charge of THE GENERAL MANAGEMENT OF PRISONS.

How dare anyone talk to us about the 6 million gas chambers, EVEN TRUE, when we know for a fact that the concentration camp that tortured tens of millions Russians WAS CREATED AND MAINTAINED BY 50 BOURREAUX OF JEWISH ORIGIN???

Doesn't it take more than A MONSTEROUS BULOT???

Let's also remember that the ideologue MARX, like Lenin (a little adopted Jew) and the members of the revolutionary government, were of Jewish origin, and that their victims were so numerous that historians are unable to agree on the number of tens of millions...

Who has been happy under this regime where alcohol soaks FORTY MILLION INDIVIDUALS? You can eat a little, perhaps, as long as you exterminate the millions of mouths that would be unemployed, through organised famines or the Gulags.

How can this regime feed the country when we know that Ukraine, which was the world's granary under the Tsars, is no longer even capable of supplying wheat for Ukraine alone?!!!

Who revolted in Prague, East Berlin, Budapest, Gdansk and Warsaw, if not THE WORKERS AND THE PEASANTS?

Communism has never defended the former or the latter, because COMMUNISM, like all forms of socialism, TAKES EVERYTHING FROM EVERYONE.

There is no end to the list of human groups exterminated by this abominable regime. One and a half million Muslims were deported or massacred:

THE MUSLIMS OF CRIMEA THE BLAKARSLES THE KARATCHAIS THE CHECHENES THE INGUSHES...

On a Bernard Pivot programme, Mme Carrère d'Encausse, a very official historian, had this to say:

"Even if the Communist experiment had succeeded, which it certainly did not, it would not have been worth the appalling cost in human lives"...

A Jewish writer recently interviewed by Jacques Chancel said after evoking this panorama: "HOW CAN THERE BE A SINGLE COMMUNIST IN THE WORLD"?

Asking the question is tantamount to formulating a psychiatric diagnosis.

In any case, it is certain that in SOVIET RUSSIA THERE WAS NOT A SINGLE ONE OUTSIDE THE "NOMENKLATURA"...

TOLERANCE, TOLERANCE!

"In 1984, the most intelligent will be the least normal. George Orwell.

There is tolerance:

For Marxism, which exterminates millions of people all over the world.

For pornography and sexual permissiveness, which degrade the essence of man and bestialise him.

For films about violence and sex.

For homosexuals, themselves victims of tolerance,

For chemically modified food. For encouraging masturbation (a factor in homosexualisation) and moral and physical degradation.

For the murderers of 5 people or the rapists of little girls. For a pathogenic, carcinogenic and teratogenic pill.

For self-service abortion.

For the trafficking of foetuses and children deemed to be unborn and after laboratory experiments, WHEN THEY BEGIN TO WALK THEY ARE THROWN IN INCINERATORS (book: "Bébés au feu"). (Whereas abortion for eugenics WAS RETENTIONED AS A CRIME OF HUMANITY AGAINST NAZISM AT THE NUREMBERG TRIAL!!)

For polluters of all kinds who make lakes and seas sterile and exterminate animal and plant species...

NO TOLERANCE FOR THE TRUTH:

For Professor FAURISSON, WHO WANTED US TO KNOW THE RECONFORTANT NEWS ABOUT THE 6 MILLION GAS CHAMBERS MISTAKE!

NO TOLERANCE FOR ANYTHING THAT IS CLEAN, GENUINELY FREE.

THERE IS ONLY TOLERANCE FOR THE INTOLERABLE.

THERE IS ONLY TOLERANCE FOR THAT WHICH EXTERMINATES US.

There is tolerance for "MUSIC THAT KILLS"... [8]

---

[8] MEYER LANSKI, circumcised on the 8th day, godfather of the U.S.A. MAFFIA, kept the F.B.I. on a leash by a blackmail file he held on HOOVER, head of the F.B.I. No fight against the MAFFIA was possible as long as Hoover was alive, not even by the goodwill of Robert Kennedy whom the Maffia assassinated (Canal+18/6/94).

MUSIC THAT KILLS

The naïve public believes that Rock 'n Roll, Rapp and the pseudo-music of these decades are harmless forms of entertainment and a passing fad of elated youth. THIS IS ABSOLUTELY FALSE.

The Beatles made no mistake when they said:

"OUR MUSIC IS CAPABLE OF CAUSING EMOTIONAL INSTABILITY, PATHOLOGICAL BEHAVIOUR, EVEN REVOLT AND REVOLUTION. ROCK'N'ROLL IS THE ENERGY CENTRE OF A WORLDWIDE REVOLUTION...".

There seems to be no ambiguity in this statement, as we shall show. Would it be possible for such a regressive rhythmic outburst to produce no PHYSICAL, PSYCHOLOGICAL, MENTAL, MORAL, SPIRITUAL effect on the individual and on the masses?

Only a mentally retarded person would assert the harmlessness of this mega-crime of lèse-humanité from which financial companies with unambiguous identities derive immense profits.

Unfortunately, such idiots can now be found in abundance, because the purpose of this "music" is precisely to produce an exponential number of mental disorders on the entire planet...

Let's examine the effects of these pseudo-musics from the concrete to the abstract.

Let's look first at the mass hysteria, riots and brawls that break out at festivals when these atrocious noises are played:

In Vancouver, during a Beatles show, it only took 30 minutes for 100 people to be trampled, assaulted and seriously injured...

In Melbourne, more than 1,000 people suffered serious injuries at a rock festival.

In Beirut, a hysterical crowd of participants could only be dispersed with the help of 5 hydraulic hoses.

In Altamont, USA, in 1969, a Rolling Stones festival attracted 300,000 people. Several young people died of asphyxiation and three of overdoses.

In Cincinnati, USA, at the Coliseum River Front, in 1975, eleven young people were trampled to death by the 18,000 spectators who broke down the barriers to enter the festival. The band, "the Who", STARTED THEIR SHOW AS IF NOTHING HAD HAPPENED...

At the end of the show, frenzied spectators invaded the stage, causing several others to suffocate.

During a rocking weekend in Los Angeles, 650 YOUNG PEOPLE DIED. The morgue's refrigerators were already full and bodies were deposited in the corridors along the walls on both sides. An awful smell of death pervaded the building. The bodies could not be identified. The victims were young people who had left the family home.

Let's sum it up by quoting FRANCK GARLOCK's 'the big beat'.

"The disciples of chaos and disorder could not have found a more perfect vehicle for promoting and inculcating their ideas and "philosophy" in the young generation of every country in the world. Yet in the countries where rock music is most popular - the USA and the UK - not only is the rate of juvenile delinquency the highest in the world, but the rate of youth crime, out-of-wedlock births, acts of violence, murders and suicides is also the fastest growing in the world...".

These most obvious facts therefore demonstrate that the revolution in pseudo-music such as rock'n'roll, etc., has caused the most perfect perversion of youth the world has ever known.

"Pervert youth and you will conquer the nation", I have heard in left-wing literature. This goes further than the phrase by CRÉMIEUX: "Own the press, you will own opinion"...

What are the physical and organic effects of this pseudo-music?

They are tragic. The most important is the progressive hypotrophy of the internal genital gland, which, as endocrinologist Dr Jean Gautier has shown, is the organ of MORAL SENSE, love of God, willpower, voluntary attention and the noblest human qualities.

INSUFFICIENCY OF THIS GEL AUTOMATICALLY LEADS TO MENTAL REDUCTIONISM, ATHEISM, and an absence of MORAL SENSE. We have known for 40 years that this gland is atrophied in people with dementia.

The most varied observations, according to temperament, have been made about the pathological effects of this repetitive, chanted music, with its ignorant lyrics.

I have to say that when I hear this kind of 'music' by chance, I feel painful, unbearable blows to the core of my body. What's even more extraordinary is that even when I cover my ears, I can still physically feel this shaking of my whole being. It's obvious, then, that to find pleasure in such scans, you have to be already disintegrated. They are then absorbed LIKE DRUGS that the addict cannot do without. They remain unbearable for anyone who has kept his body and soul healthy.

A number of effects have been observed clinically: changes in heart rate and breathing. Increased secretions from the endocrine glands, in particular the pituitary gland which, as we all know, is the body's automatic conductor. (The voluntary conductor being the internal genitalia). When the scansion is accentuated, the larynx contracts;

when the music 'descends', it relaxes. Basic metabolism and blood sugar levels change during an audition.

It is therefore possible to "play" on the human organism as if it were an instrument, and in fact some electronic music composers manipulate the brain by SHORT-CIRCUITING CONSCIOUS FACULITIES, JUST AS DRUGS DO...

The predominant rhythm of rock and pop music conditions the body and stimulates hormonal functions.

Intensity amplifies the effects: above 80 decibels the effect is unpleasant and above 90 it becomes harmful. At rock concerts, 106-108 decibels are measured in the centre of the hall and 120 near the orchestra!

Ear specialists are also discovering hearing problems in young people, early-onset deafness, which normally only affects the elderly.

There has also been an increase in cardiovascular disease and balance disorders.

Unfortunately, the 'auditory' effects are matched by 'visual' effects whose negativity is no match for the auditory effects.

From a visual point of view, the intensity of special lighting and the use of laser beams cause irreversible damage to the eyes of some people. If the beam penetrates the eye, it can burn the retina, creating a permanent blind spot.

What's more, the flashes of bright light that erupt to the rhythm of the music sometimes cause dizziness and hallucinatory phenomena.

IN FACT, THE BRITISH GOVERNMENT HAS ISSUED A WARNING ON THIS SUBJECT AND HAS DISSEMINATED IT IN SCHOOLS. The famous music therapist ADAM KNIESTE has this to say on the subject:

"The central problem caused by rock music in the patients I have treated clearly stems from the intensity of the noise, which provokes hostility, exhaustion, narcissism, panic, indigestion, hypertension and a strange narcosis. ROCK IS NOT A HARMLESS PASTIME, IT'S A DRUG DEADLIER THAN HEROIN, POISONING THE LIVES OF OUR YOUNG PEOPLE...".

On a sexual level, the low-frequency vibrations caused by the amplification of bass guitars, combined with the repetitive effect of the 'beat', have a considerable effect on the cerebrospinal fluid.

In turn, this fluid directly affects the pituitary gland, which controls hormone secretion. The overall result is an UNBALANCE OF SEXUAL AND SURRENAL HORMONES AND A RADICAL CHANGE IN BLOOD INSULIN , so that the various functions controlling MORAL INHIBITIONS ARE TOTALLY NEUTRALISED.

The psychological effects are no less serious: the DEPERSONALISING influence is extreme. People suffer deep psycho-affective trauma.

Here are the obvious findings:

Changes in emotional reactions ranging from frustration to uncontrollable violence. Loss of both conscious and reflex control and concentration.

Considerable reduction in the control of intelligence and will over subconscious impulses.

Neurosensory overexcitation producing euphoria, suggestibility, hysteria and, in some cases, hallucination.

Serious impairment of memory, brain function and neuromuscular coordination.

A depressive state leading to neurosis and psychosis, especially if music and drugs are combined.

Hypnotic or cataleptic state, turning the person into a kind of zombie or robot. SUICIDAL AND HOMICIDAL tendencies, considerably increased by listening to this kind of music on a daily basis for long periods.

Self-mutilation, self-immolation, self-punishment, especially at large gatherings. Irresistible impulses of destruction, vandalism and riots following rock concerts or festivals...

The MORAL effects follow automatically from this clinical tragedy: sex, drugs, revolt, black magic, Satanism, from another era...

In addition to the horror of the sound and light effects, there is the subliminal aggression. Subliminal aggression consists of introducing suggestive elements into texts that are reconstituted by the conscious mind and influence the victim, in other words all the young people in the world.

There's no need to insist on this very real effect, because the texts themselves can influence cynically, without any need for subliminal effects.

Here is a song text, unfortunately famous, which clearly illustrates one aspect of this monstrous crime of lèse-humanité that these pseudo-musiques constitute:

"God told me to skin you alive
I kill children

I like to see them die
I kill children

I make mothers cry
I crush them under my car
I want to hear them scream

Feed them poisoned candy
And spoil their Halloween... "

One wonders why the political and judicial authorities do not intervene to punish such crimes, where perversity is added to childishness...

In the Queen album KILLERS, if you play the music backwards you get: "start smoking marijuana".

In the song 'When Electricity Came to Arkansas', there's an unintelligible section that plays backwards: "Satan, Satan, Satan, he's God, he's God, he's God" and the message ends with a demented laugh.

We could write a book listing the subliminal, satanic, blasphemous effects, or the encouragement of drugs or bestial sexuality.

SO IT IS CLEAR THAT INTELLIGENCE, WILL, FREE WILL AND MORAL CONSCIENCE ARE UNDER SUCH ASSAULT THROUGH ALL THE SENSES THAT THEIR CAPACITY FOR DISCERNMENT AND RESISTANCE IS DIMINISHED OR SIMPLY NEUTRALISED.

In this state of mental and moral confusion, the way is TOTALLY OPEN to the most violent outbursts of repressed impulses, hatred, anger, jealousy, revenge, sexuality. Rock stars, DESPITE THEIR PATENTED DEBILITY, BECOME IDOLES TO BE PRAISED.

IT'S AN ERSATZ OF RELIGIOUS SENTIMENT PERVERTED TOWARDS BESTIALITY AND THE NEUTRALISATION OF BEING.

This bewitchment has macabre consequences: the "groupiez" or girls who accompany the "idol", indulge his every whim only to be replaced by other girls on the next tour. There were suicides provoked by the death of the "star", and murders like that of John Lennon.

Nothing can resist the inevitable erosion of the conscience, the heart and the mind of those who listen to these dreadful rhythmic musical regressions from which we can only protect our own by the PRINCIPLE OF AUTHORITY and the explanation of all this when the young person's intelligence is sufficiently developed. IN THE MEANTIME, THE ABSOLUTE IMPERATIVE OF PROHIBITION IS ESSENTIAL IF YOU WANT TO SAVE YOUR CHILDREN, BECAUSE BY THE TIME THEY ARE OLD ENOUGH TO UNDERSTAND, THEY WILL HAVE GONE ROTTEN...

The spirit of this subversion can be found in the text by the anarchist JERRY RUBIN:

"Elvis awakened our bodies, changing them completely. The animal hard rock that holds its secret in the ENERGY BEAT, penetrated hotly inside our bodies: the rousing rhythm brought out all the passions that had been repressed, held back. The back seat of a car was the theatre of the sexual revolution, while the car's radio served as the medium for this subversion. Rock marked the beginning of the revolution. We fused a new political life with a PSYCHEDELIC lifestyle. Our way of life, our acid, our freaky clothes, our rock music, that's THE REAL REVOLUTION... "

SO EVERYTHING IS PERFECTLY CLEAR.

WHO FINANCES?

This is globalism. To be sure of reaching young people indifferent to political speeches and strategies, it has entrusted the WICCA agency with the task of setting up rock production studios to ensure the worldwide distribution of the works of the most aggressive and moronic bands. Some of the best-known production studios include:

Zodiac Productions, Atlantic Productions, Capitol Records Inc. Mercury, Inter global music, aristo records, etc.

Jerry Rubin leaves no doubt about who he is.

A certain GURGY LAZARUS is cashing in comfortable billions on this immense crime of lèse-humanité. I saw him on television once.

She's so disgustingly good-looking that you couldn't imagine a worse director of Hell...

Ugly symbolism: "WE HAVE THE FACE OF OUR SOUL", said Carrel...

So all this is part and parcel of the globalist plot to lead young people towards INTERNATIONALISM CORRESPONDING TO THE ADVENT OF A SINGLE WORLD GOVERNMENT.

The successive severing of links with family, religion, nationality and cultural ethnicity means that young people lose any sense of belonging to a particular group or country, but feel that they are CITIZENS OF THE WORLD; The globalist citizen, atonic, stupefied, drugged, incapable of convictions other than those undergone by the subliminalisation of the mass media, without faith or law, without obligation to parents, God, homeland or master, as devoted as a consumer-producing votive zombie to the Immondes who manipulate him occultly, putting in his hand the bloody flag of psychedelic freedom...

Is there a SINGLE political party that has repeatedly stood up, as they all do for the arithmetical-technical nonsense *of 6-million-rooms-to-gas*, to denounce this disintegration of our global youth?

Which party screams every day against music that kills and drugs that "benefit and are managed by Jewish High Finance"????

NONE.

ABOUT DR A. CARREL AND THE MANIA FOR RENAMING STREETS AFTER HIM

How could the circumcised speculation that leads peoples to bloody tears and a degeneration unique in history, accept without hysteria the existence of a true genius whose conscience provided all the parameters of consciousness necessary for a happy and balanced humanity?

Impossible. So the stunted local councils are bowing to pressure from the circumcisocracy to rename Carrel streets; we're talking about 16 towns. I haven't been able to write to all the mayors, but I have at least made the effort to speak to the mayors of Strasbourg, Béziers and Limoges.

Mayors and local councillors, I have learned from the press that you have been forced to consider whether to remove the name of ALEXIS CARREL from the street that bears his name in your town.

I would like to draw your attention to this grotesque incident, which adds to the grotesquerie of our "syphilisation" (Baudelaire).

Carrel is the greatest mind I have known since the Greeks. His surgical prowess is far surpassed by his lucidity as a thinker, and since 1934, when 'THE UNKNOWN MAN' was published, everything proves that he was right about everything, and that the state of purulent decomposition in which we find ourselves is far beyond his prognostications, which are not pessimistic, but realistic.

ALL THE GREAT CIVILIZATIONS HAVE BEEN EUGENISTIC and none has accepted the exponential proliferation of motor and psychic freaks, delinquents and pampered criminals. NONE has accepted the GIGANT HOLOCAUST of hundreds of millions of normal children in their mothers' wombs...

NONE AT ALL.

We are ruled by Jewish High Finance and Marxism.

I'm a Jew myself and ashamed of being one when I see the role my fellow Jews are playing in the ruin and suicide of humanity, assisted by political clowns.

NONE OF THEM have the slightest intellectual authority to make you remove from your towns the name of Carrel, who at the head of the State would certainly not have been generated liberalism and Jewish Marxism:

Monstrous unemployment growing exponentially. The chemification and sterilisation of the soil.

The disappearance of a qualitative humanity.

A return to the barbarism of American cities, French suburbs and inter-ethnic massacres.

Viral diseases such as AIDS generated by the deliberate disappearance of all morality and the expansion of pornography.

Atomic and neutron bombs, Chernobyls past and future, the invasion of extremely dangerous nuclear waste

The invasion of household waste, with typhus, plague and cholera likely to lead to the disappearance of forests and the murder of agriculture and farmers.

The disappearance of the middle class and SMEs

Institutionalized ethnic mixing, with the Lebanonization of countries and endemic racism, created and willed by the pseudo "anti-racists" for whom anti-racism is just a pretext for their hegemony, for their absolute dictatorship, particularly over the mass media.

The pseudo-freedom of women, which deprives them of their status as mothers and wives and leaves their children to drugs and delinquency.

Music that kills is pathogenic, both mentally and somatically, and criminogenic in megalopolises saturated with cars and noxious gases that will soon be unstoppable.

The exponential disappearance of animal and plant species, accentuating the ecological imbalance.

The disappearance of the ozone layer, leaving mankind and nature exposed to deadly radiation.

You can be sure that the management of the State according to Carrel's conscience would NEVER HAVE ABORTED SUICIDE SUCH AS THE JUDÉO CARTÉSIANISM implacably ASSURES US.

Reading L'HOMME CET INCONNU will convince you of this, and I'll end with a quote from the book that sums up this letter perfectly:

"THE GREAT CRIMINALS ARE NOT IN PRISON BUT AT THE PINNACLE OF LIBERAL SOCIETY"...

Don't make a fool of yourself in the eyes of history by renaming a street that bears the name of a true elite, who would have ensured the healthy survival of humanity had they had the power to do so.

The Institut sur l'Homme that Carrel had created thanks to Marshal Pétain was a reasonable and necessary institution to protect humanity against those who, endowed with immense defects, were destroying it...

Yours sincerely

THE ASTONISHING CHURCHILL

All the streets bearing his name should be renamed!!

A former civil servant told the Toronto Star on 20 June 1992 that Churchill wanted 100,000 inferiors sterilised or put into camps! He revealed that secret government papers recently made public reveal that Churchill, after he was appointed Home Secretary in 1910, was troubled by the fact of moral collapse and that people of low intelligence were having more children than the educated classes. He thought this would lead to the decline of the British race.

He added: "I believe that the source that feeds the flow of madness must be dried up and sealed before the year is out"...

In an article from 1920 (photocopy attached), he published a highly intelligent and lucid reflection on the Jewish question and clearly expressed the dangers of speculative international Judaism...

There's not a street left for Churchill!

As the 1920 article (see translation) shows, Churchill's lucidity about the danger of the planetary suicide we are experiencing at the hands of international Jewry was perfect, as was his willingness to practise eugenics, like any reasonable country.

A niagara of proofs by 9 shows that he was right about everything in the face of the general Judeo-Cartesian decomposition of humanity.

Alas, Churchill succumbed. He was confiscated by international Jewry. He allowed himself to be invested by financiers and we remember how the financier Baruch influenced Churchill, who turned Colonel Beck inside out. He had made a full agreement with Hitler, which was broken, forcing Hitler to invade Poland...

It was probably this enslavement against his conscience that drove him to drink. He was literally bought by Jewry, which paid off his considerable debts.

Despite his clear-sightedness, he committed himself to an all-out war against Germany, which was heroically trying to save mankind and free it from the atrocious dictatorship of the dollar, which is now exterminating us...

In 1920, he would have allied himself with Hitler to fight Bolshevism, whose "circumcised" impulsive and ideological forces he, like Solzhenitsyn, was familiar with.

By allying himself with Stalin, HE SUICIDATED HUMANITY AS A WHOLE.

When Hitler sent him RUDOLPH HESS, that "criminal of peace", to try to achieve peace in an alliance against the Bolshevik forces, he imprisoned him without even receiving him BECAUSE HE MUST NOT BE LISTENED TO, BECAUSE AMERICAN Jewry ABSOLUTELY WANTED WAR, into which it dragged the United States, despite the best efforts of true elites like LINDBERG.

Yet he was clear-sighted, because in 1945, in front of the American ambassador, he uttered these historic words:

"We killed the wrong pig"...

ZIONISM VERSUS BOLSHEVISM, A STRUGGLE FOR THE SOUL OF THE JEWISH PEOPLE BY RT, HON. WINSTON CHURCHILL

(Extract from the *Illustrated Sunday Herald*, 8 February 1920)

"Some people love the Jews and some people don't; but no sensible man can doubt that they are, without doubt, the most formidable and remarkable race that has ever appeared on the face of the earth.

Disraeli, the Jewish Prime Minister of England and leader of the Conservative Party, was always loyal to his race and proud of his origin. On a well-known occasion, he said: "The Lord treats the nations as the nations treat the Jews."

"It is certain that when we consider the wretched state of Russia, which, of all the countries in the world, has treated the Jews most cruelly, and when, by contrast, we note the good fortune of our country, which seems to have been preserved from the awful perils of that time, we must admit that nothing that has happened since in the history of the world has been able to invalidate the truth of Disraeli's confident assertion.

GOOD AND BAD JEWS

Nowhere does the incessant conflict between good and evil, ever present in the human heart, reach such intensity as in the Jewish race. Nowhere is the duality of human nature expressed so strongly and so terribly. We owe to the Jews, in the Christian Revelation, an ethical system which, even if entirely separated from the Spiritual, would be incomparably the most precious gift given to humanity, a gift rich, it must be said, in all wisdom and knowledge fused together. It was on the basis of this system and this faith that the whole of our present civilisation sprang from the ruins of the Roman Empire. IT MAY WELL BE THAT THIS SAME ASTONISHING RACE COULD, IN THE PRESENT DAY, CREATE A PROCESS WHICH, BY DEVELOPING ANOTHER SYSTEM OF MORALITY AND PHILOSOPHY AS EVIL AS CHRISTIANITY HAS BEEN BENEFICIAL, WOULD, IF NOT NIPPED IN THE BUD, IRRETRIEVABLY REDUCE TO ASHES ALL THAT CHRISTIANITY HAS MADE POSSIBLE.

It would be almost as if the Gospel of Christ and the Gospel of Antichrist were predestined to spring from the same people, and that this mystical and mysterious race had been chosen for the supreme manifestations of both the divine and the satanic.

NATIONAL" JEWS

There can be no greater mistake than to attribute to each individual a recognisable part of the qualities that make up the national character. There are all kinds of men in every country and every race, some good, some bad, and most of them average. There is no greater error than to deny to an individual, because of his race or origin, the right to be judged on his personal merits and behaviour. In the Jewish people, with their particular genius, the contrasts are more striking, the extremes more widely marked, the consequences more conclusive.

In this fateful age, there are three main currents of political thought among the Jews. Two of these bring efficiency and hope to humanity, and to a very high degree, but the third is radically destructive.

Firstly, there are the Jews who, living in every country in the world, identify with that country, enter into its national life, and while they faithfully adhere to their own religion, consider themselves to be full-fledged citizens of the country that received them.

Such a Jew living in England would say: "I am an Englishman who practises the Jewish religion". This is a dignified and useful concept in the highest degree. We in Britain know well that during the great struggle the influence of what may be called "National Jews" in many parts of the country was overwhelmingly on the side of the Allies; and in our own army Jewish soldiers played a most distinguished part, some rising to the head of the army and others winning the Victoria Cross for their courage.

The Russian national Jews, despite the inferior position from which they suffered, succeeded in playing an honourable and useful role in national life in Russia itself. As bankers and industrialists, they energetically promoted the development of Russia's economic resources and were the very first to create those remarkable organisations, the Russian co-operative societies. In politics, their support was overwhelmingly for liberal and progressive movements, and they were the strongest supporters of friendship with France and Great Britain.

INTERNATIONAL JEWS

In violent opposition to this whole sphere of Jewish efforts, the projects of the Jewish International arose. The members of this sinister confederation are, for the most part, drawn from the unfortunate populations of countries where Jews are persecuted because of their race. Most, if not all of them, have abandoned the faith of their ancestors and removed from their minds any spiritual hope of another world.

This movement among Jews is not new. From the time of Spartakus, Weishaupt to that of Karl Marx, and then Trotsky (Russia), Bela-Kun (Hungary), Rosa Luxembourg (Germany), and Emma Goldman (U.S.A.), this worldwide conspiracy to overthrow our civilisation and reconstitute society on the basis of arrested development, envious malfeasance, and impossible equality has been constantly growing.

It played, as a modern writer Mrs Webster has shown, a definitively obvious role in the tragedy of the French Revolution.

It was the mainspring of all the subversive movements of the nineteenth century. Now this clique of extraordinary personalities from the underworld of the great cities of Europe and America has clutched the hair of the Russian people and has become virtually the undisputed master of this enormous empire.

JEWISH TERRORISTS

There is no need to dwell on the role played by these international Jews, most of whom are atheists, in the actual achievement of the Russian Bolshevik revolution. It is, without doubt, of the greatest importance. Their role here outweighs all others.

With the exception of Lenin,⁹ the majority of leading figures are Jewish. Moreover, both the driving force and the inspiration came from Jewish leaders. The influence of Russians like Bukharin and Lunacharsky could not be compared with the power of Trotsky or Zinovieff, the dictator of the Red Citadel (Petrograd), or Krassin or Rudec, all of whom were Jews. In the Soviet institution, the preponderance of Jews is even more astonishing. And the dominant, if not principal, part of the system of terrorism applied by the Extraordinary Commission for Counter-Revolutionary Combat was taken in hand by Jews, and in some remarkable cases, by Jewish women.

The same nefarious dominance was exercised by the Jews during the brief period of terror when Bela Kun ruled Hungary.

The same phenomenon occurred in Germany (particularly in Bavaria) for as long as this madness was allowed to descend upon the temporarily prostrate Germans. Although in all these countries there were many non-Jews who were every bit as bad as the worst of the Jewish revolutionaries, the role played by the latter, when one considers the insignificance of their numbers in relation to the population, is staggering.

PROTECTOR OF THE JEWS

Needless to say, the most intense passions of vengeance were exacerbated in the hearts of the Russian people. Wherever General Denikin's authority could be exercised, protection was always afforded to the Jewish population and considerable efforts were made by his officers to prevent reprisals and punish those who instigated them. This situation prevailed to such an extent that the Petlurist propaganda against General Denikin denounced him as the "protector of the Jews". The Healy girls, nieces of Mr Tim Healy, recounting their personal experience in Kiev, stated that, to their knowledge, on more than one

---

⁹ Lenin was a little Jewish orphan adopted by the Ulyanov family.

occasion, officers who had committed offences against Jews had been degraded and sent to the front.

But the hordes of brigands who infest the vast area of the Russian Empire do not hesitate to satisfy their taste for blood and vengeance at the expense of innocent Jewish populations, whenever the opportunity presents itself. The brigand Makhno, the hordes of Petlura and Gregorieff, who marked all their successes with the most ignoble massacres, found everywhere among the half-dazed populations, in a half-fury, an avid reaction towards anti-Semitism in its most foul form.

The fact that in many cases Jewish interests, like their places of worship, are exceptions to the universal Bolshevik hostility, has had the effect of associating the Jewish race more and more with the horrors now being perpetrated.

This is an injustice to millions of harmless people, most of whom are themselves victims of the revolutionary regime.

It therefore becomes particularly important to create and develop a strong Jewish movement which will distance people's minds from these fatal associations. This is why Zionism has such a profound meaning for the whole world today.

A HOMELAND FOR THE JEWS

Zionism offers a third sphere to the political conceptions of the Jewish race. In sharp contrast to communist internationalism, it presents the Jews with a national idea of an imperative nature.

The opportunity and responsibility of providing the Jewish race throughout the world with a homeland and a national centre of life fell to the British Government by virtue of the conquest of Palestine.

Mr Balfour's stature as a statesman and his sense of history were quick to seize this opportunity.

Statements were made that irrevocably decided Britain's policy.

The fierce energy of Dr Weissman, the mastermind behind the practical aspects of the Zionist project, supported by many of the most eminent English Jews, as well as by the full authority of Lord Allenby, are all focused on the realisation and success of this deeply motivating movement.

It is clear that Palestine is far too small to admit more than a fraction of the Jewish race. It is also clear that the majority of national Jews do not wish to go there. But if, as may be, during our lifetime, a Hebrew State were created on the banks of the Gurdine, under the protection of the British Crown, and which would include three or four million Jews, it would be an event in the history of the world, which would be positive from every point of view, and particularly in harmony with the most genuine interests of the British Empire.

Zionism has already become a fundamental factor in the political convulsions of Russia, as a powerful competing influence in the Bolshevik circles of the international Communist system. Nothing can be more significant than the fury with which Trotsky attacked the Zionists in general and Dr. Weissmann in particular.

The cruel penetration of his mind leaves him in no doubt that his aims of a world communist state under Jewish domination are directly thwarted and prevented by the new ideal which directs the energies and hopes of Jews everywhere towards a simpler, truer and more attainable goal.

The battle that is beginning between Zionist Jews and Bolsheviks is nothing less than the battle for the soul of the Jewish people.

DUTIES OF LOYAL JEWS

In these circumstances it is particularly important that the national Jews of all countries who are loyal to their adopted land should come forward at every opportunity, as many English Jews have already done, and take a prominent part in all measures to combat the Bolshevik conspiracy. In this way they will be able to defend the Jewish name and make it clear to the whole world that the Bolshevik movement is not Jewish, but vehemently repudiated by the great mass of the Jewish race.

But negative resistance to Bolshevism in all fields is insufficient. Positive and practicable alternatives are needed in the moral and social perspectives, by building with the greatest possible speed a Jewish National Centre in Palestine which can become not only a refuge for the oppressed of the unfortunate lands of Central Europe, but which will also be a symbol of Jewish unity and the temple of Jewish glory.

This is a task that calls for every blessing...".

* * *

Alas, Churchill did not understand that Zionism and Bolshevism were linked, that we would howl about a false holocaust and be silent about the real holocaust of tens of millions of people by the revolutionary and concentrationist Bolshevik Jews...

He didn't understand that the innocent beget the Marxes, the Freuds and the Soros. He didn't understand the tragedy of circumcision on the 8th day...

And now "this rite is going to destroy everything on the borders of nations" (Dominique Aubier).

ESSAY ON JUDEO-CHRISTIANITY, JUDEO-CARTESIANISM AND THE HOLOCAUST DOGMA

Isn't it astonishing that Eisenhower, Churchill and Pius XII never mentioned the Jewish Holocaust in their memoirs, either before or after they were written, even though the USA, England and the Vatican had a highly effective spy network?

Everyone knows, for example, that the Vatican had such an efficient network in Poland that the gas chambers could never have escaped its subtle and implacable investigations. He could no more have overlooked the trafficking necessary for the purchase and production of gas chambers than he could the trafficking and invoicing of crematoria, of which he knew everything.

This simple observation reveals the bloated statue of the impostor, confirmed by THE PSYCHOLOGICAL REACTION of those who are told the good news of the non-existence of gas chambers and the enormous inflation of the figure of 6,000,000 underlined by the arithmetical and technical demonstrations.

It is astonishing to find no mention of the Holocaust in either Eisenhower's Crusade in Europe or Churchill's History of the Second World War, both written AFTER THE NUREMBERG TRIAL. And yet we hear so much about the Holocaust from the media, even in mainstream films. It's true that cinema is entirely in the hands of the circumcised.

It is also true that Westerners are particularly ripe for Holocaust hypnosis.

The Blacks would probably have reacted differently: they would have taken great pride in this extermination and would have warned the

Jews that if they continued to whine they would exterminate ten times as many.

The Asians would have offered their humblest apologies, waiting patiently for the time to exterminate lies and liars.

We, on the other hand, treat this lie as a religious dogma worthy of perpetual adoration, without ever mentioning the 50 Jewish prison and concentration camp executioners who EXTERMINATED 60 MILLION GOYS IN THE USSR...

And yet everyone knows them, ever since Solzhenitsyn published their names and photographs in Volume II of the Gulag Archipelago.

The dogma is therefore that of the one thousand nine hundred and eighty-fourth State religion, as so well described by George Orwell in his novel "1984". The dogma is well guarded by THE ANTI-CONSTITUTIONAL AND ANTI-HUMAN RIGHTS LAW of the StalinoGayssotian inquisition.

So we must have lost all our spiritual heritage and it must have metamorphosed into stinking selfishness and materialism. We live in the media state religion of liberal democracy.

Like the Christian state religion, it has its unnatural dogmas, its demands for ABSOLUTE BELIEFS. It goes without saying that heretics will be persecuted, as alignment with Orwell's 1984 and Huxley's Brave New World becomes the sine qua non for survival.

The fundamental dogmas of this unnatural society are as follows:

All races are absolutely equal except, as Coluche said, "the Jews who are more equal than the others", and who have, it is implicit, many superior qualities (See: ROTHSCHILD, MARX, FREUD, EINSTEIN, PICASSO, OPPENHEIMER, S.T COHEN, BENEZAREFF, SOROS, FLATOSHARON, WARBURG,

HAMMER, GURGILAZARUS, DAVID WEILL, SIMONE VEIL, MEYERLANSKI, godfather of the MAFIA, et al)...

Racism is the most enormous of crimes, apart from anti-white racism, which is an understandable virtue: it is in no way a crime, not even a misdemeanour. All nations must be multiracial, EXCEPT ISRAEL (!!!) because the Jews need a homeland. The others don't need one at all, and we can negrify them, Arabise them, Asianise them ad libitum...

Paradise will come on earth when all races have disappeared, when blood is mixed except for Jewish blood, which must retain its own identity. Militarism is evil unless it is used against South Africa or an enemy of Israel.

Feminised males and masculinised females are normal and desirable, as is homosexuality.

Preserving your ethnic group is therefore a crime. On the other hand, you can massacre them or reduce them to starvation, if you are a Marxist president, in which case you will be entitled to aid and handshakes from our delicate liberal-socialist presidents.

These Marxist presidents of Africa, America and Asia will never be treated as criminals of lèse-humanité and will, like Pol Pot, enjoy complete freedom. This title is reserved exclusively for those who would prevent the Jews from doing harm, by putting them in camps or killing them by war.

Adolphe Hitler is ABSOLUTELY EVIL, AND NATIONAL SOCIALISM IS THE WORST INVENTION IN HISTORY.

It doesn't matter that Hitler gave his country a job and an ideal in just a few years. OUR PSEUDO-DEMOCRACIES, WHERE EVERYTHING IS DISINTEGRATED AND ROTTEN, ARE THE IDEAL POLITICAL REGIME.

This must be taught from nursery school onwards and ANY deviant can ONLY BE AN IRRELEVANT PSYCHOPATH WHO MUST ABSOLUTELY BE "STALINO-GAYSSOTISED"...

The Holocaust, which is in fact AN ARITHMETICOTECHNICAL INCEPTION, is the worst crime in history, but not at all the 200 million goys exterminated by INTERNATIONAL COMMUNISM, JEWISH IN ITS ESSENCE THROUGH ITS IDEOLOGISTS AND FINANCERS.

We are all guilty of the Holocaust and we can only redeem ourselves by adhering to, or even unconditionally surrendering to, the liberal-socialist democracies.

Whether this resolves itself into a BIOLOGICAL, MORAL, ECOLOGICAL, ECONOMIC, PORNOGRAPHICAL, PLANETWIDE TOXICOLOGICAL POLLUTION, is of no importance to the synarchs of the globalist Judeocracy WHO ARE ENTIRELY LACKING MORAL SENSE AND THE SPIRIT OF SYNTHESIS.

The important thing is to affirm pseudo-democracy with the equality of SOROS, WARBURG and the unemployed, who will soon be a billion on the planet according to the Club of Rome.

IT'S OBVIOUS THAT WITHOUT THE BALLOT PAPER, THE CIRCUMCISED LOSE ALL POWER SINCE WE ONLY VOTE FOR THOSE THEY MANIPULATE.

If a religious tradition took power democratically, the elections would be cancelled very democratically. For those who tell me that democracy allows you to democratically choose a regime other than your own, I remind them of the recent annulment of the Algerian elections...

Only lousy parties with a total lack of real values can get elected.

These despicable and unnatural dogmas are taught in schools, preached by governments, affirmed by the courts and added to the dogmatics of all Christian movements.

AND YET, DESPITE THE FACT THAT THE MOST MORONIC OF MORONS CAN SEE THAT THESE IMBECILIC DOGMAS ARE THE IDEAL RECIPE FOR SOCIAL AND ECONOMIC CHAOS AND RACIAL EXTINCTION, MILLIONS OF GOYS ARE BLEATINGLY EMBRACING THESE SUICIDAL BELIEFS THAT GO AGAINST ALL THE LAWS OF NATURE.

WHY?

It's simply because these easy dogmas exert a religious demagogic power far superior to that of the Established Churches. They satisfy the need to belong to a herd that has abdicated all real freedom. They nourish a certain need for order and even a confused ideal for a mass that has abdicated all freedom.

They are just as common among practising Catholics as they are among members of the Atheist Union.

The overwhelming psychological fact is how these ghosts of men submit to the filthy hazing of schools. What man worthy of the name would not rather die or kill than kiss a pig's head, as we have seen on television?

The masses have no critical sense and without spiritual guides they are lost.

Finally, these absurd dogmas demand no personal discipline, are detached from any transcendence, and encourage egoism and complacency.

Man, who has become his own caricature, wants to believe in so much nonsense. He adds to this his unconditional faith in the sham of the

Holocaust, which becomes THE fundamental dogma of the new religion. A religion he is not even aware he has adopted.

All this, and we can see it ABOVE THE OBJECTIVE OF THE MÊLÉE AND OF ANY PRIVATE PARTY, IS THE RADICAL AND ABSOLUTE ANTITHESIS OF NATIONAL SOCIALISM.

National Socialism noted: The flagrant inequality of ethnic groups.

He was legitimately concerned about his ethnic group and not at all about racial hatred (the awareness he had of the danger of International Judaism, so well expressed by Churchill in his 1920 article, had nothing to do with racial hatred, a label that the Jews imposed on him as an alibi in their fight against Hitler and have been doing since 1934).

Hitler advocated a community of peoples with a common heritage and blood. He wanted ethnic purity (as practised by the Jews, with the exception, for reasons of penetration, of the daughters of the nobility or the upper bourgeoisie), military training, discipline and responsible men and women.

He advocated motherhood as THE major virtue.

So it seems that the main purpose of the Holocaust hype, apart from the unheard-of political and financial advantages, is to SHOW US THAT HITLER WAS RIGHT IN EVERYTHING THAT IS ESSENTIAL.

Any objective mind who has studied the problem of Hitler and National Socialism knows that this organiser had in record time, led his country from the rottenness of Weimar, where EVERYTHING WAS JEWISH, to an incredible and marvellous community in harmony with nature!

Hitler even protected animals with a special code, and harming them in any way was a crime.

He had given his homeland a Germanic heritage, fundamental values and a high purpose.

THE RESULT WAS THE SOCIAL AND ECONOMIC MIRACLE WE ALL KNOW ABOUT, WHICH IN JUST A FEW YEARS, WITH 6 MILLION UNEMPLOYED, STUNNED THE WHOLE WORLD.

THE NON-JEWISH CIRCUMCISIONISTS THEREFORE DEVISED THE HOLOCAUST SHAM IN ORDER TO VEIL THE TRUTH AS THICKLY AS POSSIBLE WITHOUT EVER CALLING IT INTO QUESTION, EVEN THOUGH IT WOULD BE EXCELLENT NEWS!!

It is therefore perfectly clear that destroying the myth of the Holocaust, which in itself means nothing compared to the 60 million exterminated in the USSR by 50 Jewish executioners, is a mortal blow to the liberal-socialist religion.

Ergo: belief in the Holocaust = democracy.

What is astonishing about the Holocaust dogma is that for years after the war, NOBODY EVER SPEAKEDED ABOUT IT. Then, after 8 or 10 years, there was a hysterical explosion. When people are shown the ARITHMETIC, TECHNICAL AND PSYCHOLOGICAL absurdity of this fable (a fable, moreover, that is grotesquely conceived, because if the Jews had said that 3 million of their people had been massacred by shooting them or hanging them, the Holocaust would have been PERFECTLY CREDIBLE, despite real arithmetical inflation even with this figure), they don't want to know and react like Muslims to pork.

THEY'RE ALLERGIC TO THE TRUTH IF IT UPSETS THEIR CONDITIONING.

They remain emotional and cannot use their intelligence, like children, like hypnotised people.

The remarkable thing is that, as Hitler said, "the bigger the lie, the more they believe it". So how could it not be easy for the Jews, who dominate everything and in particular the media, to transform this absurd myth into historical truth? A truth never to be controlled, like the imprudent FAURISSON or the unfortunate NOTIN, who was not at all interested in the Holocaust but wanted to use this media example to demonstrate the conditioning power of the press, conditioning because hypnotic, like the atheist-levy-sion...

It seems that people want to feel guilty: it seems that guilt is a psychological legacy of Christianity, a structural conditioning.

When our ancestors were Christianised, all too often by force, the Church Fathers began an educational programme of submission, superstition and SELF-DEVALORISATION.

The feeling of guilt began with the stupid way in which original sin was treated, which endocrinology has shown me to be sexual but which should have been treated quite differently (a misuse of sexuality causes an exacerbation of the thyroid gland of temptation and an insufficiency of the internal genitalia. We can understand the tragic consequences when we know that the exacerbation of the thyroid gland produces pride and morbid imagination, and that the reduction in the activity of the internal genitalia diminishes love of God, the spirit of synthesis and the moral sense). The unfortunate Sisters and Brothers who accused themselves of having slept with the devil were burnt alive. These succubi and incubi were the victims of a turgid thyroid, of an inability to live up to their chastity, and they imagined they had accomplished the crime of crimes by sleeping with the devil, especially as their unsatisfied glandular state had given them a real orgasm.

So the general psychology was that we were sinners born wicked and corrupt and that we could do nothing but bow down and ask forgiveness of a Jewish God. The flesh is evil, we must hate the flesh, hate ourselves, be guilty, confess and thus be saved.

In early Christianity, the hysterical application of this guilt took a dismal turn. Young girls despised their bodies and were convinced that any sexual relationship was evil (CF: "Jesus conceived without sin": implying that the carnal relationship of Joseph and Mary, the legal spouses, was a sin!) and condemned them to eternal hell.

Men and women wandered all over Europe torturing and flagellating themselves, hating life and begging death to deliver them. It's sickening and unnatural, but we need to know the facts because they affect our lives today.

The word JUDÉO CHRISTIANISM is perfectly explicit. The origins of Christianity are Jewish. Communist brainwashing proceeds rigorously from the same psychological methodology. The Holocaust dogma is itself the product of two millennia of dogmatic sclerosis.

White people are therefore psychologically conditioned to suffer Jewish hegemony. Paradoxically, if my lucidity in the face of the facts escapes this, it is precisely because I am Jewish.

This conditioning of guilt makes it easy to manipulate whites by the media, the liberal professions, governments and the justice system, which are totally "circumcised" (the word "Jew" should not be used, as this word has only a strictly religious meaning: the normative gangsterism of Cartesian Judeo is not Jewish).

It was child's play to rush white people into racial integration, massive immigration of non-whites, the liberation of women, which was going to exterminate the concept of family and reduce children to pain, suicide, drugs, delinquency, pathogenic music...

Another child's game was to "holocaust" them...

This dogmatic belief in the absurd and uncontrolled myth of the Holocaust is a direct consequence of the psychological shaping wrought by historical Christianity.

You don't have to be a practising Christian to be deeply holocausted. The patent humanists who are Christians minus the superstition, reduced to divinising man who is going to become homonculised in three centuries, are just as infected when they are not more so since they make up the entire political class.

There are a few Christians who are conscious of the need to preserve ethnicity and who, like Churchill, have no doubt about the mortal danger of amoral, asynthetic and circumcised international speculation. But they remain influenced by the Jewish Bible.

These more or less lucid Christians base their philosophy of life and the future on the shifting sands of Judaic perversion.

Can you read a book more full of the extermination of peoples, cowardice, incest and other horrors?

History is quite clear: IT HAS ALWAYS BEEN IN CHRISTIAN COUNTRIES, AND ONLY IN THESE COUNTRIES, THAT THE JEWISH ATHEEATIC SPECULATIONISM FINANCE, MURDEROUS IDEOLOGIES AND POLLUTING SCIENCE HAS REIGNED.

Historical Christianity, which since the third century has forgotten all the rules of life that make man and unite him with the Transcendent, was the first enormous Jewish multinational that served as a nest for ALL THE JUDÉO CARTESIAN SPECULATIONS OF LIBERALO SOCIALO BOLCHEVISME.

It is perfectly understandable that, although not an avowed enemy of the Church, Hitler should have sought to protect young people from Judeo-Christian influence.

Today, a mass of selfish, materialistic, pornographic slaves (the largest fortune in England belongs to a pornographer, while the Queen is only 57th in the list of English fortunes: a derisory symbol of the inversion of all values), will never be able to reach a highly evolved human species capable of leading the world from chaos to a golden age.

When we see in documentary films and photographs the beauty of the young Germans of the Third , their clear eyes full of ideals, we say to ourselves that THEY COULD HAVE. As for us, we look at the biotypical hideousness of the holocausted undead in the underground, wrapped up in that uniform of international bullshit that is the LEVIS bluejeans. The pastoral Church has had the immense merit of the charity of monastic culture, the splendour of Vézelay and Chartres, the sanctity of Francis of Assisi and Monsieur Vincent. But the dogmatic Church has turned history into a doctrinaire sclerosis in which the fearsome notions of heresy and anathema, which Paganism had ignored, have caused seas of bloodshed and tears to flow...

Dogma, a challenge to elementary intelligence and to the moral sense, a confection of the abstruse and contradictory, inherited from the Synagogue an exclusive, tyrannical and jealous God, the theologians' God of justice, who comes from a primitive mentality where tribal justice is based on law of Talion and the practice of scapegoating.

It was inevitable that this religion of doctrinaires and theophagi, which for some 2000 years has ignored the rules that make man and unite him with God, should culminate in JUDÉO CARTÉSIANISM, i.e. the atheistic speculation of the Rothschilds of liberal finance reducing to all the pollutions and world famines, of Marx, bolshevising, robotising and exterminating men by the tens of millions, of Einstein and the genetic damage of nuclear energy, of Oppenheimer and his atomic bomb, of S.T Cohen and his neutron bomb, Freud and his pornographic abulism, Djérassi and his pathogenic and teratogenic pill, Weisenbaum and his computers that will turn men into maps, Picasso and his charnel house art...

In 5000 years of racism, UNKNOWN UNTIL NOW, those who practice circumcision on the 8th day of life (the FUNDAMENTAL cause of a hormonopsychic trauma that accounts for their CONSTANT PARTICULARISM IN TIME AND SPACE) have founded four revolutionary religions: Judaism, Islam, Christianity and Marxism. The latter, the MYSTICAL ATHEA, is the suicidal endpoint of Judeo-Cartesianism, which itself brought Judeo-Christianity to a crashing end.

There can be no doubt that Pontius Pilate, a Roman, condemned Christ to the Roman torture of the cross.

BUT IT IS CERTAIN that the Jews largely insisted that the torture take place. The Jewish community did not want there to be the slightest ambiguity as to their NON-complicity with the man who was considered a Zealot while the Romans mercilessly drowned any revolt in blood.

It is perfectly understandable that the Jewish community wanted to make it clear to the Romans that they had no inclination to revolt and that, for them, this high-profile agitator was a great potential danger.

But is this the historical problem with the Crucifixion?

In fact, it is at the very moment when RothschildoSoros-Marxo-Freudo-Einsteino-Picassism is in the process of destroying all the values contained in the symbol of Christ that the Church chooses to slouch shamefully before the globalist circumcisocracy.

It's a sad state of affairs, with the Church crushing its values while Judaic orthodoxy has not moved a millimetre. A great Rabbi once said:

"If I were a Catholic, I'd be a fundamentalist, because as a Jew I'm certainly a fundamentalist..."

We can see that the rabbinate is perfectly complicit with the speculative circumcised atheists who are all criminals before the Torah.

She says nothing and Israel receives SOROS with great fanfare...

Georges Steiner sums it all up in this pithy apophthegm: "For 5,000 years we've been talking too much, words of death for ourselves and for others".[10]

---

[10] Just a few years after this book was first written, SUICIDE HAS BECOME THE LEADING CAUSE OF DEATH AMONG YOUNG PEOPLE: *Long live Jewish pseudo-democracy...*

TOUVIER CASE

Every day a phrase from one of my friends and colleagues comes to mind when I think of the way people behave:

"Those circumcised on the 8th day will end up exercising total hegemony over humanity because of the mental inadequacy of the majority of human beings"...

A thousand-page book wouldn't do justice to this phenomenon because it would be so inexhaustive. A few symbols come to mind.

Mrs Klarsfeld, a non-Jewish woman, who for 50 years has witnessed the decomposition of humanity under the aegis of the Circumcisionists, a decomposition that owes nothing to either the Third Reich or Vichy, and who persists in pursuing, fifty years on, the pseudo-criminals of the war of two regimes that had restored honour and cleanliness to her people.

She is a silent witness to the Judeo-Cartesian macro-crimes of lèse-humanité that have become normative. And yet she knows very well that neither under Vichy nor under the Third Reich did she see a drugged child, a child commit suicide, 4 million unemployed, the immigrant invasion, the abortion of healthy children (remember that abortion for legitimate eugenic reasons was held to be a crime of lèse-humanité against Germany at the Nuremberg trials!), chemical pollution, the disappearance of forests, pornography, the tentacular Maffia, etc.

Arno Klarsfeld, who is not Jewish because his mother is not, was able to make the same historical observation and prosecute the unfortunate Touvier, without being surprised to see 50 lawyers, circumcised or Masons, lashing out at an 80-year-old cancerous old man who had only one lawyer, and this 50 years after the end of 2 regimes to which the current rot owes nothing... but where everything, absolutely everything, is "circumcised"...

Barbie, who knew he was doomed in advance in a stupid circus.

He could have dishonoured the Resistance, whose shenanigans he knew all about, and he didn't say a word.

He could put on trial these fifty years of crimes of lèse-humanité which owe absolutely nothing to Nazism, but EVERYTHING to circumcised Liberal-Bolshevism. He did nothing and let himself be condemned like a mop...

Touvier, who undoubtedly must have spared 23 Jews by allowing 7 to be shot, because it is doubtful that the Germans would have been satisfied with so little, after the assassination of Philippe Henriot, whose lucidity we can measure 50 years later when we reread his speeches, which pale in comparison with the atrocious reality...

Touvier could have justified his political option by putting the 50 years of macro-crimes, which owe nothing to Vichy, on implacable trial: after such a radically crushing indictment, he would have pulverised the courtroom, and achieved the supreme victory of being convicted anyway. He said NOTHING.

Both Barbie and Touvier behaved like accomplices to their accusers...

And the supreme demonstration of goyish silliness: Maître Trémollet de Villers, Touvier's lawyer, who, in the letter that follows this preamble, replies to me:

"I defend Touvier, not all of humanity"...

However, the adversary had naively and officially declared that it was above all the trial Vichy...!

The epicentre of the problem was therefore for Mr Touvier to justify his political option in 1940 in the face of the quintessential and supposedly democratic rot of those 50 years, owed nothing to Vichy...

We just don't get it.

As I said and as we shall see, there is not so much a Jewish question as a question of unfathomable goyish stupidity...

The Jews have the gift of decree. The Goys, the gift of bullshit...

This trial, 50 years later, of a cancerous old man who had chosen cleanliness, who had seen BRAZILLACH shot, who for me is worth 100,000 fellow human beings, who had witnessed 50 years of putrescent Judeo-Cartesian decomposition and seen our children commit suicide in a mercilessly materialistic Jewish context, inspired me to write the following letters...

LETTER TO MAÎTRE TRÉMOLLET DE VILLERS
(PAUL TOUVIER'S LAWYER)

My dear Master,

I have read "oublier Vichy" by Me Klein, and your book "Touvier est innocent".

It is difficult for me to express my indignation, which would require me to blow up a 1,000-page book to be relieved in a second. There are few words to convey the unspeakable horror I feel at this appalling affair, which shows that my fellow human beings know no bounds when it comes to arrogance, hysteria and recklessness.

It also appears that there is something immeasurable about the Goys' lack of courage and intelligence: after all, why do they put up with so many lies, how do they allow themselves to be subliminalised in this way?

Yet the evidence is there for all to see, and only hypnosis can prevent us from seeing it... After reading these books, the following immediately becomes clear: On the one hand, Mr Touvier, tried and pardoned by President Pompidou, does not have to face justice again: for him to do so is in formal contradiction with the Constitution and Human Rights.

What's more, 50 years AFTER THE WAR is unique in the history of humanity clinically highlights the prodigious hysteria of Klarsfeld and his ilk, who remain PERFECTLY MUTAL about the 50 circumcised prison and concentration camp executioners who exterminated some 60 million Goys in the USSR, led by KAGANOVICH, Stalin's brother-in-law.

WE'RE WAITING FOR THE TRIALS AND THE MEMORIALS:

It must be an oversight, negligence or simple absent-mindedness on the part of Mr KLARSFELD??

On the other hand, Me Klein's book shows with disarming naivety what you are claiming: it is about the trial of Vichy and the majority of French people who saw in the Marshal the restorer of France over and above the minor muck we had just lived through under the Third Republic.

I say "minor" because today we are wading in a major purin, since the Weimar Republic is infinitely more *serious* on a planetary scale (ecology, drugs, crime, bloody Marxist dictators propelled worldwide, Mafia, 150 wars, iatrogenism, teratogenism, nuclear waste, Chernobyl etc.).

These crimes of lèse-humanité owe nothing to the Third Reich or Vichy, but everything, absolutely everything, to the capitalist-Marxist context, where those circumcised on the 8th day reign supreme...

(I don't say "Jews" because these masters and their speculations are criminal before the Torah and the only thing that genuine Jews can be accused of is keeping a complicit silence before these impostors).

The real trial therefore lies in Mr Touvier's political choice and nowhere else.

He is unquestionably 'guilty' of this option, and that is why it is up to him to justify it with a terrible and radical indictment...

Your book includes letters from Colonel Rémy, a hero of the Resistance, and General Laurent, who would have had Touvier shot at the time of the war: both speak unambiguously in favour of Paul Touvier.

You can't expect that from hysterical people like Klarsfeld, who have learned nothing from 5,000 years of history about Jewish exactions and parasitism!

Modesty and self-effacement should guide them, especially if we know, as everyone has been able to find out since 1979, that the myth of *6-million-gas-chambers* is an arithmetic-technical nonsense, as was definitively proved by the Leuchter report, a specialist in gassings in the USA, and the counter-Leuchter report demanded by the exterminationists themselves...

NEVER in 5,000 years of history have the qualitative and quantitative parameters for potential bloody anti-Semitism been better combined than they are today.

According to your book, there is therefore a case to be made for the "banal" fact that Mr Touvier saved 23 Jews by allowing 7 of them to be shot (a very derisory reprisal by the Germans for the assassination of Philippe Henriot), but above all there is a case to be made for the reasons for Mr Touvier's political option in the light of these 50 years of macro-crimes against mankind and humanity, which owe nothing radically to either the Third Reich or Vichy...

In these fifty years, there is a gigantic indictment against my fellow hyper-criminals of lèse-humanité, an indisputable and irrefragable indictment.

What have we been witnessing for 50 years in this democratic world with its Marxmerdia and atheist-lèvy-sion?

What do we see since neither Hitler nor Marshal Pétain have any responsibility whatsoever???(I'll go back a bit further as regards the super crime against HUMAN RIGHTS that TENTACULAR MARXISM is committing with impunity).

Since 1917, the Soviet regime has maintained power strictly through terror. In 4 years Lenin massacred more than 2 and a half million citizens. Kaganovitch, Yagoda, Frenkel, Jejoff, Rappaport, Abramovici, Ouritski, Firine, Apetter, and 50 others circumcised on the 8th day, massacred 60 million people in concentration camps, forced labour camps, GULAGS (See Solzhenitsyn).

The USSR was the first country in the world to institutionalise terror as a system of government. The sole purpose of the Cheka was to exterminate anti-communists. Didn't DJERINSKY say: "We are in favour of organised terror"?

Lenin also said: "Terror must be legalised, as a principle, as widely as possible"...

5 million Russian peasants exterminated under Stalinism. Why were they exterminated? They were resisting forced, unnatural collectivisation.

Around 8 million dead in Ukraine A deliberate and Dantesque famine was organised in the middle of winter. Ukrainians were deprived of their grain and seeds.

This delightful government team of circumcised people exterminated the ethnic minorities of the VOLGA, the KAJAKS, the CHECHENES, the KIRGHISES, the TATARS...

20 million Russians were locked up in concentration camps, where they died of hunger, epidemics and exhaustion...

GERMAN CAMPS FOR JEWS AND COMMUNISTS DIDN'T EXIST THEN!

Let's not forget that the entire Soviet government team was "circumcised on the 8th day", as were the US bankers who subsidised this delicate regime for the development of human rights (Warburg, Loeb, Sasoon, Hammer etc.)...

Children were punished for delinquency with the death penalty at the age of 12!

Executions were carried out for petty theft, fleeing abroad, poor performance of farm work and strikes.

Stalin extended his empire in Asia and Europe through terror. He provoked genocides in Lithuania, Latvia and Estonia, which were repopulated by Russians.

Terror was planned in the European satellites: gulags, the death penalty, a bullet in the back of the head, as in Katyn later on (the usual, time-honoured method), the Iron Curtain, the Wall of Shame, to prevent anyone from escaping the Communist paradise...

The circumcised financiers of the USA and the Western mop politicians finance the Marxist tyrants of Asia, Africa and South America, who massacre their peoples, deliver them to famine, as in Eritrea, and torture them with flaming tyres around their necks, which is all the rage...

The countries that receive no aid are those that have a humane and decent way of life but which, O derision, violate human rights!

Chile (recently congratulated by the World Bank for its exceptional social and economic achievements!!!), South Korea, Taiwan, and South Africa, which is being Marxised using the alibi of apartheid and which will tomorrow be left to Marxist misery and inter-tribal massacres...

But the black people of Africa are all destitute, EXCEPT THOSE FROM APARTHEID!

The blacks of Mozambique are trying to join those of South Africa, where life is good. But the mines laid at the border make them explode: an atrocious wall of shame that respects the freedom of human rights.

On the other hand, the tyrants Jaruzelski, Castro, Tito, Duc Tho, Mengistu, Chadli, Brezhnev et al and their successors have pocketed billions of US dollars, as have all the atrocious bloody Marxist dictators on every continent. The "humanitarian" money they receive is used for themselves and to buy the weapons that the Kremlin delivers to them...

When you remember what Angola and Ethiopia were like! Today, red tyrants have left them to starvation, misery and massacres.

What contempt for human rights this complicity of our "bêtisentia" in the tentacular expansion of Marxism through circumcised banks, our taxes and the arms of the Kremlin...

But, as an aside, these tens of millions of uncircumcised deaths are not worth the 6 million (even real) at Auschwitz! 1000 goys are not worth ONE Jew and they can be bathed and slaughtered in bloody Marxism.

In the USSR, Marxism was good for other people: 95% of Russian emigrants to the USA were circumcised on the 8th day!

In the 25 years between 1960 and 1985, Africa saw some fifty coups d'état to install mass-murdering and starving Red tyrannies.

Our defenders of human rights have never called on democracies to protest against the establishment of these atrocious regimes that were going to massacre and starve their peoples by installing Marxist regimes.

The left, which claims to be democratic, has no objections when it comes to overthrowing a right-wing regime where everyone is happy, by a bloody Marxist dictatorship. The aberration and blindness are exceptionally highlighted by journalists who are not yet completely robotised:

MICHEL COLLINOT expressed his indignation: "When I see Chile on the world stage because General Pinochet saved it from the Communist dictatorship, and at the same time our Assembly refuses an emergency resolution on the CHADLI dictatorship, which murdered 1,500 demonstrators in one week, I wonder what degree of blindness and bad faith we have fallen into"...

GIESBERT, writing in Le Figaro, criticised "the selective indignation of the French political class and intellectuals. The President of the Republic and the Prime Minister remained silent when President Chadli's machine guns killed hundreds of defenceless Algerian secondary school pupils, while the entire French intelligentsia denounced "the horrible dictatorship of Pignochait, which used only WATER CANONS AGAINST DEMONSTRATORS"...

This is, of course, the horrible regime that was recently congratulated by the World Bank for its social and economic achievements, positive achievements that will never be seen in a dictatorship of Red mass murderers and starvers.

Duc Tho, the communist leader of Vietnam, won the Nobel Peace Prize (with Kissinger!). He had barely put the prize in his pocket when he invaded South Vietnam. A million boat people fled. 500,000 will die in the China Sea!!

Silence on human rights and closure of the banking locks for these people: if necessary, they will be forced to return to their hell, even if they prefer to die...

Have we seen a single political escapee from Taiwan, Chile, South Korea or even South Africa? Forty bloody Marxist dictators in Africa!

Long live human rights...

And Mr Klarsfeld, with his Communist leanings, is complicit in these macro-crimes of lèse-humanité...

Of course it pampers and assists the 40 bloody tyrants with money from circumcised financiers and our139 taxes distributed by our Mitterrand of the left and right, while waiting to liquidate the Ivory Coast, Morocco, Tunisia, Zaire, Togo etc. Marxistly.

It's well on the way: soon the whole of Africa, including South Africa, will be a huge famine, waiting to be a huge cemetery where human and civil rights will triumph once and for all!

We have to assume that Mr Klarsfeld, the octogenarian scourge of the vestiges of regimes that ignored such immense horrors, in his Communist vein, applauds the Indian misery in Nicaragua.

The 200,000 Miskitos, Sumos and Ramas Indians, described by the Sandinista racists as unassimilable, saw their villages bombed and their resistance fighters summarily executed. Didn't the Minister of the Interior, Tomas Borge, say:

"We are determined, if necessary, to eliminate every last Miskito in order to establish Sandinism on Nicaragua's Atlantic coast"...

That's for sure!

As Jacques Soustelle wrote in Le Monde in 1984: "villages burnt, crops destroyed, rapes, deportations"...

Long live Mr Klarsfeld's human rights...

The macro-crime of the sprawling, worldwide implementation of Marxism is in itself so horrible, so monumental in qualitative and quantitative terms (the crushing of physical and mental man) that even if the 6 million gas chambers were true (we know that this is arithmetic-technical nonsense), they would be a tiny trifle compared to this Dantean and universal crime...

There is much to be said about the crime of Freudianism, which joins the Marxist crime in disintegrating man from within. It reduces man to phallovaginal dimensions and is no stranger to the Marxist mentality that it prepares, and to the worldwide pornography that leads young people to the debility of Madona and Michael Jackson, to drugs and suicide...

This Freudian crime is entirely within the capitalist-Marxist orbit, and it would have had no chance of manifesting itself under Hitler or Pétain. It's a fact!

But this gigantic global Marxist crime is not the only major crime of lèse-humanité of this pseudo-democracy where the circumcised ARE THE ONLY TRUE MASTERS.

What horrors have been imposed on us over the last 50 years, since neither Hitler nor Pétain had any power?

Our children have been secularised, deprived of any moral or spiritual education, and given over to pathogenic and criminogenic "music that kills" (through the exaggerated physiological production of adrenalin and endorphins), drugs, delinquency and suicide by the thousands (the 2nd leading cause of death among children and adolescents). Under Hitler or the Marshals, not a single child committed suicide, drugs or alcohol. Has anyone in Nazi Germany or Vichy France ever seen a pensioner forced to shoot his son, who had become a monster on drugs?

The chemification of the soil, which becomes sterile in 50 years.

Systematic chemification of food and medicines, which affects humans at chromosomal level, leading to general degeneration and degenerative diseases such as cancer, cardiovascular disease and mental disorders.

The disappearance of a qualitative humanity with exponentially increasing overpopulation, the disappearance of any spirit of synthesis, like MORAL SENSE.

The aesthetic sense that allows us to take blue jeans uniforms or Picasso as "values" has disappeared.

A return to barbarism, as seen in South and North America and in the suburbs of France, England and elsewhere.

Viral diseases such as AIDS, which will increase in geometric progression since there is no longer any question of talking to couples about LOVE AND TRUST.

Atomic bombs as in Hiroshima and Nagasaki (unnecessary war crimes, by the way), nuclear power stations and their potential Chernobyls, sunken atomic submarines with their inevitable dangers.

Instockable and non-neutralisable nuclear waste.

Invasive household waste that cannot be dealt with in time.

The disappearance of the forests so useful for the derisory ballot papers, intended exclusively for the puppets enslaved by High Finance and circumcised Marxism. And all this with incalculable ecological consequences. Animal and plant species disappearing at an exponential rate, completing an irreversible ecological imbalance.

Disappearance of the peasant class, assassination of agriculture, the only way to ensure a self-sufficient life. The slightest politico-economic disorder can reduce a country to famine, since it can eliminate even its pathogenic, chemically-treated food...

Institutionalised miscegenation, which creates permanent and inevitable racism that automatically degenerates into Libanisation (Germany, France) and civil wars.

The pseudo-liberation of women, which eradicates their qualities as mothers and wives, is leading to a delirious number of divorces, while the children, left to suffer, become delinquents. All the children brought before the courts are the offspring of separated couples or of mothers who work intensively outside the home (Pr Heuyer). All well-to-do women can apparently make up for this deficiency. In reality, the psychological problems are obvious, although not obvious by materialistic psychology criteria. So these unfortunate young people are going to plunge into Michael Jackson and their human future will be cancelled... They'll be left with unemployment, drugs and suicide. Incidentally, young people with even a mediocre Catholic education never commit suicide!

According to the Club of Rome, unemployment will soon reach one billion. Billions of poor, starving, illiterate people.

Megalopolises will be saturated with noxious gases. Refuelling will become impossible. Forests that are already being destroyed will be further corroded by exhaust fumes.

Widespread pornography is a factor in physiological and psychological degeneration, homosexualisation (early masturbation encouraged + vitamin E deficiency) and AIDS. The ozone layer is disappearing, leaving humans exposed to deadly radiation.

Self-service abortion of healthy children, while the mentally retarded and criminals are pampered.

The pathogenic and carcinogenic pill, which causes ovarian blockages, growth arrest and frigidity (Pr Jamain).

All these crimes, without exception, are the result of murderous and suicidal Marxist Capitalism.

Anyone who has read MEIN KAMPF and seen the achievements of Hitler and the Field Marshal is perfectly convinced. There is no ambiguity here.

None of the above crimes would have been possible under Vichy or the Third Reich.

Both Hitler and the Marshal had a respect for nature. They were also concerned with human rights, not the rights of scum. The abolition of the death penalty in a context of such murderous acts against the innocent is something of an obscenity.

Let's save the rapists and murderers of little girls, let's save the murderers of old ladies, but let's massacre the Nicaraguan Indians as long as the country is Marxist!

These, my dear Maître, are the reasons for Monsieur Touvier's political choice, which I admire and respect.

I myself, at the age of 20, brought up in a circumcised financial family, joined the fight against Hitler, I believed!

But these 50 years of global horrors, with my fellow human beings pulling all the strings, have opened my eyes.

Anyone who has retained their intelligence beyond all the Judeo-Cartesian parameters that destroy it will, like me, be in agreement with the reality of the facts.

If nobody understands the basics any more, then the suicide of the planet under the aegis of my fellow creatures is bound to happen very soon.

De Gaulle said that "the French were calves". If they are zombies, then they deserve suicide, with victims and executioners mixed in.

The epicentre of this affair being Mr Touvier's political option, I remain your key witness if you wish.

To you, heart and light

Roger Dommergue de Ménasce volunteered in 1944, retired teacher after 40 years of secondary and higher education. Officer of French Merit and Dedication.

In 1994, 50 years later, the unfortunate TOUVIER was sentenced for having allowed 7 Jews to be shot and having saved 23 in 1944.

Inexpiable crime!

IN 1994 Doctor Goldstein massacred 51 Palestinians. Not a word!

Both events were mentioned on Anne Sinclair's 7/7 programme in June 1994. Tam-Tam for one, complete silence for the other.

It would be laugh-out-loud funny if it weren't so radically disgusting...

TOUVIER CASE: LETTER TO THE PRESIDENT OF THE VERSAILLES COURT OF APPEAL

15 March 1994

Mr President, Members of the jury,

On the eve of the Touvier trial, it is my duty as a Jew, a professor and a philosopher to bring you this testimony.

I radically and absolutely disapprove of this Touvier trial, this farce brought against Mr Touvier who, fifty years ago, was part of the last clean regime in France. When I signed up to fight Nazism in 1944, I naively believed that it was so that we could live under an even cleaner regime than that of the Marshal.

Fifty years on, I realise that we are lying in absolute rot and decomposition, that horror and inversion have become the norm, and that my congeners are pulling all the strings in every field, including justice, enslaved by unconstitutional and Stalinist laws...

My congeners, I don't say "Jews" but the sect of those circumcised on the 8th day, because these people are NOT Jews: all the suicidal speculations that reign in Liberalo-Marxism are criminal and heretical before the Torah.

Since my colleagues have stated unequivocally that this was above all the trial of VICHY and that Mr Touvier was merely serving as an alibi for such a purpose, I advised him, once the iniquitous part of the trial had been settled (Touvier already on trial, 50 years later, 7 Jews shot to save 23), to justify his political option 50 years later in the face of the quintessential rottenness of the current regime, undoubtedly the worst of regimes since it murders mankind and the planet in all their manifestations.

I have therefore sent the letter of which I enclose a copy to Mr Trémollet de Villers, who has the onerous task of using an alibi to defend the whole of humanity.

This letter highlights the ubiquitous and iniquitous obscenity of this legal farce perpetrated by Klarsfeldomania: give Mr Lévy the police and the courts, he will no longer be ridiculous, and that's the 20th century...

These people, with whom I disassociate myself, are concentrating all the parameters of anti-Semitism as never before in history.

Sadly, I fear that the next manifestations of anti-Semitism, which is rumbling everywhere and which their totalitarian control of the media cannot hide, will become a distressing reality that needs no revisionism...

I would add that the farce aspect of this trial, this out-of-touch maxi-jeremiad, is monumentally heightened in the face of the REAL ANGIOUS PROBLEMS that Judeo-Cartesianism forces us to face.

Under the Third Reich, as under Vichy, neither SOROS nor MARX were possible, nor, of course, the decay that their reign implies.

Please accept, Mr Chairman and Members of the Court, the assurance of my deepest respect.

What Touvier should have said
Why I chose the Marshal

Because under the Marshal there was no Soros, who can destabilise a currency with a phone call, possessing, like Warburg, Hammer and others, monstrous powers that no sovereign in human history has ever possessed.

Precisely because under the Marshal there were no bought and paid for politicians immersed in their nullity and their schemes.

Because the Marshal freed France from the most shameful guardianship, that of finance. Because under the Marshal there was no Marxism exterminating tens and tens of millions of people under the aegis of Kaganovitch, Frenkel, Jagoda, Firine, Jejoff, Appeter, Abramovici and 50 others circumcised on the 8th day.

There weren't millions of unemployed.

There was no destruction of peasants, craftsmen, small and medium-sized businesses for the benefit of the multinationals of international finance "who manage drugs".

There was even a rural restoration mission.

There were no dishevelled young people, dressed in the uniform of international bullshit, the Lévy blue jeans, given over to unemployment, despair, drugs, suicide, pathogenic and criminogenic music through the exaggerated physiological production of endorphins and adrenalin, leading to a drug-addicted mentality.

There was no stupefaction organised by MARX MERDIA and ATHÉE-LEVY-SION. There were no atomic bombs, neutron bombs or the Chernobyls of Einstein, Oppenheimer and S.T. Cohen.

There was no Freudism, which was abultifying, pornographic and preparatory to the Marxist mentality. There was not the pornography of Benezareff and his ilk.

There was no mass degeneration confined to atheism.

There was no destruction of the family by mothers working outside the home, divorce à la carte, the pathogenic and teratogenic pill, self-service abortion.

There was no monstrous, exponential growth in crime.

There was no nuclear power, not only with its Chernobyls but also with its unstorable and non-neutralisable waste.

There was no destruction of forests, animal and plant species. There was no death of the earth through synthetic chemistry.

And then there was the widespread chemification of food and therapeutics, and the exponential rise in cardiovascular diseases and cancer ( ), which continue to grow despite official research that does not address the REAL CAUSES.

There was no Maffia sprawl.

There was no life for a rapist and murderer of little girls or a murderer of old ladies: in fact, there were no such criminals under his regime!

There was no normative expansion of homosexuality and paedophilia.

There was no AIDS and the organisation of the debauchery of children under the pretext of combating this scourge, which would be entirely eradicated by the love and fidelity of the couple. [11]

There was no invasion of emigrants with the Lebanonisation of countries and racism organised BY A PSEUDO ANTIRACISM.

There was not a word of the bloody chaos of SOROSMARXISM and its 150 wars since the fall of Vichy and the Third Reich.

Nor were there any Boudarel or Pol Pot, the acknowledged exterminators of 4 million Cambodians. (To this day, they have not been bothered at all!)

Moreover, there were no bloody Marxist dictators who exterminated their own peoples and reduced them to starvation as we see in Africa, South America, Asia...

In a word, I CHOSE THE MARCHAL BECAUSE HE CRISTALIZED A FRANCE FREE OF PERRITURE...

---

[11] See next page letter to Cardinal Lustiger.

LETTER TO CARDINAL LUSTIGER, ARCHBISHOP OF PARIS

7 April 1994

Excellence,

When I see this disgusting programme about AIDS, which is nothing more than a universal incitement to debauchery, when NOT ONCE have the presenters said that the only prophylaxis for this disease is LOVE AND COUPLE RELIABILITY, when I see a mother saying: "My 10-year-old son knows that he has to use a condom to have sex"... I'm appalled and I feel like dying...

When I see this zombification of the Goys, manipulated entirely by the circumcised on the 8th day, with the complicity of the silence of the rabbinate and you, while ALL the reigning circumcised speculations are criminal before the THORA AS WELL AS BEFORE THE GOSPEL, I wonder what option there is between zombification and useless heroism.... The ONLY one who expresses ideas in line with the health of France is LE PEN and I have seen and heard you condemn him!!!

There's nothing more to be done, NOTHING. I'm sending you a copy of a page from Copin Albancelli's *CONJURATION JUIVE CONTRE LE MONDE CHRÉTIEN*. (*JEWISH CONSPIRACY AGAINST THE CHRISTIAN WORLD*) Dedicated to the Archbishop of Tours in 1909, it wasn't even cut out!

So goyish stupidity wasn't much less than it is today, since not even an archbishop understood the importance of this book, now banned by Stalinist, anti-democratic and anti-constitutional laws.

How I understand the young people who have kept a soul and who prefer to commit suicide in the face of such a world, where even you keep quiet even though we see you all the time on television.

Have I ever heard you say forcefully that the only solution to AIDS is love and fidelity between couples, that this is true freedom and not the widespread debauchery orchestrated by the Freuds, the Simone Veils, the Benezareffs and their ilk?

Did you know that any organic or mental sexual activity before puberty (around the age of 18) is a massacre of the body and mind (moral collapse, physical slouching, tuberculosis, schizophrenia, weakening of the multipathogenic immune system, degeneration of the race)?

Circumcised sexologists won't tell you that - quite the opposite, in fact. What will you say to God when you meet him soon?

"Lord, I couldn't do anything, so I supported my rotten financial and pornographic congeners with my well-timed silences! You'd think, Lord, that they wouldn't have put me where I am if they'd thought I'd be telling the elementary truth"...?

Who can I talk to today apart from THIBON, who is very old and is the last Christian philosopher with whom I get on very well despite my disagreement on dogma, but who agrees with me on the essentials of consciousness?

I don't expect any more response from you than from SOROS, BENEZAREFF or SIMONE VEIL, with whom (huge symbol!) I saw you...

Over to you, COR AND LUX

SO?

The modern world was born of money, and will perish because of it. Who is money?

Who simultaneously financed the Germans, the Allies and the Bolshevik Revolution, then came to Europe in 1919 as a peace negotiator? The financier WARBURG.

In 1940, who owned as much oil as the 3 Axis powers? The financier Hammer.

Who can destabilise a currency with one phone call? SOROS.

Circumcised finance, circumcised Marxism, circumcised science and circumcised Freudianism are four superior autisms that are exterminating humanity through the reign of antithought. The causal psychohormonal epicentre is circumcision on the 8th day after birth.

The synthesis of circumcised domination is not really planned. It is relatively unconscious because the circumcised, and this is their misfortune, are entirely deprived of the spirit of synthesis.

On the other hand, they have an uncommon talent for short-term speculation. This explains why the Protocols of the Elders of Zion are necessarily a forgery.

This synthesis of suicidal domination is only relatively developed in consciousness and is of an empirical nature (Concertations, international mutual aid, abandonment of those who will be much more useful to the cause as victims of anti-Semitism).

This dominating synthesis is therefore automatic: the disappearance of the providential elites which are the very essence of any natural theocracy, the mental inadequacy of the vast majority of human beings, the major asset of the circumcised strategy, automatically gives them all the powers since the pseudo democratic equality which they have imposed Masonically and secularly ipso facto promotes the inequality of Warburg and the unemployed...

The only solution to humanity's future in circumcised liberalomarxist chaos is the radical and absolute abolition of circumcision on the eighth day, the first day of the twenty-one days of first puberty.

This would save humanity in extremis, but I see little chance of this book being understood and of capital that is all "Jewish" implementing its awareness.

In the last part of this book, "Madness and Genius", we will now study the fundamental foundations of society, foundations without which it is necessarily reduced to the chaos and annihilation we are experiencing at the end of the twentieth century.

MADNESS AND GENIUS

(Work of Doctor Jean Gautier, endocrinologist).

The following masterly text was taught to me by Dr. J. Gautier, an endocrinologist and physiologist of genius. His work deserves a thousand Nobel Prizes and goes completely beyond Judeo-Cartesianism, whose equations all converge towards the pulverisation of Man.

The epicentre of his work, which sheds a prodigious light on our knowledge of MAN, is based on the fundamental discovery of the functional predominance of the hormonal system over the nervous system and the human being in general.

The nervous system plays only a very minor role in complex activities. Above all, it enables us to record our automatisms and acts as a bridge between our hormonal nature and our actions.

It can, of course, activate an endocrine gland, but this does not mean that it controls it functionally.

In fact, our actions are instigated by our nervous system, but it is our hormonal nature that determines the quality of our actions.

Let's take a very simple example: Chopin is at the piano, a door opens, he's going to flinch, he's an emotional thyroid, a hypersensitive person.

Khrushchev is at the piano. A door opens. He does not move. He is an adrenalian, not at all emotional and insensitive. Their nervous systems reacted differently, depending on their glandular nature.

So it is the hormonal system that is our psychophysiological master. It is the king of the organism; the nervous system is merely the prime minister.

Dr Gautier was thus able to shed light on race, heredity, glandular types,[12] the consequences of sexual mutilation at first puberty, which he also highlighted, and many other things besides, such as the role of organic endocrines.

My only merit is that I have penetrated the mysteries of his work and tried to make it as clear as possible.

The presentation that follows, at the epicentre of human survival, is not the easiest of his work, but it is fascinating.

It should be noted that Valérie Giscard d'Estaing's letter dates from shortly before the start of her seven-year term.

Yet the policy followed by this President of the Republic was the radical and absolute antithesis of the awareness expressed in these pages.

Why is this?

Because all politicians of all parties are subject to the absolute dictatorship of high finance and circumcised Marxism.

They are therefore radically imprisoned in the party's watchwords, into which they have been cast like concrete.

There are some superior minds who 'know well' but who also know that they must ignore what they know if they want to make a career of it.

---

[12] Thesis on thyroidism: "Dandyism, physiological hyperthyroidism" (1971).

There aren't many of them.

Then there are the vast majority of politicians who, having been trained from nursery school through to such absurd competitive examinations as the ENA, the Agrégation or the Polytechnique, conceptualise any of the higher psychological elaboration criteria, and who consequently believe that they are acting freely in their coterie, when in fact they are perfectly robotised. Pseudo-democratic conditioning is irreversible. The result is that all politicians of all parties are unconsciously working "freely" towards chaos and universal decay.

Any announced "change" is an illusion: change can only come about by introducing into people's lives the concepts of authentic spirituality and higher intellectuality.

Otherwise, cancer and madness will progress to nothingness. Let's get to the heart of the matter.

When it comes to posterity, human works vary greatly. Some remain, others sink.

Only CLASSICS have a right to longevity.

Human works have been created by different minds. Those that are always admired have particularities that can be found in the Man of Genius. Those that fade from human memory have something to do with the mentality of lunatics. It is easy to see that the survival of humanity depends on a perfect grasp of these two concepts.

To be healthy, we need to live in a healthy environment. This environment is both concrete - food, hygiene - and abstract - education, books, media. In other words, everything that feeds our bodies through our stomachs and our minds through our brain neurons. *In other words, the man of the current situation, fed on totally dead white bread (vitamin E deficiency), white sugar (chelating calcium from the body and teeth), food and chemical drugs (pathogenic and teratogenic), tobacco, alcohol (carcinogenic), Freud, Marx, of the science of*

Einstein and Oppenheimer, of the banking system of Rothschild, Rockefeller, Hammer, Warburg, Soros and others, who create the entire economic situation, can this man be in good health, is he not led by lucid madmen, and not by the geniuses who are essential to the balance and health of peoples?

Can Picasso's painting and all the other so-called 'abstract' horrors (when painting can be anything but 'abstract'), or the Pompidou Centre, stimulate the development of a sense of beauty in the same way as Chartres, Bach or Giotto?

Progress, as we call it, is advancing by leaps and bounds, thanks to a curious inflation of semantics. Promoted by what is known as "science", according to the same inflation, it in no way includes moral, spiritual, aesthetic and authentically intellectual concepts, and it unfortunately conditions the LIFE OF MEN IN ITS ENTIRETY.

It determines the conditions to which man cannot adapt.

It brings to the surface an ocean of practical, theoretical, financial, social and political problems that are ABSOLUTELY INSOLUBLE without returning to perspectives that are foreign to the current slumber.

Modern life, which should have brought greater ease of existence and greater well-being, IS ENCOURAGING HUMANS TO HAVE LESS AND LESS RESPECT FOR THE HUMAN PERSON.

Each individual is increasingly sacrificed to the State, to the mass-man, who has all the rights and no duties...

The slightest observation shows us that everything is going from bad to worse in this 20th century society. In the few years since Mr Giscard d'Estaing's letter, the situation has worsened considerably (3 million unemployed, 6 million immigrants, S.I.D.A., world drugs, the Maffia etc.). THE POLITICIANS ARE TOTALLY POWERLESS AND ARE AT THE MERCY OF FORCES BEYOND THEIR

CONTROL, WHICH THEIR CONDITIONING OFTEN FAILS TO RECOGNISE.

Wars, which are exclusively financial in origin, are undoubtedly only the criminal beginnings of the one that awaits us, unless biological collapse as a result of the chemification of the earth, food and medicine, and a rotten environment, make life on earth impossible in an even shorter timeframe.

It is therefore essential to know whether the prevailing ideas in officialdom are those of sensible people or whether they are the imaginary and purely speculative fabrications of unbalanced brains.

It's not enough for an idea to have some semblance of logic for it to be good and not be the source of spiritual, biological, ecological and other collapses, and hence of fratricidal struggles, persecutions and international conflicts.

Official scientists (keen on analysis and specialisation) found it extremely difficult to study human beings, so they tried to apply all sorts of investigations to them: microscopes, chemical analysis, physical and electrical measurements, laboratory data.

These laboratory data have taken precedence over observations made by man thousands of years and which had been enshrined in words, in "verbal images". They are in fact small syntheses that account for certain human properties that are quite different, but which had been recognised as having an identical origin (e.g. "sensitivity" to account for both physical and mental sensitivity).

Is the high value placed on laboratory data justified?

Who is right? The official scientist who proceeds by analysis or the human beings whose language is like a synthesis?

It is certainly not because men have been mistaken about universal phenomena that their senses have been unable to grasp, that their sensitivity has prevented them from sensing what was going on within themselves. Official scientists are therefore at a serious impasse when it comes to misunderstanding man. It would be useful to know whether their thinking is not diametrically opposed to that of the Man of Genius.

Let's look at the reality.

Not only is the unprecedented impact of science on biological man and ecology tragic, but the corollary of the progression of banal madness is staggering ('banal' madness to differentiate it from the 'major' madness that produces it) and condemns official psychiatry without appeal.

Not only are all forms of delinquency on the increase (murder, drug abuse, homosexuality, various forms of delinquency and, alas, juvenile delinquency), but after the Second World War insanity doubled in the USA. Twenty years ago (around 1960-1970), the number of insane people was forty million.

This enormous figure can only increase in geometric progression, since not only are the fundamental causes that gave rise to this dementia compounded by other pathogenic causes. In a country of 200,000,000 inhabitants, this figure is already apocalyptic.

What's more, we're going to see the normalisation of madness, crime and homosexuality, while the victims of criminals, rapists and paedophiles will no longer be of interest to anyone.

It will no longer be the crowds dressed in drooling blue jeans, topped with Afro-Look hairstyles or shaved heads who will be exhibitionists, but those who persist in dressing elegantly and retaining their personality.

Sane people will be accused of madness and subversion, prosecuted in the courts on behalf of major criminals who will open the prisons and abolish the death penalty.

In a word, murderers will be transformed into judges, since all forms of crime, even those condemned at Nuremberg (abortion on the grounds of eugenics!), will be legalised: arms sales to all Marxist countries, Marxism, the pathogenic pill, pornography, chemification, and so on.

The justice system will be clogged with delinquents, thieves and schemers at all levels, and will be unable to cope. Racism" will increase as a result of the anti-physiological and anti-psychological juxtaposition of different ethnic groups. In the USA, armed robbery by drug addicts is not penalised two years after the offence is committed. Nothing is going to get any better, and in the USA no one dares leave the house without a gun after 5 p.m.

So everyone needs to understand the importance of discriminating between madness and genius.

It is hardly reassuring to think that those who sanction our freedom are not at all aware of this fundamental problem.

Knowledge of this problem will ipso facto solve the problem of the evolution of man and the preservation of his environment.

What are we to think of these intelligent people who have an extraordinary gift, an exaggerated deformation of the mind that gives them both great talent and great mental and moral weaknesses?

Can they rule us without destroying us and themselves?

On television, a lawyer of Jewish origin spoke brilliantly in favour of the expansion of sexual anarchy, disguised as "freedom".

His presentation, however, was SPIRITUAL, MORAL, AESTHETIC AND INTELLECTUAL. And yet he won the votes of 9 witnesses present on the set (it's true that they had been carefully chosen from among morons, as their biotypology revealed at a glance).

What is a common criminal who has murdered out of misery, passion or even interest, compared to this human-shaped monster who enjoys the general esteem without the justice system being moved to take action against him for gross incitement to debauchery?

Can't we ask ourselves whether we are satisfied to have fought against Nazism during the war, only to see ourselves ruled 35 years later by the same rotten elite that Nazism was fighting against?

Would Nazism have accepted this filthy caricature of freedom that allows the manipulation of all politicians with the niagara of drugs, chemtrails, pornography, the pill, abortion, delinquency, homosexuality, Freudism, Marxism, financial scandals, the Mafia, etc.?

The problem is therefore acute: authors whose language skills and handling of feelings and ideologies are second to none often convey perverse, anti-human, unbalanced ideas.

This is why we need to study the difference between the madman and the man of genius.

There is no doubt that JEAN-JACQUES ROUSSEAU is one of the lunatics. His ideas, his style, his conceptions are commented on favourably by many professors, and yet all psychiatrists today agree in diagnosing him as suffering from full-blown dementia.

Who's right, the professors or the psychiatrists?

Could he be both mad in his life and sensible in his work? The idea is childish.

If we are capable of being so mistaken about the mental qualities of an author, we run the risk of making a very poor choice of intelligences in the official examinations and competitions that we use to train our teachers, our scholars, our lawyers and our rulers.

As things stand at present, our examinations and competitive examinations do not allow us to select people capable of aspiring to the qualities of the man of genius.

In the present circumstances, this assertion will not seem shocking to anyone, except those whose mental integrity has been destroyed by the situation we are about to analyse.

Men of genius are absent from the officialdom, and ALBERT CAMUS confided to me that since the disappearance of CARREL and his friend SIMONE WEIL, there have been none at the present time. On the other hand, there are more and more authors whose rantings run counter to man.

(A well-known author of Jewish origin recently told us, among a host of examples of aberrations, that "the maternal instinct does not exist" and that "homosexuals are neither sick nor perverted". These assertions were made despite a total ignorance of endocrinology.)

Once we know the fundamental qualities of the man of genius, we will be in a position to create a true elite capable of leading nations. What qualities do madmen and men of genius have in common?

Memory

People with dementia who have retained a certain amount of intelligence retain it well. Some can have one of the most powerful and pass with flying colours a mnemonic examination such as the internship in medicine or the agrégation in Law. Some can recite over a thousand verses. Others can remember the features of a person who has posed in front of them for half an hour and draw their portrait. Others can perform a complex addition on a simple reading.

Men of genius have a much less efficient memory and often complain about their memory. They often lack the actual memory that enables us to remember precise facts. The memory for names, numbers and events may partially lacking. This type of memory is often found in people who are very good at speaking but who lack any brilliant qualities.

Genius is characterised above all by order in the mind. The genius mind does not remember many things in great detail, but everything is organised in its memory according to the value of the ideas. Some are primary and strongly fixed. Secondary ideas are attached to these, and incidental ones to these.

THE GENIUS MIND IS HIERARCHICAL

He is trained for intellectual work, for elaboration, for discovery. They are in no way trained to speak or write with a straight face on the most diverse subjects without any depth.

On the contrary, the memories of demented people are strange, original, full of weirdness, and generally very heterogeneous. They correspond to the sensations that struck them. Their affective tendencies determine their choice of memories without discrimination by the higher criteria we will discuss later.

Judgement and will are the driving forces behind genius. Imagination.

It is very much alive in the madman as in the man of genius.

You could say that this is the most intense and characteristic dominant feature. But the quality is very different in each case.

In demented people it is: exuberant, easy, exaggerated, fantastic, anarchic, fabulist, disordered.

In the man of genius it is: disciplined, obedient to high feelings, under the effort of mind and will.

He must become aware of the whole of reality without rejecting any element that would distort objectivity, and in particular he must accept into his field of consciousness ideas that do not flatter his tendencies or ideologies. Without these conditions, knowledge cannot be achieved.

As a result, all human values are respected by its brain in time and space.

His imagination does not wander and tends towards a goal. It is an effort at discovery within the framework provided by experience. All the data in this framework is integrated. It uses the most diverse psychological elaborations to produce a specific, desired work. The demented person's imagination, on the other hand, has no limits or rules. It has no purpose. The spirit of discovery is different in the madman and the man of genius.

The madman may have an inspiration, an intuition, but his discovery will be spontaneous and unpredictable. That of a brilliant mind will be the fruit of a great effort pursued with great difficulty. Intuition helps him and willpower enables him to succeed.

Logic and Reason

Psychologists thought they could recognise valid thought by the quality of its reasoning and logic. They were partially mistaken in their assertion. These are in fact the qualities that are most developed in some mad people.

They are highly developed in persecuted persecutors.

Their logic is strong, flawless, brutal and implacable. This is why they are described as "morbid", as if such a sequence of ideas went beyond the bounds of normality, revealing a pathological state.

The logic of the man of genius is much more precarious: it's hard to be logical when you're not mad!

It is therefore less rigid, looser, fuzzier, leaving room for feeling "which perceives reality more directly than intelligence" (Carrel), for intuition.

The madman is literally the victim of a chain of arguments. He gives importance and intensity only to a systematisation that enslaves the intelligence and deprives it of any effective initiative. In many demented people, the proximity of two facts in time and space links them ineluctably in their minds as cause and effect. The genius is much less certain of this, because experience has taught him that two phenomena occurring close together may have only remote connections between them. He does not want to be a slave to appearances.

For example, I see the hypothalamus regulating the endocrines, so it's the nervous system that controls them. But observation based on narrow analysis leads to error.

In reality, it is the nervous system that will be functionally controlled by the hormonal system, as it is the first to be constituted.

This is just one of thousands of examples.

The madman uses only his sensations in relation to phenomena. The genius substitutes his mind and never concludes on a strictly analytical and quantitative observation.

He knows that if he did, he would lose his field of vision of total reality. He is therefore constantly acting with intelligence and understanding.

The madman argues his interpretation solely on the basis of his senses and emotions, and so tightly, so far removed from the facts, so implacably, that his mental imbalance becomes clear.

Think of the lawyer who preached anarchic sexual 'freedom' in an argument that defied the most elementary mental equilibrium.

In this respect, it should be remembered that the use of sexuality before puberty (around the age of 18) leads to a thyroid imbalance which causes the individual to fall into decay, to lose all moral sense and to become abulic, making him or her an ideal prey for the insane.

What demented people lack:

Voluntary attention. Willpower.

Higher psychological elaborations. The moral sense.

This is the fundamental identity of madness.

It's worth noting in passing that this identity can easily accommodate the high mnemonic and analytical skills required in competitive recruitment exams...

Our elites!

VOLUNTARY LOSS OF ATTENTION

Psychiatrists, even in the current state of decay, are in complete agreement: the insane have no attention, only attraction and preoccupation.

It's a good idea to define ATTENTION.

It's not enough to focus your mind for a long time on something that pleases you, that gratifies you, that attracts you, to show that you're paying attention.

Objectivity, natural forces and beings present themselves to us in two forms: one that is pleasant, easy and useful, and which attracts us; the other that is difficult, painful and harmful, and which provokes in us a tendency to flee, while at the same time giving rise to a state of fear and anxiety that translates into preoccupation. There is no real attention in these cases.

True attention helps us to focus our minds on sensations that are boring, painful, unpleasant, tiring and sometimes harmful; it can also enable us to turn away from sensations and ideas that are pleasant, easy and give us pleasure, in the interests of true objectivity, moral sense and altruism. True discovery can only be made through powerful attention, since it must take into account ALL aspects of a phenomenon, from its highest spiritual aspect to its most modest material aspect.

INTELLIGENCE

In the genius, it manifests itself in beauty, harmony, order, measured thinking and courage in the face of conformism.

The madman will manifest himself in excess, disorder, exuberance and imbalance.

FITNESS FOR WORK

The genius recovers all his faculties when he sets to work. The madman is inconsistent, moody. He cannot direct his work. One day he works furiously, and the next day he can do nothing. He is the plaything of his tendencies and vitality.

THE VARIOUS ATTENTION DEFICITS IN THE MADMAN

Some people are inattentive to everything. These are the intellectually unstable: their senses are not fixed. Mongolians and myxedematous people are not attracted by anything. Other defectives are attracted only by strong sensations, but their thoughts are quickly diverted by the slightest thing seen or heard.

These are the maniacs, the idiots, the precocious and senile demented. Others, depending on their functional and organic state, present sentimental twists that modify their attention with their way of seeing.

Thus, a circular madman in a state of agitation will have optimistic ideas, and in a state of melancholic depression, he will have pessimistic ideas.

It's the functional state that determines the quality of attention.

The demented person may be set in his ways: it will be difficult to get him to stop his work, even for a meal. Senile dementia sufferers perpetually tell the same stories. Melancholic and persecuted people have a delusional preoccupation, an idea of revenge for example, which remains dominant and from which they cannot free themselves. This dominance of their mind means that all sensations, ideas and events are distorted and interpreted to feed their delusional theme of systematisation. In addition, some maniacs or general paralytics have such deficient attention that they judge elements which are harmful to them as beneficial and visseras.

Melancholic people see what is good for them as bad.

Since mad people have no control over their sensations and ideas, they have no way of paying attention.

Unfortunately, this lack of attention is not only characteristic of the insane. It is also characteristic of pseudo-intellectuals who have their say in the media, and of official scientists, whereas it is normal in children, primitive people and normal people in a dream state.

Loss of Willpower

Psychiatry agrees that mad people are abulic. We also need to define willpower.

An action taken over a long period of time and with perseverance may not involve the exercise of the will at all. This is the case if this action pleases you, flatters your senses, your passions, your convictions that you do not want to question even in the face of the facts your social and material interest, but is not directed towards moral sense and objectivity.

Willpower, on the other hand, consists of doing painful, tiring things that go against our natural tendencies and convictions. This is because of a higher idea of altruism and a sense of morality towards a goal that is not selfish and remote.

In everyday life, willpower is used to prevent us from harming ourselves, for example by not smoking (which is very difficult because smoking is precisely the cause of abulia) or by not harming our neighbours.

When we do good out of respect for the human person, we are making an act of will.

For a scientist who writes and discovers in order to find out more, make a profit or put himself in the limelight, there is no such thing as will.

The will of the scientist only appears when, with perfect probity and impartiality of investigation, he promulgates from the knowledge he has acquired only that which will be of benefit to man from the point of view of his moral person. This altruistic element is essential to the concept of will.

In fact, in all beings we can find a persistent impulse to act strongly which is similar to obsessions: *this kind of obsession is very marked in abutlics.*

People with dementia have no will of their own because they think only of themselves.

They are fundamentally selfish. They have no feelings for others. They think only of satisfying their own tendencies. They obey only rewards and punishments. Teaching and reasoning have no influence on them.

It should be noted that small children - up to the age of 18! They are related to the demented. But if reasoning is of little value, *example and authority are the two breasts of true education.*

"I wash and I'm brave because Dad washes and he's brave.

"I don't touch matches because Daddy forbids it" (and not "because I can start a fire", which is incomprehensible to a very small child).

Without these two principles *there can be no education.*

It's obvious that the more spiritually and intellectually evolved parents are, the better education they will give their children. So they can lead their children to Carrel and Chopin instead of disco, drugs, Marx and Freud. I would remind you that there are no delinquents or suicides among children who receive a Catholic education, even a mediocre one. On the other hand, I have known many brothers in masonry whose children have committed suicide...

LOSS OF MORAL SENSE

People with dementia have no concept of right and wrong. Altruism is an EMPTY word for them.

They have no kindness, they are liars, hypocrites, wicked, perverse, ready to beat other sick people, to tear and steal their clothes, or whatever they feel like. They have no modesty, and think only of satisfying their reproductive instincts when they have them. They cannot resist their hallucinations or impulses. They are capable of any crime.

LOSS OF HIGHER PSYCHOLOGICAL ELABORATIONS

We need to talk at length about this ability, which has been little known since the collapse of real values.

The following discussion is based on physiological studies: it is in fact psychic possibilities which are conferred by glandular functions. Let us say from the outset: there can be no *true intellectual* without the handling of these elaborations which alone allow access to *knowledge.* The demented person is *totally deprived of* this.

The recruitment of a true elite should based on these mental possibilities, not on analytical speculation or reductionist, suicidal ideologies.

This is never the case with the demented.

ABSTRACTIONS

We have practically everything to learn in psychology.

When mathematicians and physicists realised that numbers could not be used for certain mathematical reasoning, they came up with alphabetic symbols to replace them. Philosophers, for their part, realised that most of the sensory and sentimental data we possess makes certain intellectual elaborations, such as *synthesis*, more difficult.

But they did not seek to perfect the ideational elements.

This is how it came to be believed that perfectly defined knowledge, such as laboratory data, microscopic visions, figures and algebraic formulae, could be used for psychological elaborations.

This is a definite and serious mistake.

All exact data contains within itself the values that are intimately attached to it. They form certain characteristic elements which only allow them to be possessed in the mind in the form of a definite entity *which cannot be used for psychological elaborations.*

They are therefore forced to remain as they are and can only be used for *scientific applications.*

Great scientists such as *Carrel* and *Leconte de Nouys* have warned us *against this fundamental error.*

So it is not surprising that the mind cannot, with measurements, indicate by intellectual elaboration the shape to be given to an aeroplane or a ship to increase its speed. This can *only* be achieved *through experience.*

It so happens that our ordinary ideas differ little from sensations, comparable to microscopic visions, chemical analyses, mathematical or physical measurements, whereas the other ideas are ideas-feelings, which stem from previously established metaphysical conceptions and distort the interpretation of all phenomena.

In conclusion, higher psychological elaborations cannot be carried out with sensory ideas but with abstractions.

What is an abstraction?

It seems to be a thought that contains within itself a quantity of objectivity, of feelings, of thoughts, a sort of complex like "crowd", "country", "charm", "altruism". Physiology teaches us that abstraction is something quite different.

Each verbal image corresponds to a word, made up of a number of organic functions. Sight, hearing and touch all provide elements for the word. The whole face and particularly the mouth, the tongue, the lips and the pharynx have served as the resonating organs for pronouncing the word, cooperating with the pharynx which gives the voice.

But that's not all.

Each verbal image is the fruit of an emotional state, i.e. a set of organic functions: pulmonary, cardiac, digestive, eliminatory etc. as well as all the metabolisms which modify their rhythm either more or less, according to the verbal image constituted.

All these phenomena are directed by the hormonal system.

In the ordinary circumstances of life, the word, with all the endocrine participations which link its various sensory and muscular functions, has a great advantage because of the emotional state which presides over it and which is like a potential behaviour. It can be triggered, if need be, with a rapidity that can never be achieved by reasoning of the mind. It can thus help to safeguard the subject's existence, hence its usefulness.

But this sensory and emotional participation in the word, which is its great advantage in the life of relationships, is highly detrimental when it comes to examining a phenomenon relating to man.

The word must be intrinsically intellectual and relate strictly to the phenomenon under consideration. The word must be free of all the functional elements that the observer's personality might bring to it.

This word must cease to be a verbal image and become purely ideological, no longer arousing any vital state in the researcher, or any of his feelings.

Freed in this way from the preconceived ideas and metaphysical theories that he favoured, the word then became an appropriate and impartial appellation that would bear the name of abstraction.

Discrimination of Abstract Values

The analytical tendencies of the positive sciences have accustomed us to considering each element making up an objectivity, a force, a thought, as having a similar ideative value.

The weight, size, consistency, chemical and atomic composition, and the various physical and chemical properties of a body are, for the chemist or physicist, elements that have an equivalent ideal value in their eyes.

When we want to establish *a notion of identity*, or better still *a synthesis*, we need to select the features that have a predominant value, and distinguish the most important from the secondary ones.

The same is true of the ideas and abstractions we are presented with. *This discrimination is absolutely essential in certain cases, and in particular in everything to do with man.*

One of the most important examples needs to be mentioned here, because it lies at the crossroads of human knowledge and evolution.

It is the functional omnipotence of the *hormonal system*. Which sheds light on man: race, heredity, sexuality, the different natures of men and women, the mentality of the sexually mutilated, the child, education, and so on.

Official endocrinologists have recognised that our nervous system *is entirely duplicated* by our hormonal system.

This means that there is not a single physiologically considered function that cannot be achieved with both the hormonal and nervous systems.

We are *perfectly* aware that certain functions, such as reproduction, the functioning of the female genital tract, puberty and heredity, are carried out without the intervention of the nervous system, and that it is our endocrines that do this.

In these conditions, the question arose as to which of these two systems was functionally predominant.

Here we have a considerable discrimination of abstractions: two different systems whose causal mode is in opposition: the glandular system acts by chemical phenomena and the nervous system by physical excitations.

To solve *this vast problem*, it is *essential to abandon one's personal opinions, feelings and conceptions and concern oneself only with the facts, otherwise one will fall into a serious error.*

This ability to discriminate is rarely found in human beings, and even less in academics whose mnemonic-analytic training leads them to fix obsessively on what has been learned through analysis, *without being able to go any further in time and space.*

For example: "I see the hypothalamus regulating the endocrines", *so* it's the nervous system that directs the hormonal system...

This analytical reasoning is rigorously logical and will convince anyone with an analytical mind.

The unfortunate thing is that this logic is absurd and that the synthesis that encompasses this observation *will lead to a radically opposite conclusion.*

It should be noted that this kind of flawed logic currently rules the entire planet, and that it is only natural that *this logic* should be *the formula for humanity's suicide.*

It is obvious that if it were otherwise, if our leaders were given the mental potential to rise from the idea-sensation to a true thought, *we would not be in such great ignorance about all the processes of human relational life.*

Clearly, therefore, there can be no question of asking an insane person to demonstrate such mental capacity.

The demented person has no idea what discrimination is, because in some cases he cannot even distinguish between what is useful to him and what is harmful.

He cannot form abstractions because he cannot keep an idea in his mind for long (meditation), especially if it is unpleasant and requires effort. *He cannot form abstractions and meditate on them.*

NOTION OF IDENTITY

Official scientists are keen analysts.

They believe that by dividing up all the particularities and properties of a body as much as possible, they will arrive at a more complete knowledge of the objectivities and problems. As this analysis work has been extensively codified, a list of investigations has been provided so that researchers can discover all the particularities inherent in an entity.

So analysis has become above all a question of manipulation and routine, and *absolutely not of intelligence*.

A mediocre subject, a relative lunatic even, with a degree and a bit of skill, can be capable of analysis.

While analytical methods are easily applied to material entities and constant forces, they are hardly applicable to human beings.

In human beings, laboratory research can be carried out on the somatic whole and on the physical and chemical functioning of the various organs, because there are certain constants there. *But none of these modes of investigation is applicable* to life in a relationship.

This means that true knowledge of man radically escapes the analytical method.

This philosophical truth, elementary to the culture of a normally constituted adolescent, is *ignored by official academics with diplomas.*

Thus, within official *psychiatry*, human manifestations such as madness and genius escape official knowledge because *the criteria that define them are* unknown.

The variability and instability of human functional and intellectual metabolism pose radically intractable problems for laboratory tests.

The human being is in a state of continual transformation, undergoing an organic evolution that is constantly progressing. His thinking is always changing and evolving. In this way, they become the seat of continuous physiological modifications. These are inherent in the appearance of the verbal images from which emotions arise. *For analytical investigations, therefore, Man remains radically elusive.*

Endocrinologists have experienced this more than anyone else. They have carried out a considerable amount of experimental research which, for the most part, contradicts each other.

Only those relating to the removal of glandular organs have given virtually consistent results. But these findings have not been given their full weight. And in all their consequences.

Endocrinologists are therefore only very slowly explaining some organic functions and *still know nothing about man.*

Analysis is therefore an almost non-existent means of achieving knowledge.

It can undoubtedly be *an invaluable aid*, but if set up as an absolute, *it will be the source of all kinds of confusion.*

The modern world, in all its aspects, is a perfect example. It has to be said, moreover, that the sheer quantity of data accumulated makes it impossible to discriminate or see clearly.

For the majority of beings, marked by the current system of instruction and who are therefore closed to Knowledge, *we need to recall Cannon's experiences.*

He demonstrated the predominance of the endocrines in our emotions and feelings.

When a cat is confronted with a barking dog, the adrenal secretion causes it to become combative.

If we remove the cat's entire sympathetic system, it retains its combative tendencies. A dog deprived of its sympathetic system is still endowed with all the qualities of a normal dog.

So how do you explain the fact that the adrenal glands, deprived of any nerve connection, *continue to function normally?*

For 20 years, biologists have been faced with a problem that analysis will never be able to solve.

So we find ourselves *in a regression in our knowledge of man*, and this Cartesianism inaugurated by Spinoza's materialism (circumcised on the 8th day), which Descartes would have repudiated, *is a paralysis on the road to knowledge of man and knowledge tout court*. Modern science is too harmful to mankind and the planet, too destructive of moral and spiritual values, *and hence of organic and mental health*, for us to have the slightest consideration for it.

We are going to show that the mentality of those who conceived it is close to insanity and that it is the perfect antithesis of the brilliant concept.

If analysis cannot lead to *knowledge*, the same cannot be said of *the notion of identity*.

This concept is continually used by doctors when making a diagnosis.

The doctor looks for a series of signs. He selects the most salient, the most characteristic, and then draws from his memory the identical signs corresponding to the pathological description.

What is astonishing is that the doctor who uses this mode of psychological elaboration when examining a patient is incapable of practising it when dealing with abstract data.

This is as far as abstraction goes. A spectacular example of this is *the tragic story of Doctor Semmelweiss.*

Using a *concept of identity*, this Hungarian doctor discovered the reason why women in labour were dying in hospitals in proportions that were sometimes as high as 100%. He observed some very simple facts: in the room where the midwives, *who washed their hands*, looked after the mothers-to-be, the proportion of deaths was relatively low. This was not the case in the ward where women in labour were cared for by doctors who came to treat them *without washing their hands, after having taken part in dissection sessions.*

In the latter case, mortality commonly reached 95 to 100%.

Semmelweiss had an epiphany, confirmed by the fact that one of his friends had died after an anatomical puncture, *showing exactly the same symptoms as women in labour who died like flies.*

He informed universities all over the world (something that no researcher who was not a doctor and a professor could do today), and *reduced the mortality rate of women giving birth in his own hospital to 0%, but nobody in the universal medical world understood him, and he received nothing but jeers.*

He ended up going mad and committing suicide by inoculating himself with the disease from which women in labour were dying en masse, as if to give a final desperate demonstration of his fundamental discovery which, after him, would save millions of women.

Thanks to him, hygiene, obstetrics and modern surgery were born.

This example might lead us to believe that madness is close to genius. This too would be a hasty analytical conclusion, despite its obviousness. *But this is not the case.*

Man is only sane to the extent that his hormonal system is in balance. Disruption of this balance can lead to madness.

In an evolved being with thyroid tendencies (emotional, sentimental), the internal genitalia *must remain active. It is the most sensitive to counteracting influences.* Semmelweiss had to contend with a tide of bad faith and foolish confraternity worldwide. He had to combat malice and animosity. The result in his mind was a thyroid preoccupation that unbalanced his internal (or interstitial) genitalia.

The real culprits in his madness were his peers, whose stupidity knows no excuse.

You might think that today, notions of identity presented by original researchers would be better received.

It took me 15 years to find three people to form a jury at the Sorbonne for my thesis: "Dandyism, a physiological hyperthyroidism". Today it would be impossible to defend it. (25 years later.)

The elites capable of developing a notion of identity and those capable of understanding it have completely disappeared.

Humanity's suicide is therefore certain, because it cannot survive without true genius. The notion of identity is linked to feeling, in other words to the internal genitalia.

But this endocrine is not favoured by technocratic, analytic-mnemonic competitive examinations (agrégation, internat, E.N.A., polytechnique etc.).

Nor by secular education deprived of any religious, moral or spiritual basis.

Nor by widespread vaccinations, which damage the internal genitalia and the immune system, and prepare the way for madness, cardiovascular disease and cancer, all of which will increase *at* the same time as *useless official* analytical *research*.

Nor by chemising the soil.

Or food chemification.

Neither by the therapeutic chemification nor by the generalised ugliness of residential buildings.

Not through regressive, pathogenic music or pornography.

Neither the Marxist nor the Freudian influence.

Nor by the disintegration of the family, and the working woman outside the home giving their babies to the crèche...

The interstitial is therefore lower than at the time of my thesis and much lower than at the time of Semmelweiss.

As a result, these concepts, like this entire book, *can only be understood by those who have miraculously retained a perfectly healthy genitalia.*

Since they are so rare, it seems that humanity is condemned to irreversible decline.

SUMMARY

The study we are currently carrying out is a synthesis.

For an analytical mind that can never see the whole, that remains a victim of sensation-ideas without being able to rise to a true thought, it will always be *the analytical contradiction* that it will see and never the synthetic whole.

By placing such minds in official positions in politics and academia, they have circumcised them on the 8th day, knowing full well that they can manipulate them "freely".

They automatically do what Warburg and Marx want them to do.

It is this inability to synthesise that has given rise to the suicidal phrase: "you must not generalise". It's obvious that analytical (pituitary) minds don't have this ability, so they can only produce false syntheses by generalising from a lack of fundamental parameters.

Only synthetic minds (more or less interstitial thyroid) can generalise: saints, geniuses, great artists, true philosophers who are never stuck in a system or ideology and aim only for objectivity.

This psychological elaboration enables us to consider a number of states and phenomena and to select the fundamental and common signs: *we are currently in the process of synthesising mental illnesses.*

Synthesis is par excellence the superior psychological elaboration that will enable us to understand man and to know universal phenomena. People with dementia are as incapable of synthesis as they are of identity.

We now know the defects that characterise people with dementia. *We can also identify the physiological functions to which these deficiencies correspond.*

There's a lot of talk about the internal genital gland. In one of my son's philosophy textbooks, I read that this *endocrine* gland was found to *play an important role in courage and moral sense.* Who will link Gautier's work to the teachers of lycées? Certainly not 'international de-education'...

This gland is THE HUMAN GLAND.

It confers courage, generosity, a sense of morality, altruism, a spirit of synthesis, a spirit of sacrifice, love of God and mankind, a disinterested ideal. Highly developed, it can enhance higher psychological elaborations: *synthesis, notion of identity.*

Since the patient lacks all these qualities, we can conclude that he has INSUFFICIENCY OF THE INTERNAL GENITAL SYSTEM...

This atrophy can be seen in people with dementia.

It should be noted that the term "mad" applies not only to people interned for spectacular psychopathological manifestations, but also to people speaking on television, preaching obscenity, to perverted ideologues, to ignorant sexologists, psychiatrists who claim that "the term mad has no scientific value", to statesmen, to members of the technocratic elite, endowed with major technocratic powers, such as arms manufacturers for the whole world, to financiers who have no concern whatsoever for the true progress of Humanity, to advisers preaching the right to suicide and euthanasia, and so on.

INTELLECTUAL ACTIVITIES WHERE THE QUALITIES OF GENIUS ARE TOTALLY LACKING.

Unless you have been gulled by officialdom, unless you have lost all personality, and unless you have been irreversibly marked by the madness of the situation, which is the case of the majority and particularly of those who have undergone Freud-Marxist academic deformation, *we will admit that the man of genius must possess what the madman lacks, and that in him the internal genitalia must be in perfect condition.*

Do we find in the positive sciences the qualities that characterise the man of genius? If we don't, we should not be surprised to see a geometric increase in the rotting of the environment, the biological and mental collapse of human beings, cardiovascular diseases, cancers, multiform delinquency, madness, criminality and homosexuality (which will become normative in the case of the latter).

This can only be a logical consequence, as we've already said: *nature never forgives.*

When the superior is not up to the job, the inferior destroys the superior, which destroys itself. Nothing lives without order, without synthesis, without *hierarchy.*

Until the last century, we lived in illusion, singing the praises of science. This century has disillusioned all those who had not been deprived of their intelligence by the system itself.

The environment has gone rotten, man has collapsed biologically and mentally, to the point where you can scarcely believe what you're seeing if you watch these physico-chemical amalgamations on television, in the Underground or at university, wearing Lévis bluejeans, topped with a cauliflower or cock's crest hairstyle of perfect sexual ambiguity.

Chemical medicine is pathogenic and teratogenic (Dr Pradal, an expert at the WHO, has won 17 cases against chemical drug manufacturers). It causes a proliferation of mental and motor disabilities (which Dr Alexis Carrel absolutely refused to accept, and for which he had all the streets bearing his name renamed). Yet people as official as JEAN ROSTAND had denounced this medicine as a "purveyor of madmen". We are in the process of creating a race of intelligent animals, because the time of sub-humans is over. The decline is accelerating. Man has been deprived of his freedom ("the true passion of the 20th century is servitude", said Albert Camus). We have enslaved him spiritually, closed off his conscience, violated his free will and made him a serf, destroyed his sense of morality, pornographed the whole world and, to cap it all, even childhood itself.

People who are still thinking have woken up from a nightmare.

They realised that they had been deceived, that they had literally been hypnotised, from the first and especially the second world wars onwards.

We have seen the following phenomenon: the concept of science and its achievements have so devastated people's consciences that they are clamouring for anything that will destroy them. The hypnosis is so successful that they don't realise the cause-and-effect relationship between this science and their destruction.

Since humans no longer have any criteria for knowing whether an achievement is brilliant or harmful, they could only wait for the results of these discoveries to establish whether they are perverse, harmful or deadly.

More often than not, perversion shapes psychologies such an extent that the masses can no longer be aware of anything.

We must therefore urgently recognise the works that are genius or akin to genius and reject the others.

This fundamental data contains the happiness of humanity.

The symbiosis of synthesis and moral sense produces genius. We must therefore prevent harm to those who put forward perverse ideas, even and above all with a dialectic that seems logical and reasoned, and not based on a broadening of consciousness that encompasses as many facts as possible.

Then we'll have true liberalism for saints, geniuses and great artists.

THE EVILS OF MODERN SCIENCE

This science has only a few immediate scientific truths that are relatively certain because they are measurable and material.

As far as the interpretation of the forces it studies is concerned, it is reduced to Hypotheses, in other words approximations, sometimes errors, since one hypothesis is replaced by another.

So scientists are working in error.

What's more, because it lacks a sense of synthesis, it is ipso facto unaware of the deadly consequences of its discoveries.

This inferiority stems from the exclusively *analytical* nature of science. For an analytical brain, error is presented as truth or as a possibility, and truth is inaccessible to it *because it requires higher psychological elaborations in order to be perceived.*

As we can see, humanity will continue to flounder in a state of suicide as long as it is deprived of true elites.

If science proceeded by notions of identity and by synthesis, it would arrive at certainties on which other, increasingly complementary certainties would be based.

A comical idea of modern scientists is to believe that living organisms function physically and chemically as they do in our laboratories. The idea is both childish and insane.

This assimilation leads us into the greatest error. The torpedo fish does not produce electricity like the dynamo and organic light is cold. The chameleon's mimicry has nothing to do with our photoelectric cells. As for the marvellous cellular combinations that allow the most astonishing chemical decompositions and reconstitutions, such as the distribution of albuminoids, fats and sugars from food, and their convergence in a sort of crossroads where these substances are presented in a similar form, to be then distributed according to future vital needs, either as albuminoids, fats or sugars, *this is far beyond the intelligence and imagination of the most fertile of our chemists.*

This way of seeing things corresponds to the analytical turn of current thinking: it is an *assimilation,* not a *truth.*

If we had made this clear, we wouldn't have so many academics who take what they learn at university for granted and believe, with a naivety that leaves us dumbfounded, that *analytical* data accurately reflects organic processes, *which is not true.*

True philosophy teaches us that discovery is qualitative.

But since Spinoza's error, it has been precisely *quantitative.*

Organisations take quality into account: a little alcohol leads to excitement, a lot of alcohol to torpor, sleep and death.

There are no chemical interpretations here, as they would not be sufficient.

MODERN SCIENCE IS ANALYTICAL, QUANTITATIVE AND MICROSCOPIC.

TRUE SCIENCE IS SYNTHETIC, QUALITATIVE AND MACROSCOPIC.

All the university students who will follow the Judeo-Cartesian collapse will be perfectly familiar with this philosophical reality, which is the key to knowledge.

So the analytical minds of modern science cannot know whether their discoveries (chemistry, radiation, vaccines, etc.) will harm *humanity* or not.

True intelligence has postulates that cannot be demonstrated. The truly scientific proof of madness is the use of chemistry in food, in therapeutics, in genetic or atomic experiments. *All* this proves that men are mad. That's why they *don't consider mad people to be mad!*

On the other hand, they find intelligent people crazy: "in 1984, the most intelligent will be the least normal" said Orwell in his novel 1984.

It was only *after* Hiroshima and Nagasaki that Einstein and Oppenheimer wept bitter tears over "their devil's work".

That didn't stop Samuel T. Cohen from doing even better with the neutron bomb. All these lunatics *are macro-criminals of lèse-humanité* who would not be tolerated by any country with a regime based on elementary traditional values.

The madness continues: we know that radioactive waste can be stored and not neutralised. We know that Chernobyl-type dangers are constant. We know that genetic damage can be immeasurable. But the Professors Sunflower (of whom JACQUES BERGIER was a perfectly apt symbol) continue to lead us to the worst.

How insane do we have to be to use the "energy crisis" as an excuse to commit suicide? All this means that there can be no dialogue with a false elite if we want to save humanity.

If a human group does not rise up *to neutralise all the parameters of global suicide, humanity is lost.*

Modern science is accessible to almost anyone with a university degree, *because analytical perspectives are accessible to everyone and has a large number of demented people.*

Not long ago I read in the newspaper that a remarkable inventor had developed an aeroplane of great merit. This man, Colonel, had murdered his entire family with an axe...

Psychiatric criteria are so lamentable that this man, examined on the basis of analytical criteria, would have appeared perfectly healthy, like the gendarme who murdered five people in the 1980s.

True science is only accessible to those who are capable of practising higher psychological elaborations, and of understanding the discoveries that flow from such potential.

The true scientist is neither a materialist nor a spiritualist: he is an *idealist-materialist*. He will be able to embrace a problem even in its most remote incidences in time and space. The true scientist is constantly concerned to act altruistically and to protect mankind from everything that destroys him morally and physically. *His ultimate goal is the knowledge of mankind, the only perspective from which genius can manifest itself.*

The other activities can only converge towards fame, which is physiologically quite different. The man of genius is preoccupied with truth and probity. He is detached from all considerations of personal interest, as was DOCTOR ALEXIS CARREL; he is impartial and independent, never demagogic, like a supreme judge. He observes the facts according to the importance of the phenomena. He gives each phenomenon its own value and consciously *discriminates against abstract values.*

These considerations therefore apply to science itself.

Science must be the combination, the synthesis of all the great efforts, of all the wonderful discoveries that enliven humanity *morally, spiritually and materially.*

Science must therefore have all the qualities of genius.

Its aim is the knowledge of man, his perfection.

It will therefore have to train men of genius, behind whom there will be an elite of famous men gifted with a moral sense.

Science will strive with all its resources to rid mankind of all the defects akin to insanity. It will give human beings the place where they will be happiest according to their abilities, serving a society worthy of the name and not, as I write, lying in effervescent putrescence.

Superior psychological elaborations are therefore something quite different from the pitiful analytical elaborations of our time, which converge towards destruction in every field.

By splitting up, cutting out and looking for the differential and different characteristics of each entity at different levels of observation, the latter can only lead to fragmentary knowledge that is suitable only for industrial applications, the manufacture of devices, objects, rockets, etc.

These perspectives will never lead to the intrinsic knowledge that alone is linked to human happiness.

This is never the purpose of analysis.

Modern scientists also have another comical idea: they believe that the universe was conceived by an *exclusively mathematical* mind. So nature would have taken into account only the mathematical principle to make the universal work.

By applying calculations to everything around him, the modern scientist is committing an enormity. He is exactly like the general paralytic who would judge what is favourable or unfavourable according to his mental state.

Mathematics corresponds exactly to the analytical mentality, i.e. exaggerated subdivision, excessive compartmentalisation.

If we have any sanity left, we can see that a single thought, a single *synthetic conception*, has presided over the construction of the world around us.

We have proof of hormonal actions that act on a number of organs at the same time to obtain the most diverse functions, according to a hunting principle of quality and not quantity.

Modern scientists are therefore unable to study our personality, even if it is morbid, because they use concepts that *go against our nature*.

One very serious consequence of the "analytical psychosis" is *excessive specialisation*. Each category of modern scientist works on increasingly circumscribed questions with different scales of observation.

The various specialists end up never agreeing with each other and no longer understanding each other.

Finally, the sentimental states they experience encourage them to create neologisms that increase mutual incomprehension. This tendency towards neologism, which can be found in abundance in books on psychiatry, is not proof of superiority: it is particularly developed in early-onset dementia.

MODERN SCIENCE HAS NO BRAKES AND NO END IN SIGHT

It moves forward like a drunken man driving a 25CV. *It is merely the product of the inventive frenzy of technicians who have not the slightest idea in their work of the moral and spiritual improvement of mankind.*

Drowned in the thick fog of profitability, they seek out the new, the strange, the spectacularly unknown.

The attention span of the man of genius is exceptional and allows him to be impartial.

He rejects any feelings or preconceived ideas that might obscure the truth. He is never the victim of a feeling-idea that might lead him to jump to a hasty conclusion after simple analytical reasoning.

It is in this way, and only in this way, that we can gain access to knowledge.

Let us now look at a few glaring examples of the lack of attention paid by scholars:

In many psychiatric treatises, *the insane* are said to *have an atrophy of the internal genitalia.*

So it's a known fact.

You'd think some doctors or physiologists would have been concerned.

Not in the slightest.

The authors were only concerned about *the* highly inconsistent *brain damage.* But:

These lesions occur in *healthy* subjects. They are not specific to mental illness. They are uncertain.

They are polymorphous.

Their extent does not correspond to the benignity or seriousness of the mental disorder. There is therefore *a double failure of attention* here.

Psychiatry has been bent on finding the causes of mental illness in highly untrue brain lesions, and *has neglected the constant sign of atrophy of the internal genitalia.*

The consequences are simple and tragic: *psychiatrists have no idea what mental illness is.*[13]

They therefore only use empirical methods to "cure" them: chemistry, mutilation, etc. Pathogenic and teratogenic psychotropic drugs, lobotomies, electroshock ("which suppress the symptoms and aggravate the disease", says Professor Baruk) are all used.

They are therefore unaware of the causes of the staggering increase in madness.

In the U.S., the psychiatrists' control group commits suicide more often than the control group made up of their patients!!!

Here's another example of their lack of attention: biologists have found that our limbs move thanks to nervous excitations that are very easy to reproduce with electric sparks. They have also found that all our functions can be carried out by nervous instigation, *even our endocrine glands.*

They therefore concluded that the nervous system is functionally anterior...

But they were deluded.

---

[13] This is, of course, the physiological cause. The deeper causes are failure to respect the laws of life: poor nutrition or deficiencies, failure to respect psychological and moral laws, masturbation, tobacco, alcohol, coffee, abuse of starches and meat, etc. All violations of the laws of life can be generalised. Early masturbation and alcohol can wipe out entire human groups.

When it came to explaining complex phenomena such as:

Sleep, puberty, reproduction, races, heredity, they realised that the concept of the predominance of the nervous system *did not provide them with a satisfactory explanation for everything concerning man.*

If doctors and physiologists had not allowed themselves to be obsessed by their analytical conclusions about the omnipotence of the nervous system, *they would have considered the evolution of the foetus with complete impartiality.*

They would then have noted that in the third month of intra-uterine life, there were only *three* organs that were constituted and able to function:

Adrenals, pituitary gland, thyroid.

This is enough for even a child to *understand that the hormonal system controls the whole of the human being, and consequently the nervous system.*

At this point, the nervous system *is not even in its infancy.*

They would have been able to see that it is the hormonal system and *not* the nervous system that functions *at the beginning of life.*

They also noted that a month later, the foetus's heart began to beat*: however, there can be no question of definitive innervation of this organ.* In fact, there is barely an outline of the lymph nodes.

Yet we were naive enough to claim that it is the nervous system that ensures the minute pulsations of the foetal heart!

You don't need to be a doctor, physiologist, philosopher or psychologist *to understand that this is physiologically mocking us.*

In fact, the adult heart beats at 70-80 beats per minute... and *it is precisely in cases of hyperthyroidism that it reaches 140 beats per minute!!*

These basic observations would have led *us* to understand *that the foetal heart beats at the instigation of thyroid hormones...*

We have known for a long time that the Rœsh plant-man and the myxedematous person no thyroid for operative or congenital reasons. However, they all have the particularity of having no verbal images, no sensitivity, no emotions, no relationships and no intelligence.

Careful observation tells us conclusively that all these qualities come from the thyroid gland.

A patient who has undergone total thyroid surgery loses his intelligence, his affectivity and his verbal images.

Despite this blatant evidence, and despite the fact that the nervous system is in no way able to compensate for these deficiencies, the authors have never had the idea of asserting that it is *the thyroid that is the gland of our emotions, our sentimentality and our intelligence.*

What about Freud?

It's impossible not to mention FREUD if we broach the subject of the lack of attention of modern scholars.

The worldwide acceptance of the ravings of this sex maniac can only be explained by Judeo-Cartesian decay.

We won't dwell on the frightening perversity of this 'work', which is obvious to any sane mind at the moment, especially as the effects and consequences of Freudianism are obvious to everyone: suicides after psychoanalysis, aggravations, widespread abulism as a result of new Freudian educational imperatives, encouraged pornography and masturbation, etc.

Let's just look at the lack of seriousness with which such a delirious theory has been constructed. We will confine ourselves to *physiology*, which is impossible not to do if we are talking about *psychology*.

When Freud was at the Salpêtrière, he noticed that patients whose functional system he did not know (they were hyperthyroid patients, but it is impossible to diagnose this *quantitatively*) had major sexual preoccupations and mythomaniac tendencies taken to extremes. From this he developed a concept which he gradually extended to the whole of psychology. His approach is that of certain maniacs and melancholics prey to delusional systematisation. Freud saw that the preoccupation of hysterics was most often sexual. Knowing that this preoccupation can be found in certain children (clearly thyroid patients, which Freud was unaware of). He concluded that *the fundamental factor in psychological life was sex!*

It is true that in his practice he saw many children circumcised on the 8th day who displayed this particularity, as did teenagers at puberty.

He ended up by asserting that the achievements of famous men were due to the sublimation of their reproductive instincts.

Freud told us that man possesses a sexual *instinct*.

He never tried to identify what an instinct is. He has never sought to discover whether the human sexual drive *corresponds to the fundamental identity of instincts* (incoercible, rigorous periodicity, depending on the species). He has not subjected the rut of animals to a similar examination.

Freud told us, free of charge, that from birth the child already inherited all the perverse sexual tendencies of the adult.

He did not try to find out the physiological reasons why the child was suckling and which organ, if removed, would abolish this phenomenon (the thyroid).

He didn't look any further into the reasons why he ran his hands over his genitals (urine corrosion), why sexual preoccupations were very strong in some people (thyroid) and non-existent in others (hormonally balanced).

He never sought to identify the organ that gives the child all these tendencies: the thyroid gland. In talking about children, Freud was never concerned with *glandular predominance*, of which there are four, nor with the glandular evolutions through which he passes, i.e. the *three puberty periods*.

These glandular states have a profound effect on children's mentality. Freud never sought to understand the feminine feeling of modesty. Instead, his influence practically destroyed this fundamental feminine characteristic, so perfectly in tune with the nature of the true woman.

He talks a lot about homosexuality, but *he has never had the curiosity to recognise the conditions in which it manifests itself:* interstitial insufficiency, early masturbation, widespread chemotherapy and vaccinations, multiple deficiencies, particularly in vitamin E...

He never told us how female jouissance was achieved, which does not disappear with the removal of the ovaries.

Not a word either about male enjoyment, which is physiologically very different.

Freud told us that sleep is a return to foetal life.

He has never carefully considered the functional slowing down of all the glands. He did not even see that the rifle-dog position is the best way to relax the muscles.

His dream symbolism betrays a sexual obsession of a markedly pathological nature.

Unless you are sexually obsessed (due to Freudian influence!), it would never occur to anyone to interpret a raised object as a phallus and a hollow object as a vagina! For the clinician, such an interpretation would betray *a serious thyroid imbalance.*

Such was the case with Freud and with those who accept his rantings uncritically. *They cannot meditate on the scientific facts we have just mentioned.*

It should be added that any mental state of exacerbated sexual obsession forbids abstract thought and meditation. It only allows the imaginary prolixity and torrential verbosity of our official sexologists and 'philosophers', which is different. This logorrhoea is all the more unbridled for not being by moral sense and common sense.

There's no need for this kind of symbolism, because we've all had erotic dreams with *no need for transvestites.* So we don't need this symbolism to "provide a release for sexual repression".

Freud overlooked a number of curious and interesting dreams. For example, those provoked by external influences, dreams of lightness, of running an easy or difficult race, of falling into a void, and so on.

Freud's *fabulation* lowered man to the level of the beast by plunging him into the cesspool of the lower unconscious.

In the words of EMILE LUDWIG, a circumcised man with a sense of morality, which is rare among the pseudo-elite:

"It plays a major role in the misfortune of our contemporaries, who are deprived of a sense of morality and true freedom"...

ATTENTION, WILLPOWER AND THE MORAL SENSE OF MODERN SCIENTISTS

The chapter on the lack of attention from official scientists is inexhaustible. The laboratory has developed greatly. It has taken on absolute importance.

"There are no more discoveries, only experiments and conclusions", said a naive professor on television.

The general naivety is to believe what is said in newspapers and on television, and especially in schools at all levels.

They think that without the laboratory we won't be able to discover anything about our nature, which is not true.

Of course, the laboratory can be of great service *in pathological practice*, but to believe that it is the sine qua non of discovery *is a considerable illusion*.

The human race demands practical, synthetic work by synthetic minds.

Carrel showed us that analytical laboratory data can only lead us to the dust of information by taking us further and further away from man.

Laboratory scientists have abandoned findings that have been made by man for thousands of years. They are the most important for human beings because they were made on their own scale of observation. If we are to escape from our collective hypnosis, we need to understand that: *All interpretations and conceptions that manage to explain a human phenomenon to us and are in contradiction with laboratory data lose nothing of their value. On the other hand, the most brilliant laboratory conceptions that contradict thousands of years of human observations are necessarily false.*

Man must be observed with the human eye and the various other senses.

We know that Pasteur discovered that an attenuated microbial culture could confer a *certain* immunity (and not a certain immunity). This led to the development of serums and vaccines. However, Pasteur died saying: "Claude Bernard was right, *the microbe is nothing, the terrain is everything*".

This statement by Pasteur, which gives Pasteurism a reasonable dimension, has been ignored by Pasteurians who are much more Pasteurian than Pasteur himself...

Vaccines are being imposed on us without any concern for our health.

However, we all know that there are religious orders that lead healthy moral and dietary lives and can treat plague and cholera patients without contracting these diseases.

History cites numerous cases, particularly in the Middle Ages.

Modern scientists do not ask themselves what influence the abnormal and brutal penetration of thirty or so injections of attenuated cultures during childhood and adolescence might have on our personality. *Can these putrid products really be harmless to our organism?*

This way of making vaccinations compulsory *lacks any moral sense*. It has no respect for human personality, independence or free will.

It is therefore characteristic of madness.

Such injections can disrupt metabolisms, especially in middle age, and facilitate the onset of functional disorders.

What's more, we know that the internal genitalia is very sensitive to adverse influences. It therefore becomes hypofunctional.

Its role in the functional and intellectual balance of the individual is immense. *Its weakening facilitates cellular disturbances leading to the degeneration of the race, the formation of tumours, and functional changes which can result in diseases of the vegetative organs. Finally, we know its role in personality and intelligence deficiencies, and therefore in the onset of mental disorders.*

The modern scientist's attention span is therefore extremely limited. What about his willpower?

As we have said, we see specialised scholars.

They often delve into a small question, a tiny problem (the formation of the hind legs of some crustacean).[14]

As a result, they clutter up science with futile data, creating an enormous traffic jam that hinders personal and brilliant minds.

So it's even harder for them to make the discovery.

The lack of willpower freezes the current scientist in mediocrity, in the absence of *knowledge of Man*, in compartmentalisation, in neologisms and above all *in the confusion of hypotheses that contradict each other.*

Genius will therefore have to get to work, rid itself of the robotic thinking inflicted on it by the Western university system, which is the very root of this global decline, *since it ignores all the criteria of knowledge, replaced by a Cartesianism that Descartes would have rejected.*

He will have to stop playing to the halls of memory and analysis, within the reach of every primitive. He will have to fix his mind on the main and major ideas on which the secondary ideas will automatically be grafted.

He will have to give up all current official competitions *because he will be paying for the material comfort that he will be able to derive from an irreversible conformist intellectual sclerosis.*

---

[14] I'm not making anything up

True intellectual activity can only be achieved by the will, which is physiologically the internal genital gland.

It can command all secretions to act in the brain.

The adrenals for practical ideas, the pituitary for analytical and mathematical reasoning, the thyroid for imagination, intuition and the aesthetic sense.

In short, it is not possible to disassociate the man in order to discover him: *he must be considered in his entirety with a synthetic rather than eclectic mind.*

Willpower is essential to the meditation that leads to discovery. It enables us to fight against *the misconceptions* we hold dear, and to use new information to challenge those we thought we had already established in our minds.

It has to be said that new ideas have always suffered from misunderstanding and ostracism. The genius lives alone, misunderstood. Sentimental, they often suffer cruel disillusionment. The only thing they get out of their work is *hardship, injustice and ridicule,* when they are not gambling with their lives.

The same cannot be said for the authors of false, fabulist and perverse ideas, who have no difficulty whatsoever in imposing themselves in a supposedly falsely "democratic" world.

What more can be said about the *moral sense of* modern scientists?

We said that in ancient Egypt, when a scientist made a discovery that could harm mankind in time and space, the Priestly Caste *forced him to symbolically swallow the parchment on which it was described.*

Egypt did not make any great material progress, but it did not pollute its country or its continent. It was able to survive for millennia, develop its agriculture and livestock farming, and build monuments such as the pyramids, which are responsible for transmitting to us theoretical notions that we are not about to acquire.

In other words, neither Rothschild, nor Marx, nor Freud, nor Einstein, nor Picasso et al could have done any harm in Egypt. Hegemonic finance, communism, Freudian madness and atomic and neutron bombs were no more common there than Chernobyls.

What we have known are above all *famous people*.

They did have a few interstitial characteristics, since their works were beautiful, harmonious and creatively imaginative.

Or he had a great aptitude for scientific analysis.

They cannot claim the title of genius because genius owes its mentality to the internal genital gland.

In youth, this gland regulates the relationship between the glandular system and the nervous system. *Hence the immense importance of a good education, which today is being destroyed in the name of the pseudo-secular ideal that allows the mass production of delinquents, criminals, thugs, terrorists, drug addicts and suicides.*

The internal genitalia establish the accuracy and sincerity of verbal images. It conditions the emotional and sentimental proportion that goes into each verbal image and ensures its correspondence with reality and ideas. It therefore contributes to the truth of language and the rectitude of the mind. In adolescence, it gives us control over our feelings and sexuality.

It acts on all the endocrines to reduce their functional extravagance.

It therefore stabilises the character, giving it courage and willpower. In adulthood, it can condition the activity of other glands on the brain. It forces each hormone to act on the brain's nerve cells. It can provide all the intellectual qualities of the human mind. It can develop greatly during the menopause, and produce outstanding intellectual qualities: *this explains the veneration of the elderly in all civilisations.*

In conclusion, the internal or interstitial genitalia, in its maximum development, carries within it the fundamental qualities of genius: *moral sense and superior psychological elaborations.*

The thyroid-interstitial will therefore present human development in its maximum qualities. (Pius XII)

PSYCHOLOGICAL ROLE OF THE SO-CALLED ORGANIC ENDOCRINES

Let's look briefly at the famous men and recall the psychological role of the so-called organic endocrines:

ADRENALS:

force attack, objectivity, materialism, compilation, practicality and down-to-earthness. Stalin, the ring wrestlers.

PITUITARY GLAND:

strength, resistance, analysis, mathematics, logic, moral composure. de Gaullehospital interns, agrégés, modern scientists.

THYROID:

pure intelligence, intuition, imagination, sense of beauty, sensitivity, emotions, feelings. Chopin, the great long artists, the great mystics (Francis of Assisi).

INTERNAL GENITAL:

synthesis, moral sense, notion of identity, love of God, nobility of spirit, physical and moral courage, great altruistic and human feelings. Alexis Carrel, ancient Greek civilisation in general.

***

We could define genius physiologically by saying that it is *the voluntary application by the internal genitalia of the thyroid hormone to cerebral activity*. (Other hormones too, but the thyroid is the endocrine of intelligence, intuition, imagination and feelings).

The adrenals have made a number of composers famous, including *Beethoven*. They also give us practical intelligence, a tendency towards industrial and military applications, as well as chemical research. They also have a tendency to compile.

Since the thyroid is the gland of the imagination and verbal images, poets, novelists, historians and writers owe it a great deal. Plastic artists too.

Among thyroid intellectuals, there were the classics who synthesised the particularities found in many men. Their active interstitials controlled their thyroid. This was the case with *La Fontaine*.

Those who had a lively thyroid with an interstitial that acted MORE on literary form than on imagination were the romantics.

Those whose thyroid did not obey the internal genitalia were independents, symbolists, impressionists and sometimes hysterical mystics.

Inadequate internal genitalia can lead to homosexuality, as in the case of Oscar Wilde.

The pituitary gland is the gland of the *positive sciences*.

This is what drives today's scientists. It tends towards estimation, comparison, quantitative analysis and calculation.

It is this that is currently driving the tragic development of modern science, according to the interests and fantasies of scientists.

We don't owe it much thanks. *Its physiological independence from the internal genitalia creates its malfeasance.* We spoke of the designer of an extraordinary aeroplane who killed his entire family with an axe.

You can be a perfect atheist and still create atomic and neutron bombs, because that's all down to the pituitary gland.

A brilliant pituitary designer can be a raving lunatic, unable to link his analyses to *any higher concept or synthesis.*

Physiologically, the pituitary gland mainly excites the *reproductive* genitalia (the organ of reproduction), which is in opposition to the internal genitalia. This is why today there is an explosion of analytical minds and no minds of synthesis.

The famous man is therefore fundamentally driven by *a* predominant endocrine system.

It gives them a special aptitude. Unfortunately, this ability can be *an excess of the mind to the detriment of fundamental human concepts.*

Speculative intelligence is therefore *the antithesis of pure intelligence.*

It's easy to see why *finance doesn't think and science doesn't think either.*

Genius is a complete spirit. He is *universal* in the synthetic expression of his creation.

All his work takes account of all the realities that make up reality.

His sentimentality is directed towards human problems where his finality converges. The famous man turns away from the human entity. This is the category of intellectuals who officially reign.

The absence of a spiritual structure means that they inevitably work like sorcerers' apprentices against man. As a result, physics, chemistry, technology, chemical nutrition and chemical medicine all converge to destroy man and his environment.

It is obvious that we must include in the latter category the designers of social plans who conceive for statism and the man-mass, without worrying in the least about their attack on freedom and respect for the human person, which they constantly betray in the name of human rights.

The modern scientific concept is therefore suicidal.

Thus, contemporary history clearly shows us that ignorance of the hierarchical order based on the supremacy of spiritual authority over temporal authority *necessarily* leads to imbalance, social anarchy, confusion of values, *domination of the inferior over the superior*, biological, intellectual, moral and aesthetic degeneration, oblivion of transcendent principles *and then negation of true knowledge* coming from the mind that penetrates notions of identity and synthesis, and not from the mind that is wrongly called 'scientific'...

There remains only one alternative: the suicidal reign of Wall-street and Marx or traditional dictatorships that put men, women, children, nutrition, morality and the environment in their proper places.

Everything else, as Hitler said in Mein Kampf, *can only lead to total destruction.*

WHAT DOES IT MEAN TO BE A FASCIST?

> *"Dictatorship is the normal reaction of a people who do not want to die".*
>
> *"The great criminals are not in prison, but at the pinnacle of liberal society.*
>
> *"The liberal bourgeois is the elder brother of the Bolshevik.*
>
> Dr Alexis Carrel.

If it means having a religion that teaches good and evil, not to eat just anything, to practise controlled breathing and true prayer,

If it means respecting the family, loving your children, giving them an education that makes them real men and women,

If it means having your wife at home, so that she's queen of the house, looking after her home, her husband and her children, who won't become disco customers, drug addicts, unemployed, delinquents or suicides,

If it means refusing the systematic violence on television and in the cinema, if it means refusing the "music that kills", criminogenic through exaggerated physiological stimulation of adrenalin, "toxicogenic" through exaggerated physiological stimulation of endorphins,

If that means rejecting degrading, filthy pornography,

If that means rejecting nuclear power with its unstorable and non-neutralisable waste,

If it means refusing to fool around with genomes and all forms of monstrous genetic manipulation,

If that means refusing the WARBURGs who simultaneously financed Germany, the Allies and the Bolshevik revolution, in order to come to Europe in 1919 as peace negotiators (for the Treaty of Versailles!),

If it means refusing to sell hidden weapons to everything that is being exterminated on the planet,

If it means giving the right to speak to those who have something to say (Faurisson, Zundel, Notin, Roques etc.), without forcing them to remain silent through Stalinist and Orwellian laws that are anti-democratic and anti-constitutional,

If this means rejecting the global destruction of the forest, particularly for the niagara ballot papers, which is essential for ecological balance,

If it means refusing to accept the disappearance of animal and plant species,

If it means refusing to wipe out the peasantry, reduced to economic distress by shameful speculators and sold-out politicians, when peasants, like the destroyed craftsmen, constitute the first vital social body of a nation,

If it means refusing to let synthetic chemistry kill off the earth,

If it means refusing systematic vaccinations that destroy the immune system, causing degeneration, cancers, cardiovascular and mental diseases,

If this means rejecting pathogenic chemistry as a principle of health, even though it affects humans at chromosomal level, causes serious illnesses and is teratogenic,

If it means refusing the demonising dictatorship of Soros and all the financiers circumcised on the ⁸ᵗʰ day, who possess gigantic powers that no sovereign has ever enjoyed in history,

If that means rejecting Marxism (like pornographer Freudism), which has exterminated 200 million victims throughout the world and continues, in Africa, Asia and South America, to massacre populations and reduce them to starvation,

If that's refusing the monstrous, tentacled MAFFIA,

If that means denying life to rapists and murderers of little girls, as well as to any heredoalcoholic or syphilitic lunatic, idiot or profound moron,

If that means rejecting the normative expansion of paedophilia, homosexuality, sexual laxity and AIDS...,

If that means saying no to institutionalised miscegenation, which automatically generates Lebanisation and bloody racism, as well as incoercible social unrest,

If that means saying no to the mop politicians, unconditionally subservient to finance, who are going to reduce the whole of Europe to unemployment with their globalist treaties and who are free of any real spiritual or moral discipline,

If that means refusing to wear the uniform of international bullshit that is the LEVIS blue jeans,

So yes, I am a fascist and proud of it...

THE WORLD OF TOMORROW

We are bogged down in *pseudo-progress*.

Soil depletion leads to collective physiological and psychological decline, in particular through hypotrophy of the endocrine glands, which are insufficiently supplied with vital substances such as iodine, *magnesium*, etc.

These vital deficiencies give rise to all the aberrations of behaviour, all the collective and individual madness, all the victories of the most insane ideas and ideologies. *We are all involved in atheistic speculative materialism.* We cannot suddenly extricate ourselves from it.

A hand must be extended to those who are stuck in the abyssal swamp *of Rothschildo-Marxism* and who dream of extricating themselves from it imperceptibly and painlessly.

Our feet will remain in the chemical mire of materialism for some time to come, but our heads must reach for the blue of heaven, and refuse to enter into dialogue with an increasingly unconscious, increasingly insane world.

The day after tomorrow, each ethnic group will live in the country that formed it. It will produce the basic elements necessary for its subsistence, and will stay away from anything that is pathogenic, carcinogenic, teratogenic or *artificial*.

No more nitrates that kill the earth and mankind, no more massive antibiotics that cause quantitative rather than qualitative populations to grow in geometric progression, whose countries have been drained of their natural resources by colonialism in all its forms and the lie of progress. Man will then be a craftsman, free to create with his heart and his mind, whether he is a carpenter, a poet or a philosopher.

No more mass production of soulless objects that do nothing for happiness, which is a neuro-endocrine-psychic balance.

Man will radically eliminate the sexual mutilations that distort the mind in the first month of birth. Man will extricate himself from the conditioning of all sclerotic dogmatism, from the doctrinaire spirit of decadent religions and the degenerate ideologies that they have more or less arranged. Neither simple belief in the Eucharist nor Marxist economic frenzy will make a man organically and mentally healthy, a HAPPY man.

From an early age, the child will learn a suitable diet that tends towards raw and vegetable foods, hygiene, natural health and controlled breathing, because the breath is the divine agent of prayer and self-control.

He will learn meditation.

Man will return to a simple diet, from which toxic substances such as alcohol, coffee, tobacco, white sugar, white bread, Coca-Cola, etc. will be banished, with a focus on fruit and vegetables, especially raw, and a little fresh cheese and eggs until he has regenerated.

It avoids food mixtures.

Man will strengthen his natural immunity through the constant presence of the mother in the home, the *irreplaceable* epicentre of family equilibrium. He will use wheat germ, pollen and the natural magnesium contained in dried fruit, for example.

The child's character will be formed by the application of the laws of life, courage, nobility of feeling, spiritual ideals, tolerance for all that is great, beautiful and true, and in no way for all the forms of putrescence that preach intolerable tolerance.

It is therefore these natural means that will stand guard on the threshold of health, rather than physico-chemical processes that are radically alien to the concept of health.

Man will refuse the media hype, and will seek the truth by being a permanent revisionist over and above all the subliminal and hypnotic stultifying processes of the press, radio, television, publishing and perverse and conditioning teaching.

The day after tomorrow, man will never again lose sight of the happiness-generating concepts of *synthesis and moral sense*.

He will know that only a disinterested intellectual spirit is subject to rectitude and not to expediency and the elementary forms of profit.

It will abandon an involutionary, *microscopic, analytical, quantitative* science for an evolutionary, *macroscopic, synthetic, qualitative* science.

Man will know *that there can be no freedom without authority.*

He will submit to the authority of the transcendent, to the divine laws designed to preserve the health of his body and mind, because he will know that if you slavishly stoop to a pseudo-freedom you are subject to the crushing totalitarianism of your baser instincts, of materialism with its pornography, its drugs, its gulags and its pulverisation of the psyche...

UBU EMPEROR

A retired Jewish teacher, very ill and very old, who suffered a stroke, has been charged with anti-Semitism and fined €500.

This professor belongs to the international de Menasce family, which owned one hundred and fifty billion francs at the beginning of the last century (cotton, Egyptian bank).

The professor had written a letter to the son of a concert pianist friend. The imprisoned son, a hormonal patient (paedophile), had written him a geopolitically lucid letter to which he had replied.

The letter contained the sentence: *"The goyim have chosen my fellow creatures as their masters, and they're going to die for it"*. Quite legitimately, the prison governor opened the letter and, displeased with the sentence, sent it to the public prosecutor in Châteauroux, who had the teacher charged. The result was a fine for anti-Semitism. What's more, this teacher has an adopted daughter who has been disabled for life by a vaccination, for whom he is the sole provider, and who does not even enjoy the status of an industrial accident victim!

The impecunious professor borrowed the fine from friends and paid it himself.

But this is not about religion or race.

All his fellow members of the upper middle class are agnostics or atheists. He himself is agnostic.

Race? There is no such thing as race, apart from white, black, yellow and red.

There are only ethnic groups that are the result of hormonal adaptation over a millennium to a fixed geographical environment. Now, the "Jews" - a term used for convenience and which will be clarified later - are spread all over the planet and have never lived in a fixed geographical location: even in Palestine, where they have not lived for more than three centuries. They take on the physical appearance of the country in which they find themselves.

Their constant particularism in time and space, their sometimes caricatured features, their enormous speculative powers deprived of a moral sense and a spirit of synthesis, essentially spring from a poorly understood hormonal operation: **circumcision on the 8th day after birth,** i.e. on the first day of the first puberty which lasts 21 days. Circumcision on the first day of puberty hypotrophies the **interstitial** gland (gland of the moral sense, of the spirit of synthesis, of altruism), but because of its inability to harmonise the balanced whole of the glandular system, over-stimulates the pituitary gland.

It's this pituitary hyperactivity that foments financiers and ideologists: you have to be circumcised on the 8th day to extort 50 billion dollars without scruples, not to mention science, atomic, hydrogen and neutron bombs and specialised medicine. The thyroid is also the gland of imagination and automatism: you have to be circumcised on the 8th day to be a pianist as extraordinary as Horowitz or a violinist of unequalled virtuosity like Yehudi Menuhin.

We must therefore say, to the exclusion of all racial and religious concepts: **the sect of those circumcised on the 8th day rules the World.**

It was this particular circumcision that made them a group of predators, persecuted and driven out of every country they found themselves in, **without exception, long before the advent of Christianity.** (See Bernard Lazare's book: *L'antisémitisme*).

At the same time as this grotesque affair of a Menasce charged with anti-Semitism, the economic collapse broke out. The Israeli writer

Shamir stigmatised American Jewish billionaires, whom he accused of having collapsed the pyramid, in an article published on the Internet and unambiguously entitled *"gallows birds"*[15]...

Madoff then joined the other circumcised billionaire financiers, extorting 50 billion dollars - a phenomenon unique in the world and beating all the Jewish usury records in history.

Only a person circumcised on the 8th day can be capable of such a frightening feat. **Those circumcised on the 8th day are therefore predators**, as *Benjamin Franklin* historically understood.

So Mr Madoff will pay his bail and his fine with the stolen money, and the state will be his accomplice by endorsing him!

Meanwhile, Mr Zundel was forcibly abducted from his wife's home in the United States and sentenced to six years' imprisonment for having proved the imposture of the Holocaust.

Law has become the bloated caricature and antithesis of Justice.

By its very existence, *the Fabius Law* (one circumcised on the 8th day) proof par neuf of the imposture. When you control television and the media, you don't need *Orwellian laws* to expose the truth: evidence and arguments are enough.

The Fabius Gayssot law (a communist who only has some 200 million corpses behind him, victims of Marxism) is the most revisionist law there is, since it is an admission of imposture...!

This law was declared unconstitutional, anti-human rights and anti-democratic by many legal experts, and Mr Toubon, who became

---

[15] Those circumcised on the 8th day are guilty, but not responsible: their hormonal and secular determinism is absolute.

Minister of Justice, declared that it was a step backwards for law and history and would never be applied!

It is enforced by robots who are more concerned with their own feeding troughs than with truth and honour.

If Madoff ever had the miraculous idea of denouncing his Jewishness, he would be charged with anti-Semitism!

It's all very well knitted by the *demon* dictatorship served up by the hedonistic larvae of the world. But a fantasist can get thousands of spectators to repeat: *"The Pope's a cocksucker"*... Several times in a row, of course...

The fingertips of all the prosecutors in France won't budge!!! There is no protection for religion!

Decidedly, this world of larvae, accomplices in their own suicide as the professor became acutely aware during his interrogation by the police - whose ignorance and unconsciousness exceeded all bounds - deserves to disappear, for simple reasons of asepsis...

The Fabius-Gayssot law is radically dictatorial, categorically anti-democratic and therefore has no constitutional existence. It is incapable of standing up to arguments and evidence masterfully put forward by international revisionism...

It is proof by nine of an absolute sham.

Justice itself will eventually collapse before its house of cards[16]...

---

[16] Revisionist professors and intellectuals have as many rights as the pornography that is spreading around the world and the billionaires in dollars who are the major swindlers of circumcisocracy on the 8th day.

DID YOU SAY ANTI-SEMITIC? NO?

> "The Jews, that handful of uprooted people, caused the uprooting of the entire globe." - Simone Weil

> "The lie of progress is Israel. - Simone Weil

> "As for circumcision on the 8th day, don't worry about it: it's beyond comprehension." - The Talmud

> "Who would have thought that a rite could go so far and risk destroying everything on the frontier between nations." - Dominique Aubier (about his book on circumcision on the 8th day, aimed exclusively at Jews)[17]

Everything that follows has been subjected to the sieve of the most absolute accuracy of history and current events. Only totalitarian international de-education can plunge the world into the most radical ignorance.

THE ULTIMATE SYNTHESIS OF THE GEOPOLITICS OF THE LAST MILLENNIA

For thousands of years before Christianity, **the Jews were expelled** from all the countries where they were found, because of the **vampirism** and **exorbitant usury they practised**. When Christ did exist, they were not blamed for the crucifixion. When, during the Middle Ages, they were still excluded from all the countries where they were found, was not the crucifixion that was the cause of their general ousting, it was only the icing on the cake. The same causes. The same

---

[17] This book leads to the same results as endocrinology with regard to Judeopathy.

effects: **vampirism and usury were the perennial root of the evil.** It is perfectly clear that not all countries, in different languages, at different times, in different placesused the word to expel the Jews: the root of anti-Semitism is therefore **in** the Jew and not in the anti-Semite.

What are the causes of this universal expulsion of the Jews, in ancient times and in the Christian era?

An overview of history tells us so.

Not only did the Jews monopolise the currency exchange business, but the real source of their wealth was usury or , which brought them great advantages. Little by little they came to be the real bankers of the age and the lenders to social classes. By lending to the emperor as well as to simple craftsmen and farmers, they exploited both the great and the small **without the slightest scruple.** We can get a rough idea of the proportions reached by their traffic by examining the rate of interest authorised by law in the 14th and 15th centuries.

In 1338, Emperor Ludwig of Bavaria granted the burghers of Frankfurt a special privilege *"in order to protect the Jews of the city and to look after their safety with all their heart"*, thanks to which they could obtain loans from Jews at 32.5% per annum, while foreigners were authorised to lend up to 43%. The council of Mainz took out a loan of a thousand florins and they were allowed to claim 52%.

In Regensburg, Augsburg, Vienna and other places, the legal interest rate frequently rose to 86%. But the most vexatious interest charges were those demanded by the Jews for minor loans, which small traders and farmers were forced to take out.

"The Jews pillage and plunder the poor man," says the rhymer Erasmem d'Erbach (1487); *"this is really becoming intolerable, may God have mercy on us. Nowadays, Jewish usurers set up fixed premises in the smallest towns; when they advance five florins, they take pledges that are six times the sums lent.*

Then they claim the interest on the interest, and again on the new interest. In this way, the poor man is dispossessed of he owned".

At the same time, Tritème said: *"It is easy to understand that among the young and the old, among the educated and the ignorant, among princes and peasants alike, there is a deep-rooted aversion to usurious Jews..."*.

This is an undeniable historical fact, and Christ had nothing to do with it. During the Christian era, the phenomenon continued and all the countries of Christendom ended up being expelled by the Jews for the same reasons: monopolisation, vampirism, major and merciless usury.

In 1789, Benjamin Franklin, a democrat and a Freemason, made it clear in his preliminary speech for the drafting of the American Constitution that he wanted to make the following statement:

"In every country where Jews have settled in large numbers, without exception, they have debased its moral grandeur, depreciated its commercial integrity, ridiculed its institutions, never assimilated, built a state within a state, ridiculed religion and undermined it. When they tried to thwart their plans, they financially strangled the country, as they did in Spain and Portugal.

If you grant citizenship to Jews, your children will curse you in your graves. If you do not exclude the Jews in the Constitution of the United States, in less than two centuries they will swarm, dominate your country and change the form of government...

"If the civilised world wanted to give them back Palestine, they would find a pressing reason not to return because they vampires and vampires cannot live on the backs of other vampires..."

Israel, the only country where there are no Jews! They live in all banks of the world, particularly in the United States, and have no desire to go to Israel, which for them is nothing more than a bridgehead to dominate the Middle East and take its oil.

Everything Benjamin Franklin said has come true in full.

Twenty-two (22) Bush ministers were as Jewish as the current government.

The general collapse of the economy was castigated by a Jew, Isaac Shamir, an honest Jew, who condemned *"collapse of the pyramid"* by the billionaire Jews of the United States. The article about these billionaire Jews had an unambiguous title: *"Gallows Jesters"*. Among those it stigmatises are: Tom Friedman, Henri Paulson, Ben Bernanke, Alan Grennsberg, Maurice Grennsberg, **Lehman Brothers**[18] Merrill Linch, Goldman Sachs, Marc Rich, Michael Milen, Andrew Fastow, George Soros and others...

The icing on the cake was that Maddof, a Jewish swindler, stole 50 billion dollars: it was just an unfortunate accident - the depositors wanted their money back. Had this not been the case, Maddof would still be operating underhandedly in a hushed international silence.

The *Federal Reserve* **is a private body** of gigantic power (including some of the billionaires mentioned above) which has led every war, from the First World War in 1914-1918 to the invasion Iraq less than 100 years later. The whole of international finance is involved in modern warfare. The members are always co-opted: in 1913 their names were Rothschild, Lazard, Israel Moses, Warburg, Lehman Brothers, Kuhn Loeb, Chase Manhattan Bank, Goldman Sachs...

All Jews. These people demand that we pay interest on fictitious loans and can confiscate everything.

The Bolshevik revolution was entirely Jewish: tens of millions died. Everything about it was Jewish: American Jewish bankers, Jewish

---

[18] The Lehmann brothers' financial collapse and 28,000 unemployed were mentioned on the TV news, as were Israel's war crimes and crimes against humanity against the Palestinians. (September 2009)

politicians, Jewish administrators, prison and concentration camp executioners such as Frankel, Yagoda, Firine, Appeter, Jejoff, Abramovici and fifty others led by Kaganovitch.

A Jew, Laurent Fabius, had the law that bears his name promulgated. The law prohibits talk of *"gas chambers and six million"* because of the absoluteness of the Nuremberg Tribunal, which was fallible because the Katyn massacre, which was blamed on the Germans, was Soviet, as a revisionist Russian president denounced! (Gorbachev).

A future Minister of Justice said that if this law were passed it would be unconstitutional, anti-human rights, anti-democratic and that the judiciary would never apply it. It was promulgated and applied by the trembling larvae of magistrates who are on their stomachs in front of this upside-down Justice and the totalitarians who have them democratically promulgated.

What followed was even more devastating: Ernst Zündel, who was convinced that the Shoah was a sham and had taken part in several trials in Canada, had married an American woman in the USA.

Under the false pretext that his immigration papers were not up to date (he was American by marriage), he was abducted, imprisoned in Canada, sent Germany without the slightest official legal procedure (and therefore illegally) and sentenced to 5 years in prison for trying to prove the imposture of the Holocaust.

A hundred or so writers, engineers, lawyers, professors and historians were imprisoned without the slightest chance of defending themselves or providing irrefutable proof of their statements:

This is what we call **democratic freedom of expression.**

They include Mahler, Sylvie Stolz, Wolfgand Fröhlich, Gerd Honsik, Walter Lüftl, Vincent Reynouard, Professor Faurisson, German Rudolf, Dirk Zimmerman, Kevin Kälter, Fredrick Töben, Arman Amaudruz, René Louis Berclaz, Jürgen Graf and others.

A book entitled *The Jewish Mafia* shows that the Russian and American mafias are Jewish. Among the Jewish mafiosi, there is one who alone owns 170 billion dollars.

All the owners of Russian oil are Jewish. One of the most important, Kodorkovski, was sent to Siberia by Putin.

All the most famous writers have denounced the Jews, even Napoleon I, who was commissioned by the Revolution and by Rothschild to liquidate the monarchies of Europe, referred to the Jews as *"that cloud of crows"*. (Incidentally, a book about the emperor is entitled *Napoléon antisémite*).

Among the great writers who denounced the Jews are:

Karl Marx *("Suppress traffic and you suppress the Jew")*, Jaurès, Ronsard, Voltaire, Kant, Malesherbes, Erasmus, Luther, Schopenhauer, Vigny, Balzac, Proudhon, Michelet, Renan, Dostoyevsky, Hugo, Drumont, Wagner, Maupassant, Jules Vernes, Simenon, Jean Giraudoux, Marcel Aymé, Céline, Montherlant, Léon Bloy, Mauriac, Proust, Musset, Chateaubriand, Mme de Sévigné, Racine, Molière, Shakespeare, Dickens, Walter Scott, etc.

In Israel's defence, it must be said that the economic and technical situation recent centuries has encouraged Jewish atrocities for which the goyim, veritable hedonistic larvae, **bear a great deal of responsibility.**

The Jews make too much of it because of **the enormous speculative possibilities**, deprived of moral sense and spirit of synthesis, conferred on them by circumcision on the 8th day.

All Jewish pathology stems from this, and it's easy to understand if you know about the great discovery of the **functional anteriority of the hormonal system over the nervous system and the existence of the first puberty, which begins on the 8th day and lasts 21 days.**

After all, if you know
these basic parameters
history and current affairs,
why on earth,
are you anti-Semitic???

* * *

"If the Jews, with their Marxist profession of faith, take over the reins of humanity, then man will disappear from the planet, which will start spinning again in the ether as it did millions of years ago."

- Adolphe Hitler

That's where we are now, and at the top of our game horror, the Jewish laws (Fabius) condemn in justice to the real elites who are vainly trying to proclaim the truth (Faurisson, Zundel, etc.).

Genrikh Yagoda

Frenkel

Ouritski Moisséi Salomonovitch

Paul Warburg

Armand Hammer

Edgar Bronfman

Mayer Carl von Rothschild

Sir Zacharias Basileios

Carl Djerassi

Simone Veil

Bernard Maddoff

Thomas Friedman

Pablo Picasso

Sigmund Freud

Albert Einstein and Oppenheimer

Adolf Hitler

Karl Marx

Other Titles

ABORTION
GENOCIDE IN AMERICA

BY JOHN COLEMAN

I MAINTAIN THAT WHEN A WOMAN AGREES TO AN ABORTION IN A NON-LIFE THREATENING SITUATION, SHE HAS TAKEN LEAVE OF HER SENSES AND SHOULD BE ADJUDGED "TEMPORARILY INSANE."

ABORTION SHOULD BE EXPLAINED AS EUPHEMISM FOR "MURDER BY DECEPTION"

BEYOND the CONSPIRACY
UNMASKING THE INVISIBLE WORLD GOVERNMENT

by John Coleman

All great historical events are planned in secret by men who surround themselves with total discretion.

Highly organized groups always have the advantage over citizens

THE CLUB OF ROME
THE THINK TANK OF THE NEW WORLD ORDER

BY JOHN COLEMAN

The many tragic and explosive events of the 20th century didn't happen by themselves, but were planned according to a well-established pattern...

Who were the planners and creators of these major events?

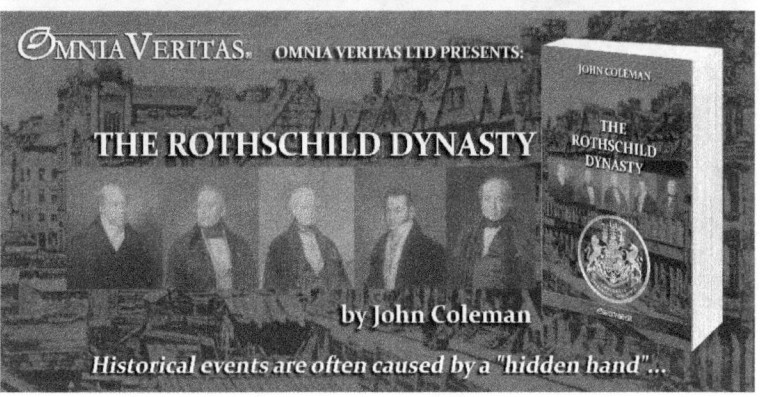

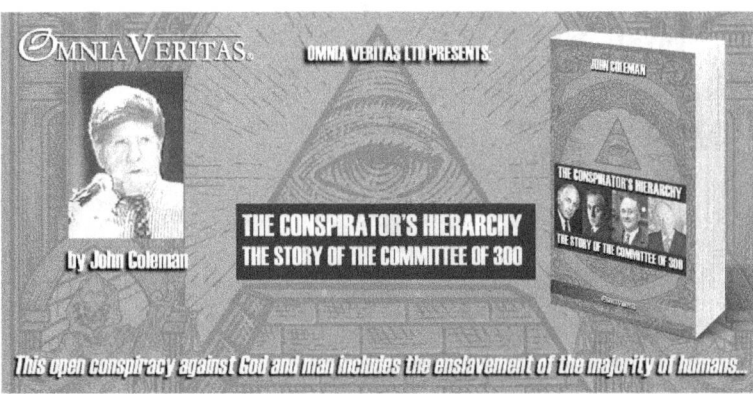

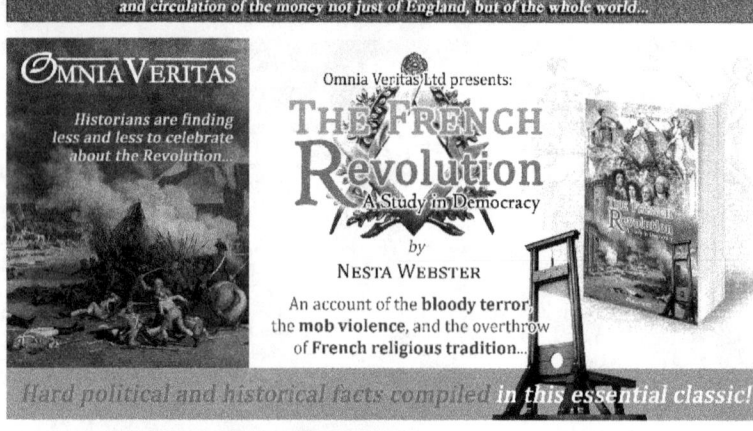

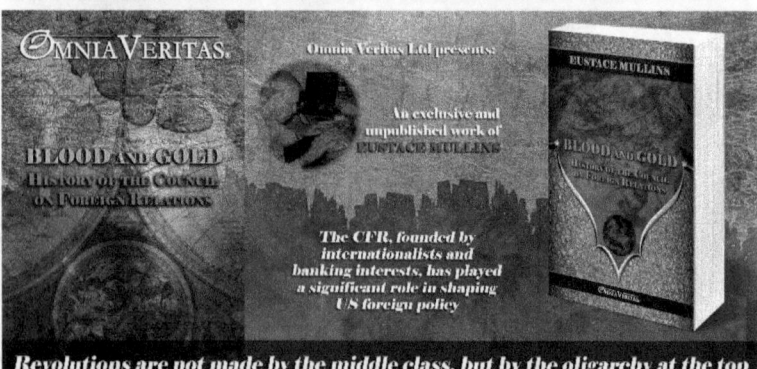

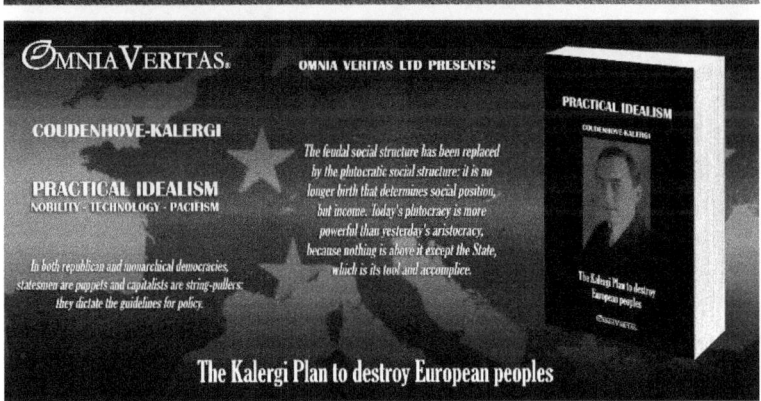

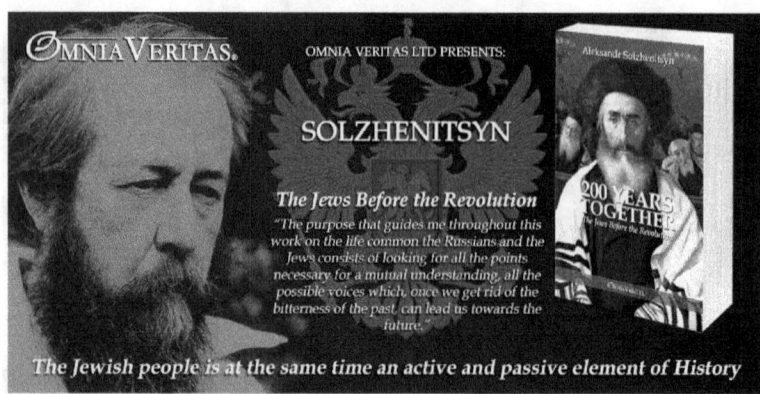

www.ingramcontent.com/pod-product-compliance
Lightning Source LLC
Chambersburg PA
CBHW050130170426
43197CB00011B/1778